HO...
LIBRARY - NAPLES

P9-DHA-405

STATE OF
CONFUSION

STATE OF

CONFUSION

STATE OF CONFUSION

STATE OF

CONFUSION

STATE OF CONFUSION

POLITICAL MANIPULATION AND THE ASSAULT ON THE AMERICAN MIND

DR. BRYANT WELCH

THOMAS DUNNE BOOKS
ST. MARTIN'S PRESS
NEW YORK

THOMAS DUNNE BOOKS.
An imprint of St. Martin's Press.

STATE OF CONFUSION. Copyright © 2008 by Dr. Bryant Welch. All rights reserved.
Printed in the United States of America. For information, address St. Martin's Press, 175
Fifth Avenue, New York, N.Y. 10010.

www.thomasdunnebooks.com
www.stmartins.com

Book design by Jonathan Bennett

Library of Congress Cataloging-in-Publication Data

Welch, Bryant, 1946–
    State of confusion : political manipulation and the assault on the American mind /
Bryant Welch.–1st ed.
        p. cm.
    Includes bibliographical references and index.
    ISBN-13: 978-0-312-37306-1 (alk. paper)
    ISBN-10: 0-312-37306-6 (alk. paper)
    1. Manipulative behavior–United States–History–21st century.   2. Political
culture–United States–History–21st century.   3. United States–Politics and
government–2001–   I. Title
BF632.5.W45   2008
155.8'973–dc22   2008011065

First Edition: June 2008

10   9   8   7   6   5   4   3   2   1

DEDICATION

To my family

My father, Ervin Welch, whose love, wisdom, and integrity have been the constants of my life and who taught me through his example that government can be as good as we are willing to make it

My wife, Debbie, the most beautiful woman I know, who has for over forty years done nothing less than make my world feel familiar

My sons, Lucas and Tucker, who have taught me that sometimes things just work out very, very well through no fault of my own

My artist sister, Marilyn Hotes, who I hope has not absconded with all *of the family creativity*

With love and gratitude

CONTENTS

ACKNOWLEDGMENTS

My thanks go to Tom Dunne and his staff at Thomas Dunne Books and St. Martin's Press for making this book possible. In addition to Tom Dunne, I have benefited from the suggestions of editors Mark LaFlaur and Erin Brown and their assistant, Lorrie McCann. My agent, William Clark of William Clark Associates, lent his credibility to the project. I was most fortunate both to have him represent me and for his guidance throughout. Walt Bode's diverse professional editing skills and extensive experience in the publishing field were also invaluable throughout the preparation of the manuscript.

I am fortunate to have lived in the worlds of psychology, law, and politics. They provided the experiences that shaped this book. In the psychology community, Dr. Richard Wolman made many helpful suggestions for the chapter on religion; Dr. Toni Thompson and Dr. Pam Winton did the same for the section on education. Dr. Nancy McWilliams read the entire manuscript and lent her vast clinical expertise and support to the project. Early in the development of the ideas for the book, Dr. Gil Gerard provided helpful theoretical input. Chuck Zapiec shared his unique perspectives on religion and has been a wonderful friend throughout this process. Jean Perwin, Esq., provided legal assistance. Ervin Thompson, M.D., made valuable comments about the manuscript.

While this book reflects my own idiosyncratic view of the mind, it evolved from clinical supervisors who, while personally very diverse, shared a wonderful capacity to foster independent clinical awareness and judgment. I am especially indebted in this regard to David P. Rogers, Ph.D., who showed me that the inmates often have far more humanity than those who run the asylum, to William Burlingame, Ph.D., for his extraordinary professional judgment, and to the late Mary G. Clarke, who had a Zen-like wisdom witnessed by everyone who knew her and who taught me the folly and destructiveness of all attempts to fit patients into the procrustean bed of psychological theory.

In the 1980s, I filed a successful class action antitrust suit against the medically controlled American Psychoanalytic Association to open psychoanalytic training to clinical psychologists and social workers. Immediately after the "cessation of hostilities," I trained at one of their institutes, the Washington Psychoanalytic Institute. I am grateful to the Washington Institute and to my supervisors there, Richard Waugaman, M.D., and John Kafka, M.D., not only for their clinical skill, but also for the openness and kindness with which I was received. Most of all, I am indebted to the late Roger Shapiro, M.D., whose professional influence shaped the psychological thought in this book more than any other person. Roger enabled me to experience the mind in ways that I never could have without him. He helped me see that our inner emotional experiences often hide in the unrecognized recesses of our mind and take flight from our awareness in amazing and highly idiosyncratic ways. Most importantly for this book, he helped me see that our ability to experience our own true self is ultimately a quasi-political psychological struggle that takes place inside each of us.

I learned much about Washington politics and organizational dynamics while working at the American Psychological

Association. Dr. Faith Tanney, Dr. Nathan Stockhamer, Donna Daley, Clifford Stromberg, Arnold Schmeinder, Ph.D., Helen Desmond, Ph.D., and Patrick Griffin made enormous contributions to the ideas expressed in this book from that period, and I consider all to be invaluable friends.

My fellow psychologist/attorney Bruce Copeland, J.D., Ph.D., not only spoke the bizarre language that results from mixing psychology and the law, but he carried a special burden during this period by serving as my best friend. Other psychologists who should be acknowledged include Dr. Rebecca Goz, Dr. Harry Whitehorse Parad, and Dr. Marc and Judith Mann.

In the legal arena, I learned invaluable lessons working with distinguished attorneys James Overholser, Mathew Quint, Robert Jenner, and Kenneth Curtis. The legal world is a jungle full of predatory monsters. Thus, their friendships are appreciated even more than their considerable legal acumen.

I met and benefited from knowing hundreds, if not thousands, of wonderful psychologists across the country. They are without question an extraordinary blend of understanding, intelligence, and kindness. I do not believe any profession has loftier values than psychology.

At the same time, it is important in making the acknowledgments for this book to say that along the way I encountered evil as well as goodness. It was not until I got to Washington that I encountered the kind of clever and often diabolical political manipulations that have ultimately proven so valuable to understanding political deception and manipulation. These occurred in many places, even in the inner sanctum of the American Psychological Association. While those experiences were at times distressing, at this point in my life, I would not have missed them for the world. They, more than any others, helped me finally understand and conceptualize the pages that follow.

My wife, Debbie, is an extraordinarily talented designer and builder. More than anyone, she was the architect of this book. My recurring personal mental image while writing the book was to framing a house. What made it especially difficult was the sense that I had to drive every nail with my head. Debbie provided badly needed support and stability, and read every chapter, critiquing and suggesting. She is an integral part of every line, and without her, the book simply would not have happened.

STATE OF
CONFUSION

CHAPTER 1

THE ASSAULT ON THE AMERICAN MIND: GASLIGHTING

I don't want to just end the war; I want to end the mind-set that got us into war.

—SENATOR BARACK OBAMA

merica is rapidly becoming a nation psychologically unable to confront its problems. From the White House, from the media, and from the pulpit, Americans have been deceived by predatory political forces into fighting a disastrous war, squandering our national wealth, destroying our standing with other nations, and neglecting badly needed initiatives at home. It is a series of failures that will haunt America for generations to come. And the consequences will not end simply because George Bush leaves office.

America has been gaslighted. Gaslighting is an insidious set of psychological manipulations that undermine the mental stability of its victims. These techniques have invaded our media, infiltrated our churches, and attacked our most basic free institutions. For millions of Americans, the techniques have altered the way they think, feel, and act. It has been nothing less than an assault on the American mind.

State of Confusion explains from a psychological perspective how and why these manipulative and destructive techniques are now deeply embedded in our political system and why they have

1

had a progressively debilitating effect on the American mind. If they go unchecked, America will be less and less able to respond rationally to the very real crises facing us.

Why did Americans become so vulnerable to divisive political tactics? Why did America get dragged into such an unwise war in Iraq? Why have fundamentalist religious groups, Fox News, and hate-filled right-wing radio played such influential roles in America's political landscape? Why are long-accepted scientific ideas like evolution under siege? These questions and others puzzle people from all points on the American political spectrum and from all points around the world. *What has happened to the American mind?*

I have an unusual background that I hope will shed additional light on both how to answer these questions and how to attack the problems confronting America. I am a clinical psychologist and attorney. I have spent half of my thirty-year career treating patients in intensive psychotherapy. The other half I spent in Washington, D.C., much of it in a political position with the American Psychological Association. There I had the opportunity to study politics and politicians firsthand as few clinical psychologists have. It is the synergy of these combined experiences in both psychology and politics that has shaped the concerns I am raising in this book.

The term *gaslighting* comes from the 1944 movie *Gaslight,* starring Charles Boyer and Ingrid Bergman, in which a psychopathic husband, coveting his wife's property, tries to drive his dependent young bride insane by covertly manipulating her environment, making her increasingly perplexed and uncertain. Among other things, he raises and lowers the gaslights in the house while denying to the wife that there has been any change in the lighting. While he feigns genuine concern for her, he cleverly isolates her from any contact with the rest of the world that might interfere with his propaganda-like assault on her sense of reality. He fires the trusted elderly maid and replaces her with a younger one whom he can seductively control and who is naturally competitive with his young wife.

With a combination of seduction, deception, isolation, and bullying, the husband so warps his wife's reality sense that she gradually begins to accept his "reluctant" suggestion that she is losing her mind. She becomes almost totally dependent on her husband to tell her what is real and what is not real, in spite of periodic clues that he is lying. Just as she is on the brink of a complete nervous breakdown, she is rescued by a perceptive Scotland Yard detective who has become suspicious of the husband and uncovers his machinations. When the detective exposes the husband's deceptions to the wife, she regains her mental stability and is able to forcefully confront her husband as he is taken off to jail.

In the mental health profession, *gaslighting* refers to a series of mind games that prey on our limited ability to tolerate much ambiguity or uncertainty about what is happening in important areas of our lives.[1] It is a highly destructive form of psychological manipulation that undercuts trust in our sense of reality and results in confusion and perplexity. If the victims of gaslighting do not come up with a resolution for the perplexity, they will act in an increasingly primitive and irrational fashion. This is what has been done to large segments of America.

In the search for a resolution to their perplexity, people often become extremely vulnerable and dependent on someone else whom they regard as omniscient and to whom they look to "clarify" confusing events. This makes them vulnerable to manipulators and

false prophets. Many Americans have succumbed to demagogues' manipulations. Political operatives like Karl Rove, media
sources like Fox News, Bill O'Reilly, Sean Hannity, and Rush
Limbaugh, and religious leaders like Ted Haggard and Jerry Falwell have all contributed to the assault on the American mind.
But they are merely the current players in America's state of confusion. We will never be free from the control such people acquire until we understand how and why their techniques work.
To do that, we must understand the mind.

Psychotherapy with patients provides a microscope for learning
how the mind really works. It taught me that the mind functions
very differently from the way we think it does. It does not follow
rules of logic, for example, moving from A to B to C. Nor is it
cognitively driven, with decisions based on the thoughts we may
tell ourselves are the reasons for our actions. Instead, what we
psychologists see with patients on the couch is a mind made up
of a series of loosely associated symbols, feeling states, fears, and
wishes that are connected in highly idiosyncratic fashion. Our
mind moves from one to the other according to each person's
own rules and oftentimes in a seemingly chaotic manner. At their
core, most people are driven by very primitive feeling states–fear,
sexual perplexity, and envy, for example–of which they are at
best only dimly aware. These are the things that shape people's
view of reality and are driving America's political behavior. They
transcend logic and even financial self-interest.

Minds are like snowflakes. People walk about in far more different realities from one another than they realize. In marriage
therapy and in politics, I have seen in exquisite detail two people
who think they know one another talk right past each other,

often with disastrous results. Whether it is between a married couple or two belligerent nations armed with nuclear weapons, no two parties can understand each other without deep appreciation for the infinite variability of the human mind.

In group therapy, I have seen how psychological contagions can make groups behave in the most bizarre and irrational ways. H. G. Wells said, "Human history becomes more and more a race between education and catastrophe." Anyone who has studied psychological group processes can appreciate this.

During my seventeen years in Washington, D.C., I lobbied and managed myriad psychologically related issues in the public arenas for organized psychology including the Clinton Administration's ill-fated health care plan, homosexuality, and psychological trauma. As an attorney, I also fought against large HMO insurance companies in court rooms around the country on behalf of mental health patients who had suffered the all-too-often-fatal effects of our current system of managed health care.

When I moved to Washington, D. C., to enter the political world, I was initially struck by the contrasts between clinical work and political work. In the treatment setting, two people are working as hard as they can to achieve greater self-understanding. This requires tremendous candor and honesty. In the political world, in contrast, smoke and mirrors predominate and are often weapons of choice. In therapy, people are searching for their true motivations; in politics, they are often trying to obscure them.

But ultimately the experience that I brought from the therapeutic consulting room to the Washington political world was invaluable. I began to see that transcending that difference between the political world and the therapy world was the human mind, working the same in both the clinical setting and the political.

Psychological concepts such as resistance, symbols, and transference were extremely helpful in learning how to develop a political legislative campaign. Understanding and being able to read the nature and depth of certain emotional states, like envy and narcissism, helped avoid pitfalls that could invite political opposition from people whose support was badly needed. In a relatively short period, using this understanding for organized psychology, we were able to make substantial advances for mental health treatment through our legislative initiatives, legal battles, and public relations struggles.

At first I had thought using these psychological tools was just the only way *I*, given my background, could make sense of political things. With time, I concluded it was the only way political things *do* make sense.

But there was another part of the psychological world in Washington for which I was not so prepared. There is a widely known and very old saying in Washington: "If you want a friend, get a dog." That is an overstatement, but not as much as one might think. And the reason for that is because Washington is a beehive of deception where one can never be sure of what is real and what is not real. Who is sincere and who is just very good at pretending to be sincere? It can get very confusing. In Washington, gaslighting reigns.

Gaslighting exploits weaknesses in the human mind and has a debilitating effect on the victim's ability to think rationally and to function independently of the gaslighter. It can take many forms. In all instances, however, it involves the clever manipulation of "reality" by a predator that undermines the victim's independent mental functioning for the gaslighter's own political, financial, or psychological motives.

I have treated many patients who have been painfully gaslighted in family, work, or organizational settings. I have seen whole organizations undercut by manipulative CEOs. But when gaslighting is done to an entire country as it has been done to the United States, the stakes are chilling. The political use of gaslighting has led to a psychologically impaired and unstable American electorate. The resulting policy decisions have had devastating implications for all Americans and the world.

Many individual victims of gaslighting I have treated become anxious, depressed, confused, and demoralized. Others, however, have tried to avoid that painful uncertainty by letting someone else in their life proclaim a "reality" for them that fills in the void in their own reality sense, often with disastrous results. In marriage therapy, for example, it is not at all unusual to see a spouse become so dependent on the other that they let their spouse convince them that they are responsible for all of the spouse's own problems, even his or her philandering. The victims are unable to tolerate the uncertainty that comes from challenging their spouse based solely on their own perceptions of reality. Over time, this pattern tears them down further. They become weaker and weaker unless and until it is interrupted, like in the movie *Gaslight*.

This same process takes place in political dependency, where people will accept the most bizarre and illogical arguments in order to maintain a dependency relationship. Once Americans adopt the irrational beliefs and become dependent on the gaslighter, they are highly unlikely to reconsider their beliefs, no matter what the consequences and no matter what the evidence to the contrary. This is why it was so easy to retroactively adjust the rationale for the Iraq war so many times. With remarkable ease, America's cause went from eliminating weapons of mass destruction to evicting an evil dictator to spreading democracy, because the idea that our leaders might have been wrong, incompetent, or worse was simply too disconcerting a proposition for many Americans to consider. An already traumatized and confused nation, bombarded by messages from people on whom they had become increasingly dependent, was simply too weak to rebel.

But why is there such dependency? A fundamental aspect of human psychology is the mind's effort, its outright *need*, to have a reality it feels certain of. The reality it creates may or may not be accurate. That is less important. From the point of personal psychological need, it is better to *feel* certain than to *be* right. The mind simply cannot function well without this certainty, and, if it feels uncertain, it will seize on almost anything for help. This is the pressure point of maximum vulnerability in the human mind, a point that right-wing ideologues have learned how to press—and that progressive liberal forces are only recently even addressing. *American politics is now a battle to shape what Americans perceive as reality.*

Making reality a political battleground means that in America reality is up for grabs, and the long-term risk is that voters will become the prey of anyone who seems to provide security, strength, and certainty.

In using the term *gaslighting*, I am not implying that American politicians, or even the gaslighters themselves, are consciously and ruthlessly trying to drive voters insane. Instead, I contend that the political gaslighters have consciously and ruthlessly tried to impose a reality beneficial to their own cause without regard to the long-term psychological effect their behavior has on the individuals they are trying to influence. Many have been very successful in their efforts to distort Americans' perception of political reality. As a result, at present, the way many Americans' reality sense is being shaped is making them psychologically sicker and less able to confront reality. For example, it was only after America was forced by TV to see the undeniable incompetence and indifference of Bush to the Katrina storm victims that a majority of Americans were able to acknowledge that their emperor had no clothes.

In America today, psychological gaslighting exploits people already confused and perplexed about an increasingly complex world. Their world is made more confusing by leaders deliberately misleading them and making them struggle with explosive, but only subliminally recognized, psychological states like sexual perplexity, paranoia, and envy.

In an age of gaslighting, few things are presented as they are. In fact, they are often presented as exactly the opposite of what they are. Political conservatism, long associated with fiscal responsibility, has become a façade for tax cuts for the rich and burgeoning deficits. The Clear Skies Initiative permits increased pollution. The president campaigns against our "addiction to oil" one day, and quite literally the next he cuts the funding for alternative fuels. The list goes on, and examples multiply daily.

Ostensibly "real" news networks, like Fox, say to us that "we report and you decide," but they provide us with artificial news, while comedy shows labeled as fake news shows, such as *The Daily Show*, expose falsehood with rapier-like humor. A decorated war hero running for president against a man with a questionable military record is attacked and branded a liar who is unfit to lead. American ideals of freedom and democracy are used to rationalize the overthrow of foreign governments and the brutal treatment of innocent people who will now hate America for generations. Sadly, America's reputation is changing from the upholder of humanitarian ideals to that of world bully.

After the 2006 election, a seemingly sobered George Bush implied to the American people that he had heard their cries for de-escalation of the Iraq War. He spent well-publicized time "listening" to experts from the military and Congress. He carefully reviewed the reports of the Hamilton–Baker commission on Iraq.[2] He delayed his announced new plan to change course. Despite all of this posturing, he then *expanded* the war with a troop surge.

While this bold duplicity makes some sputter in disbelief, it makes others simply deny the reality of the situation, ignoring the incongruity of it all in order to maintain their dependency relationship on the president. Because the mind is able to turn away from conflict that is unpleasant, it is as if these people are able to erase part of their own memory and avoid confronting reality. Needless to say, this is not a healthy coping mechanism because, for reasons I will discuss, each time the mind turns away from reality, it becomes weaker and functions less effectively. Unfortunately, this approach to psychological conflict is increasingly widespread in contemporary America.

When the mind's reality sense is repeatedly manipulated by clever people with devious intent, victims' mental ability to function effectively is eroded, and they become disoriented. Rationality falls by the wayside. People behave erratically and, because of their own ever increasing uncertainty, they become dependent on demagogues and ideologues who speak confidently and appear to offer escape from the uncertainty. This has happened to millions of Americans who, lured by moralistic bromides, have turned to neoconservative spokesmen, ministers, and politicians and become dependent on them, even enthralled by them.

It is remarkable how many of these prominent political and re-ligious spokesmen to whom conservative Americans have looked for help have themselves been exposed for serious hypocrisy, how many preach morality, but practice what they themselves have labeled immorality. What is even more astonishing, how-ever, is how dependent and willing to overlook hypocrisy and de-ception millions of their followers are. *This reluctance to see the gaslighters for what they are is the cornerstone of the gaslighting rela-tionship.*

In March 2007, former House Speaker Newt Gingrich, shortly after publishing his new book *Rediscovering God in America*, ad-mitted that he was having an affair with a younger employee at the same time he was leading the impeachment of President Clinton for not being forthcoming about the same offense.[3] Gin-grich had the chutzpah to imply that his willingness to risk being exposed as a hypocrite at the time of the impeachment was a profile in political courage. He made the peculiar announcement in an interview on James Dobson's show. Reverend Dobson, a leading spokesperson for the religious right and founder of Focus on the Family who was blessed with the exclusive Gingrich in-terview, praised Gingrich for his forthrightness.[4]

The self-described "culture warrior" Bill O'Reilly, who also brutally attacked Clinton for the Lewinsky affair, published a book, *The O'Reilly Factor for Kids,* advising young boys not to treat girls abusively. While denying any wrongdoing, he settled a law-suit brought by a much younger female subordinate alleging bizarre sexual and abusive behavior on O'Reilly's part.[5] His rat-ings increased substantially after the settlement.

Rush Limbaugh, after frequent rants about drug addiction, es-pecially targeting baseball player Darryl Strawberry and musician

Kurt Cobain, was himself discovered to be addicted to oxycodone, reportedly illegally purchasing over thirty thousand
pills.[6] He returned to the air shortly thereafter with seemingly no
ill effects to his career.

Ted Haggard, president of the National Association of Evan-
gelicals, an umbrella organization for evangelical Christian
churches representing 30 million Christians, and an outspoken
opponent of homosexuality, who met with President Bush on
monthly telephone conference calls to advise him on spiritual
matters, initially denied, but then admitted, that he was having
sex with a gay male prostitute while using methamphetamine.
Haggard contended that after three weeks of counseling he was
"totally heterosexual," but his claim was rejected by church elders. He is now reportedly pursuing an online degree in psychology so he can "help others."[7]

Self-annointed moralist William Bennett, secretary of education under President Reagan, sanctimoniously presented himself
as the personification of virtue by decrying illegal drug use and
other immoral behaviors. He was discovered to have a serious
gambling addiction at the same time he was marketing his book,
The Book of Virtues.[8] He resumed his moralizing a few months
later.

In the movie *Gaslight*, the gaslighting husband fired the elderly
maid and carefully controlled any outside influences that threatened his own control of his wife's reality sense. Similarly, today's
gaslighters have extended their reach throughout American society in multiple ways to increasingly control information Americans receive about the world. They have invented a 24-hour-a-day,
7-day-a-week cable pseudo-news channel, courted and coopted

evangelical religious leaders, and viciously attacked their opposition with smear campaigns. At the same time, professions that have
historically played important roles in helping us define our political
reality are all under attack; mainstream media, law, education, and
even science have all suffered a precipitous decline in influence.
Thus, the American mind is on one hand assaulted by powerful
new forms of deception and, on the other, abandoned by traditionally supportive institutions. Given the complexity of our present situation, this could not have occurred at a more difficult time.

The most recent assault on the American mind has taken
place in three specific emotionally charged psychological states:
paranoia, sexual perplexity, and envy. These are the true "battleground states" in American politics today. Whoever carries the
day in addressing and harnessing these psychological states will
control and shape the American political landscape for the coming decades. Any political party or movement that fails to consider them in its campaign strategy handicaps itself significantly.

The genie cannot be put back in the bottle. The methods of
gaslighting are now deeply and permanently ensconced in our
political system and will not go away. The forces are there, the
techniques operative. Unless we learn about these techniques
and how to defend against them we will continue to suffer from
them. But when we do understand how the mind works—how
certain states of mind affect us in our political behavior—it provides us with a powerful and consistent explanation for America's
behavior in today's political world.

In the chapters that follow, we will discuss both the psychology
and the political structures that make gaslighting work. Psychologically, we will see how the mind creates its reality, why it is so vulnerable to demagogues, and what the current forces operating on

the American mind are doing to it. In addition, we will discuss how gaslighters like Karl Rove, Fox News, right-wing radio shows, and some parts of the religious right go about their work, and why they have been so successful in leading America astray. Most important, we will see how critical it is that these forces be understood before America reaches an even more dangerous level of instability in a world that is becoming increasingly chaotic.

American politics now and for the future will be the politics of reality. Any party that does not try to articulate a reality that appreciates the needs and complexities of the human mind will become increasingly obsolete. A nation armed with nuclear weapons suffering the psychologically regressive effects of gaslighting as it is grappling with the post-9/11 loss of its island-fortress security is a highly combustible combination that is terrifying in its potential consequences. This book sounds an alarm to these dangers, describes the psychological dynamics behind them, and suggests remedies to prevent their potentially devastating consequences. An understanding of the human mind is the key tool of the new political architect. We will begin at the starting point of it all: the human mind.

CHAPTER 2
THE MIND: REALITY SENSE, PERPLEXITY, AND REGRESSION

Reality is unforgivingly complex.

—ANNE LAMONT, Bird by Bird

The human mind is a wonder. It miraculously converts, organizes, and interprets a vast and infinitely complex bombardment of stimuli—from both inside and outside the mind—into a cohesive, subjective experience people call "reality" and psychologists call our "reality sense." This is done unconsciously, far from our awareness, so efficiently and effectively that the very notion of "creating our reality" feels foreign to us. We assume that our senses simply perceive the world as it is objectively. Nothing could be further from the truth.

A reality sense is more than just a person's beliefs or values. It is one's total subjective experience of life. It is what you would experience if you could literally inhabit another person's mind and body. Of course, the most we can do in this regard is to use our imagination and our empathy. Performing such an imaginary exercise—inhabiting someone else's reality—in a meaningful way requires the kind of empathy a good actor uses in performing a role. Good actors do not "act like" the characters they are portraying; they *become* them. This kind of empathy lets them feel the pressures, inhibitions, exhilarations, and other emotional currents of the mind and body of their character. Highly developed empathy can even let one begin to see the nonrational way feelings, memories, habits, superstitions, and beliefs are connected in the other's mind. These are the elements that compose a person's reality sense and are critical to understanding why each person acts the way they do. This empathic experience, if done properly, is profoundly visceral. You feel it in your own body. It is what good therapists try to do with their patients in psychotherapy.

If you can truly imagine and experience, without judging, what it would actually *feel* like to inhabit a mind and a body that differs from you in important areas—along religious lines, for example—you will come away with a sense of just how breathtakingly different personal realities are in America.

A growing group of Christians live in and experience a world that is literally as described in the Bible. These are not people who just pay lip service to fundamentalist Christian reality. For them, the world *is* five or six thousand years old and was created in six days by God, who stands over them and actively intervenes in their daily lives, often in response to prayers.

If these Christians stand in proper relationship to God and their faith is adequate, they will be rewarded with an everlasting life after death of immeasurable joy, peace, and beauty that reunites them with loved ones who have already died. Understandably, this is far more important than anything that happens to them in this world and is a wonderful salve for many of life's hardships.

Religious fundamentalists can have a deep and personal relationship with Jesus that is warm and tender and envelopes them with a rich protective tapestry of love. The inner subjective reality for these people is that God had a son who was brought to life on Earth by a virgin birth and who was endowed with divine powers, including the ability to rise from the dead. This son of God, Jesus Christ, will return to Earth when the time is ripe, after which there will be a precipitous but glorious ending to the world that will be rapturous in nature for those who have believed in him. While no two minds ever share exactly the same reality, for our purposes, we will call this the fundamentalist reality.

At a very different extreme from the Christian fundamentalists are people for whom there is no all-powerful being that actively intervenes in their daily lives. Instead, the universe and everything in it evolved over millions and millions of years, making their own personal lives far less significant in the context of the larger cosmos than in the biblical reality. They evolved from simian ancestors and their personal life ends with biological death. The world, or at least the planet Earth, may end, but it will not be from divine intervention and will most decidedly not be rapturous for anyone around to experience it. Humans are essentially alone in an endless universe, and this aloneness can only be alleviated by connection with other human beings, here and now. For the sake of convenience, we will call this secular humanist reality.

The differences in personal reality are brought into sharper relief if you consider how one group's world must feel to the other. For the fundamentalist, for instance, the secular humanist reality *feels* profoundly nihilistic and devoid of meaning. It feels like a rationale for hedonism stripped of moral values—indeed, of any value at all. Above all, it is a world sapped of the experience of ecstasy that religion with its celebratory joy brings to many fundamentalist Christians.

For the secular humanist, on the other hand, entering the reality of the religious fundamentalist is like Alice's experience entering Wonderland—a world characterized by magical thinking not unlike a child's belief in Superman or Merlin. To the humanist, the fundamentalist world feels as if it is built on psychological denial and driven by self-indulgent wishful thinking that is rationalized and protected from tests of reason by calling it faith. For the humanist, loving God and Jesus in the particular way fundamentalists do feels like an idolatrous affair with God and Jesus rather than a true experience of love for all mankind that makes the Golden Rule come naturally.

Before leaving this exercise in trying to experience other people's sense of reality, be aware that unless you have found some part of the other's reality rich and rewarding, you have missed the *experiential* objective of the exercise designed to give a three-dimensional aspect to much of what we will discuss in this book. If you are a secular humanist and cannot appreciate what it would feel like to have a benevolent figure like Christ watching over you, for example, then you have missed a major part of the fundamentalist experience that you need if you are to begin exploring the fundamentalist mind-set and what creates, affects, and motivates it.

Similarly, the reality of a secular humanist offers rewards different from the fundamentalist's reality. Human love becomes all the more poignant and tender by virtue of the seemingly nihilistic background. In secular humanist reality, to love thy neighbor is not just important—it is life's highest meaning, the precious substance that gives life its value. Death is an approaching wall

that gives immediacy and a romantic poignancy to the importance of loving others right here and now.

The point is not that one is right or wrong, better or worse, or
even that they are "just different points of view." It is that they are
very, very *different* and will lead to profoundly different experiences of, and reactions to, any given event. If one is living in their
Father's house designed as He wishes, one is much less likely to
assume the same responsibility for addressing problems than one
does if living in one's own house. In the former case, it is presumptuous to even think of altering the existing order. In the latter, it is immoral not to do so.

Thus, when the late Jerry Falwell and other conservative fundamentalist clergy opposed environmental interventions in response to global warming, they were speaking to very different
mind-sets than Al Gore's.[1] In fact, fundamentalists are more
likely to see Al Gore as presumptuous for thinking he has a right
to intervene in God's world. The secular humanist, in contrast,
saw Reverend Falwell as equally arrogant by virtue of being so
disdainful of their reality.

The process by which our minds actually weave our reality sense is
complex and leads to an infinite array of potential outcomes. In
creating its reality sense, the mind must operate in Janus-faced
fashion, looking out and looking in at the same time. It looks out at
external reality where it filters and selects from an infinite array of
sensory information, processing what and how much information
to take in and what information to exclude. However, the mind
must also look inward at the important psychological needs we all
have. These include self-esteem needs, sexual needs, and security
needs. All of these internal and external factors must be integrated

to create a cohesive experience that constitutes our reality sense. It is nothing less than our subjective sense of who we are and how we experience our existence.

None of this is an easy process in the best of times. But it can all be greatly complicated under two conditions. First, if the external world undergoes rapid and significant changes, then the mind has to integrate the new information into the person's reality sense. As a general principle, the more significant and extensive the change, the more difficult it is for some minds to accommodate. For some, change is almost always bad for that reason. It is too taxing and stressful. Second, if there are threats to one's feelings of self-worth, personal security, or sexual adequacy, the reality formation process is similarly burdened because the mind has to manage these as part of its reality creation process.

The swiftness and vastness of the change we experience today is intense. Technology alone outstrips many people's ability to assimilate the change it brings to their lives. Mass communications have so shrunk the world that Marshall McLuhan's global village of the 1960s is no longer just a futuristic idea.[2] It is a reality that requires people to process increased contact with different cultures in a much more immediate and complex world.

In American culture, the changes have been equally dizzying. Americans feel that their children are being bombarded with stimulating invitations to a potential lifestyle that can quickly drag them out of the parental orbit into a world that feels very dangerous and beyond parental control. For recreation at the movies or on TV, they see sexual behavior that their parents for the most part never confronted.

The change to which Americans have been subjected has also affected their personal feelings of safety. Americans today have watched planes fly into the Twin Towers and have seen the giant buildings topple as people just like them jumped screaming from the buildings. They have seen the bodies of American servicemen burned in public demonstrations and angry mobs of menacing-looking people spouting hatred toward America directly into the camera.

Many Americans are perplexed and overwhelmed when it comes to making sense of all this. Understandably, they are looking for help. They are looking for greater simplicity and clarity, not greater complexity. In a world that is growing increasingly complex, this makes them very vulnerable. And therein is the rub.

Wondrous though the mind may be, despite all its constructive power, it has limits, and its limitations make America vulnerable to political manipulation and to terrible miscalculations on political matters. We ignore those limitations at our peril.

The problem with the mind is this: the mind's strength—the power to weave a coherent reality out of the booming, buzzing, multifaceted confusion we live in—is also its shortcoming. The mind not only *can* create a reality sense; it *must* do so. When it cannot maintain a comfortable sense of a cohesive world, the mind—and the rest of the person along with it—becomes very agitated and perplexed. And it is here that the mind gets into trouble, submitting to irrational beliefs, implausible explanations, and illogical solutions.

But why is this psychological state of perplexity so intolerable that it overthrows reason, judgment, and common sense? *Perplexity,* like many words in the mental health field, often loses its psychological significance because of its everyday usage. True perplexity can be extremely painful and even terrifying, depending on context, degree, and the stakes.

Perplexity is the mind's heart of darkness. It is the emotional result of not being able to distinguish with confidence what is real from what is not. In a state of perplexity, the world is frighteningly chaotic—without rationality, predictability, or safety. The victim of perplexity feels that they have no ground to stand on, as if they are in a panicky free fall.

The reality sense the mind provides is what separates us from that psychological abyss. When the mind is perplexed, to stave off its own disintegration, the mind begins to manufacture, piece together, edit, delete, and selectively attend to reality in whatever way it can to shape a reality sense that it can convince itself is "true." Oftentimes, as we shall see, it does this in some very counterintuitive and problematic ways. The reality we ultimately weave does not have to *be* a "correct" reality; it simply must *feel* like a correct reality, one that eliminates the perplexity.

Perplexity is difficult to tolerate in its own right, but it is especially so if it arises in areas of insecurity such as people's understanding of important events in their external world or their feelings of self-worth, their sexuality, or their personal security. We do not tolerate uncertainty or perplexity in these areas well at all.

When the mind's cohesive reality sense feels threatened, the mind will take extraordinary steps to preserve it, even if it means forsaking logic, personal morality, or common sense. Often it retreats—"regresses," psychologists say—to a state that leaves it feeling less perplexed, but also functioning less effectively.

In psychological regression, the mind unwittingly returns to earlier developmental levels of mental functioning that are less demanding. One's thinking is more concrete, like a child's, is more likely to be ruled by superstition than logic, and is less likely to be analytically sound. People are literally more simple-minded. Some who have noticed this phenomenon refer to a "dumbing down" of America. This is psychological regression.

All of us, not so long ago, had minds that actually believed in ghosts, goblins, the tooth fairy, and many, many other fantasies. Our maturity since that time is only a matter of degree. Adults desperate for a secure reality oftentimes prefer similarly simple, magical answers over competent but more taxing assessments of complex political issues.

When people regress, they also become more dependent on others for the exercise of judgment, for an interpretation of external events, and for a moral code. Gaslighters are quite willing to fill this void and meet that need. Effective gaslighters cater to the emotional needs of people in this condition by presenting messages that make them feel better temporarily, but that over the long haul are in the gaslighters' interest, not the victims'.

People plagued with self-doubt about what is real and what is not crave two things: certainty and simplicity. Logic and analysis are much higher-level mental functions that are simply too taxing for an already perplexed mind. Thus, listening to George W. Bush was much simpler than listening to Al Gore or John Kerry. Listening to the powerful simplistic certainty of Bill O'Reilly for an overwhelmed and confused mind provides more certainty and support than listening to a dispassionate news analysis. In addition, the emotional experience that O'Reilly provides, the anger and disgust, provides pseudoclarity for a perplexed mind and tends to justify people's feeling that there is someone else to blame for their distress—liberals, democrats, the poor, or the French.

If the gaslighter does his or her job effectively, because of the dependency needs of the audience, be they voters, viewers, or parishioners, a state of thralldom soon develops between spokesperson and beguiled audience. Simplistic angry messages are handed out to meet the cravings of an audience that wants above all to feel certain. Once those beliefs are absorbed, the new believer is highly unlikely to reconsider them no matter what the cost and no matter what the evidence to the contrary. When people escape from stressful perplexity, they are loath to revisit it.

It is quite difficult to reason with people when they are in a regressed state, clinging to a reality that someone else has given them. The more irrational people's thinking, the more rigid they are in defending it. People literally would rather fight than switch when it comes to their reality sense. Galileo, whom Einstein called the father of modern science, was condemned to house arrest from 1633 until he died in 1642 for his support of the Copernican notion that the Earth went around the sun and not vice versa. He was ordered to recant his views, which he did, but still the established order did not feel safe unless he was confined. After all, important aspects of reality were at stake. The rigid society of the seventeenth century could not tolerate such a radical shift in its reality sense, and therefore it renounced physical reality in favor of psychological comfort. Three hundred and fifty years later, "justice" was meted out when Pope John Paul II expressed "regret" at the Catholic Church's treatment of Galileo.[3]

When Americans were confronted with a terrorist threat, they had to construct a new reality in a hurry to account for the changing world that was obviously upon them. They were told Iraq was the appropriate target for their concerns about terrorism. They were told Saddam Hussein was close to Al Qaeda and

by virtue of his WMDs was an imminent threat to America, war-
ranting the first openly acknowledged preemptive war in American history. It was not simply the cunning of the Bush
administration that sold America on this. Americans' inability to
acknowledge areas of uncertainty and massive ignorance about
the Middle East in general made them vulnerable to anyone with
an "explanation," to clarify what was real and what was not real,
no matter how fantastic that explanation was.

The increased dependency on others to define their reality for
them and the inability to think and function independently only
grow worse with time. The mind becomes so dependent on and
pays such irrational obeisance to anyone who can protect it from
perplexity that it steadfastly overlooks incompetence or severe
character flaws in the admired charismatic leader. An irrational
form of political loyalty emerges that binds the beguiled victims
to the beguiling political gaslighter.

Political gaslighting is a sophisticated psychological art form
that has combined with mass media techniques to become a very
powerful political instrument. The current group of political
gaslighters has correctly and astutely understood that Americans'
reality sense is more vulnerable to some forms of manipulation
than to others. These exist in the emotional, not the cognitive,
realm of the mind. There are three highly charged emotional
states—envy, sexual perplexity, and paranoia—that are the targets
of the current assault on the American mind.

If people already psychologically taxed by a rapidly changing
world cannot establish a reality sense that leaves them comfortable in these three areas, they become especially perplexed—and
that is central to the current wave of confusion and irrationality

afflicting America. Whoever controls the psychological turf in these areas of paranoia, envy, and sexuality will be the dominating force in American politics for the foreseeable future. These are the current battleground states in which the American mind is being manipulated, making America's national behavior highly dysfunctional and volatile. We will begin with the most dangerous, paranoia.

CHAPTER 3
STATES OF CONFUSION: PARANOIA

We don't see things as they are, we see them as we are.

—ANAIS NIN

On September 11, 2001, I stepped out on my back lawn fifteen miles from the Pentagon. Two planes had struck the World Trade Center towers, the Pentagon had been hit by a third, and there were rumors of another attack along Constitution Avenue in the District. Like most Americans, I felt disorienting anxiety. There was a frightening sense of anticipation that was so diffuse it was inescapable. The concept of political terrorism took on an immediacy I had never experienced before. I felt certain my world would never be the same. In the days that followed, as I looked back on my own fear, I began to realize how vulnerable America was to the dangers of a paranoid response to 9/11.

Paranoia is more complex than the everyday usage of the term suggests. Literally, *paranoia* means "a mind outside itself," a concept that is quite different from the slang term connoting a state of irrational suspicion. Ultimately, paranoia is about the boundaries between you and me, between one person and another. True paranoia is a fascinating form of mental confusion over psychological boundaries that occurs to some extent in all of us.

Ironically, paranoia uses the same mental mechanisms that let us empathize and understand one another. Under stress, those mechanisms run amok, and the mind confuses emotional experiences that are actually inside us with experiences that are outside us. This is where the notion of "a mind outside itself" arises.

September 11th was not just a crisis of national defense; it was also a psychological crisis from which America has yet to recover. It disrupted our psychological equilibrium and required us to make internal psychological adjustments to process the enormous anxiety. For a world armed with nuclear weapons, paranoia is by far the most dangerous of the battleground states. If the world does ever have a nuclear holocaust between or among nations, paranoid mechanisms will almost certainly play a major role in the disaster.

In some cases, the mind responds to a psychological crisis by developing higher levels of functioning to meet the new challenge. However, if it feels overwhelmed by the crisis, the mind resorts to more primitive or regressive psychological mechanisms, such as denial or projection, that may be so out of touch with reality that they lead to inept and even self-destructive behavior. The consequences can be devastating for the individual, group, or nation involved. Emperor Nero, for example, reportedly fiddled while Rome burned, an extreme example of psychological denial.

In going to war in Iraq, America was befuddled by another form of psychological self-deception: paranoid projection. Americans were given only flimsy evidence that Iraq was an imminent threat to the country, and yet many of us succumbed to psychological manipulations from President Bush, Vice President Dick Cheney, and Secretary of Defense Donald Rumsfeld. This was due to malfunctioning paranoid mechanisms in the mind caused in large part by psychological trauma from 9/11. Americans of all political persuasions have to learn about these mechanisms or be manipulated by other incompetent or evil leaders in the future.

Paranoid mechanisms let us "step outside our own mind" to project uncomfortable and confusing feelings we have onto others or to blame them for our own problematic emotional predicaments. They can create psychological distortions in many other ways as well. A perplexed mind, instead of staying perplexed, will "resolve" the distress of an unknown enemy by finding an enemy, even if it is not the real one. The perplexity, at least temporarily, is over. If I feel threatened but am not sure of the real source of the danger, my mind rearranges my sense of reality to find a tangible threat and make me more comfortable. And while I may blame, kill, hang, or bomb the wrong person, I am less perplexed and less anxious.

Obviously this type of thinking can have some very serious consequences when it is acted out on a world stage. America's decision to go to war in Iraq was made at a time when mentally destabilizing paranoid mechanisms were at play in the American psyche. Some of America's leaders actively exploited these fears for their own objectives while others were too paralyzed by their own paranoid insecurities to stand up to them.

Paranoia is such a pejorative term that it is easy to simply dismiss it as a sign of mental illness and assume it is something healthy people do not have. That is not true. In using the term *paranoid mechanisms,* I should make clear that I am not referring to serious mental illnesses such as paranoid schizophrenia, which involve much more serious psychopathology. Instead, I am referring to psychological mechanisms that exist in all of us. Paranoid mechanisms play a very adaptive role in the world. For example, they are at play in all forms of human empathy. To understand other people and anticipate what they will do, we have to "read them." We have to take our own mind outside itself and put it in them. We have to empathize with what it is like to sit inside the other's mind. To do this well requires an exquisite sensitivity to the other person.

Unfortunately that sensitivity is not always accurate. People's ability to read others is limited at best, and what people read in others can easily get confused with their own inner feelings, wishes, and wants. Mothers, for example, are known for their empathic powers and often can correctly read their children's needs in situations where there appear to be no discernible behavioral or verbal cues to what the child is feeling. The mother may not always be right, however. It is still true in many cases, as the old saying goes, that "a sweater is something a child puts on when the mother is cold."

Ultimately, people see other people through the prism of what is happening in their own mind. This potential for confusion, between what is us and what is someone else, is the core mechanism at play in paranoia. In the same way I think I know what someone else is feeling when I am empathizing with them, I can get confused in that process—confused by my own needs or emotions. In my mind I attribute things to others that are not there, or more precisely, are not really there to the same degree I think they are there.

I may seize upon a kernel of truth to justify my distortion. For example, Saddam Hussein was a tyrant, and he did no doubt hate the United States. He was not, however, America's most dangerous national enemy. That conclusion was fed to Americans by an administration that had been eager to go to war with Iraq even before 9/11. Americans fell for it, however, because of the paranoid mechanisms induced by 9/11.

The best way to understand paranoid mechanisms is to see them at play under the microscope that intensive psychotherapy provides. Don Wilcox* entered intensive psychotherapy treatment after a long-standing difficulty staying in intimate relationships with women. He had had several relationships that were initially promising but invariably failed. As Don described it, when he got close to women they seemed to "become bad" or hateful figures in his eyes, causing him to leave the relationships, oftentimes precipitously. Eventually, however, he realized that these feelings were overreactions on his part to the inevitable foibles, flaws, and misunderstandings that characterize all relationships, and he was puzzled by his own strong aversions that seemed to arise just as he got close to women.

As he began to explore in treatment his experiences with women, he noticed that just before he broke away from one of these relationships, he had had a panicky feeling that he could not clarify or explain. As he talked about this one day, in my efforts to imagine what it felt like inside his world, I began to get an image of a very raw and sensitive component to the young man's experience of his own body. This was not a feeling I had ever had before, and so I wondered if possibly it was something I was sensing in him. When I described my image to him, he said it described exactly the vague feeling he noticed in his body at the time of the experience with the women. That clarification of the feeling led him to a series of memories from his childhood of very similar experiences.

*For obvious reasons, all clinical vignettes I use in this book are disguised, and for efficiency, some of them are actually composites of several cases.

For complex reasons, Don had developed very negative feelings about his body at an early age and begun to loathe his body. He then "projected" the self-loathing onto others. In his mind, he did not loathe himself; others loathed him. As an adult, he felt judged and violated by the women and left the relationships abruptly, feeling very betrayed and angry, much to the surprise of the puzzled women.

By leaving the relationship, of course, Don was able temporarily to stop the painful feelings. This seemed to confirm his sense that the other person had been the cause of the feelings. In truth, though, he had only substituted new feelings of loneliness for the painful discomfort he felt when he was around another person in a close relationship. After this problem arose in several relationships, he realized there must be something he was doing to contribute to the pattern, and he sought treatment.

Don's vignette illustrates that the apparent walls separating one person from another are not nearly as thick as one might think. Our minds have a porous psychological skin, the permeability of which will vary from person to person, as will the degree of sensitivity they feel when the psychological skin is touched or penetrated. Don confused feelings that were actually in him with feelings he thought were in the other person when he blamed women for the discomfort he felt in intimate relationships.

Don's story shows that our ability to differentiate our own feelings from someone else's feelings is limited. The psychological boundaries between people are not firm. This is because the same mental membrane that faces out also faces in, and it is easy under pressure to confuse what is inner with what is outer. Obviously this can be the cause of massive misunderstandings and confusion, as it was for this young man. This is a very common psychological occurrence, the significance of which goes largely unappreciated. It can occur between nations as well as individuals.

Don had enough perspective to consider the possibility that his feelings were not reality based. As a result, with therapy, he was ultimately able to see the situation more objectively and not project his own feelings onto his relationship. Eventually he was able to form a viable intimate relationship with a woman, whom he married.

As a therapist, it is my job to be sensitive to these projections and diplomatically interrupt them. The sooner I can pick up on the way the patient has felt slighted and empathize with his reaction, the quicker that potential toxin in the emotional climate can be disarmed. Unfortunately that type of intervention is not available on the world scene, where the effects of these kinds of misunderstandings are potentially cataclysmic. Instead, the paranoid process goes unchecked. Groups of people continue to project blame for their fears and uncertainties onto others and make them diabolical monsters. This is an ongoing dynamic. Projection takes what hostility actually exists, magnifies it, transmits it back to the other, who does the same thing, and a minor issue becomes a major one. It is a primary reason why relations between countries can reach such levels of intensity that leaders can convince people to go to war, as Bush did with America. Iran, Iraq, and North Korea become the Axis of Evil, and the United States becomes the Great Satan. Hate confirms hate and leads to more hate. It can become a never ending story, as the world has seen in Northern Ireland, Eastern Europe, Africa, and many other places. In these contexts, paranoid projection is an ongoing, dynamic process between two groups that hate each other. A chilling and potentially catastrophic example of this is the growing tendency of many Americans to equate all Muslims with terrorists.

One of the most difficult and important jobs in psychotherapy (and all intimate relationships) is sorting out exactly which feelings are truly in the patient and which are in the analyst. This is also an important exercise to perform before a nation goes to war. Because of the fact that everything we experience, whether it is from outside us or inside us, we experience in the same mind, there is much greater confusion between what is inside us and what we think is outside us than we recognize.

Why did the psychological mechanisms by which Americans construct their reality fail us so badly after 9/11? If there was ever a time Americans needed to use all of our rational faculties, it was then. Yes, of course, Americans were lied to by leaders. But why were so many Americans so determinedly gullible?

The capacity for self-reflection that Don showed in his recognition of his relationship difficulties was noticeably absent in many Americans, and those voices that did encourage such reflection were vilified and dismissed as weak and unpatriotic. The president, the vice president, and many other Republicans characterized debate about the war as providing aid to the enemy. Karl Rove, for example, accused war critics of wanting to provide "therapy" to terrorists.[1] Of course, no one was recommending therapy for terrorists. Rove was trying to create a straw man for people to hate so they would not have to think about complex issues.

Don could have done what many people do when their paranoid distortions are confronted: they shoot the messenger, become angry, and reaffirm their own distortions. When the United States was told by almost all of its allies that the Iraq venture was unwise, Americans attacked, threatened, and cajoled them. America's oldest ally, France, was vilified, and some French businesses in America were vandalized. The rest of the world was cautioning America, and yet Americans thumbed their noses at them and determined to send young soldiers and billions of dollars to Iraq.

This paranoid mind-set made America much more susceptible to Bush's ongoing manipulations about the war. Having a target for the paranoid fear and rage generated by 9/11 was more important than having an accurate rationale for the particular target America selected. Americans went to war for paranoid reasons, and reversing that course has been very difficult. Saddam Hussein, in his prolonged, defiant, saber-rattling resistance to the United States, misunderstood the paranoid psychological state of America and paid for that with his life.

In paranoia, the critical point for understanding is the line of demarcation between the inner world and the outer world, the line between what is in me and what is outside of me. This line is the point of maximum sensitivity in all of our relationships, for better and for worse. It is called a psychological boundary.

Our psychological boundaries raise fascinating psychological issues. They are the point at which all human intimacy and understanding occurs. They are also the point at which we experience other people as annoying, hostile, and intrusive. They play a large role in paranoia and can be very dangerous if not appreciated and respected.

For example, most Americans underestimate the psychological impact our military bases in the Middle East have on people in the Middle East. Americans would not take well at all to having Saudi Arabian military bases in Nebraska, Ohio, New York, and Colorado. Planting a military base in another's country, when understood in the context of the paranoid nature of the mind, especially the extreme sensitivity that exists around psychological boundaries, is the equivalent of poking a sharp stick in the other's eye.

This is true for all people and all nations. Because the mind needs to be open to the external world in order to understand the world and to connect with other people, we have sensitivities at the boundary line between what is us and what is the external world. This is how we make meaningful contact with others and absorb the world around us. This sensitivity can vary greatly from person to person. For many, the very experience of boundary contact feels abrasive and leaves them feeling a terrifying loss of control. Countries like North Korea are seen as extremely paranoid because of their widely perceived hypersensitivity to foreign influence and mistrust of the world beyond their borders.

For most people, the sensitivity to boundaries is less dramatic, but for those whose psychological boundaries are not firmly established, they will be especially hypersensitive to any boundary incursions no matter how minor they may seem. In contrast, people who are excessively impervious to goings-on at this boundary will be seen as lacking in empathy and concern for others. For everyone, however, boundaries are very important matters. Problems in boundary relations will preempt the effective functioning of the mind, making one feel threatened and needing either to withdraw or attack.

This is why boundaries and the space between people are hazardous to negotiate and require much caution. They must be open so people can connect with others and understand the world, but because of this very openness they can make people feel very vulnerable. This is why all cultures have customs designed to "detoxify" the tension that people's hypersensitivity to boundaries creates. For example, when two strangers encounter one another in close quarters, they feel awkward if there is not some way to comfortably, but not too intimately, suggest friendliness or courtesy.

The Japanese deferentially bow when passing one another, as if to make certain that one's own presence is not intended to give offense to the other. In America and other parts of the Western world, people discuss the weather to offset the tension that they feel when two strangers meet on an elevator or in a similar space. It is also why the law attaches such significance in criminal and civil law to trespass and assault and why people have such seemingly irrational fights over minor property disputes. Good fences do make good neighbors and for good psychological reasons.

From a psychological perspective, the most significant aspect of 9/11 is that the assault penetrated our national boundaries. When psychological boundaries are penetrated, it can be intolerably fragmenting, frightening, and enraging. If it is extreme, as 9/11 was, it leads to an enormous emotional upheaval creating instability, impaired judgment, and even perceptual distortions.

Of course, the 9/11 attack was terrible. But to put this danger in perspective, for the forty years of the Cold War, Americans lived in a world where their enemies could not only knock down two buildings, damage a third, and kill thirty-five hundred Americans; it was a world in which nuclear annihilation threatened death for the entire nation on very short notice. The Cuban Missile Crisis was the apex of that threat, but even it did not have nearly the residual psychological impact on the nation that 9/11 has had.

Only in 9/11 and Pearl Harbor have America's national boundaries been violated. In World War II, Pearl Harbor was the only event FDR could use to persuade the American people that a madman was intent on world conquest in Europe, a message that did not resonate with Americans despite Hitler's nearly complete occupation of Europe, until America was attacked *by Japan.*

More than any other single fact from 9/11, the psychological assault on our borders is what triggered the paranoid process that led to our irrational response in Iraq. Opponents of the Iraq war were baffled by public acceptance of the nonsensical argument that America had to fight the enemy "over there" so that we would not have to fight them "here," inside our personal space. In truth, the enemy was not even in Iraq when America went there, and the war in Iraq had little, if any, apparent connection with Al Qaeda's ability to hit America at home again. But the argument is a lot more understandable in its perceived credibility if one keeps in mind the hypersensitive role boundaries play in our assessment of personal risk. Americans were so susceptible to Bush's arguments in support of war with Iraq because psychologically they were using Saddam Hussein as a bromide, an attempt at relief from anxiety at not having the real external target to fight back at "over there." Hussein became the enemy and the uncertainty was at least partially resolved.

A frequent complaint prowar commentators make about antiwar groups is that those who wish to end the war do not fully appreciate the extent of the threat posed by Al Qaeda and terrorist groups in general. That message resonates for many Americans who support the war effort. However, there are very few Americans who misunderstand or minimize the terrorist threat. In truth, what is not fully appreciated by either side is the degree of terror prowar advocates feel over having their psychological boundaries penetrated. This gives the war an added urgency and has contributed in no small measure to America's irrational national response to post-9/11 events. It also made it difficult for America to admit its mistake in Iraq.

Paranoid mechanisms create a very serious danger that a country just attacked will respond to the attack irrationally. In these situations, leadership is a matter of life and death. Had Kennedy and Khrushchev not been sufficiently free of paranoid thinking during the Cuban Missile Crisis, America would in all probability have had a nuclear conflagration. Robert Kennedy said in describing American statesmen managing the crisis, "The fourteen people involved were very significant—bright, able, dedicated people, all of whom had the greatest affection for the U.S.... If six of them had been President of the U.S., I think the world might have been blown up."[2]

If one looks at the issues confronting President Bush at the time of his decision to invade Iraq, in this regard, this problem becomes even more striking. The very idea of an attack on our country creates enormous pressure to find the enemy. But consider the case of a man who also has to psychologically assess the degree of danger the country is under from a foreigner that he has never met, but who a few years previously tried to kill his father. This was the situation that President Bush confronted when he had to determine how to prioritize the role of Saddam Hussein in America's war on terrorism.

There is strong evidence that a war with Iraq was a primary

item on the Bush agenda even before 9/11. President Clinton's secretary of defense William Cohen (a Republican) reported that in the transition of power between administrations, the Bush representatives discussing national defense showed interest only in Iraq.[3] And there was a now-less-than-funny joke making the rounds before 9/11 that Bush had two objectives: "Cut taxes, and get Saddam."

Regardless of Bush's *conscious* intentions, it is very hard to believe that he would be in a position to objectively assess the intentions and character of someone who tried to kill his own father. No judge, no matter how honest, would ever be allowed to sit in judgment on a defendant with such a personal history of involvement with a defendant. That issue, of course, has nothing to do with Bush's integrity. The issue is to what extent he was able to assess objectively the kind of threat Hussein posed to America and the extent to which Saddam Hussein, not Al Qaeda, warranted the expenditure of resources at a time when America had so many other threats to its safety in Afghanistan, in Pakistan, and at its own borders.

In this country, however, the only question even briefly raised about this matter was whether Bush was *deliberately* going after a personal vendetta in pursuing the war. The absence of any discussion of how he was *unintentionally* affected by the history between Saddam Hussein and his father was testimony to America's limited appreciation of the power of unconscious motivation. It is hard to imagine anyone even trying to vet this problem in the Bush White House, and it certainly was not well vetted in the media. It was almost as if even raising the issue was an embarrassment around which one had to carefully tiptoe. Grappling as America was with the emotional effects of 9/11, Saddam Hussein was transformed from an evil, but relatively limited, frustration into a life-threatening menace by virtue of the mechanisms of projection.

But the problem runs much deeper than issues related just to George W. Bush. We all use paranoid mechanisms to explain away many of our vague and unpleasant feelings. Enemies play a very important role in this because people can attribute all manner of unpleasant feelings they have to an enemy. As strange as it may seem, our enemies actually help us maintain a cohesive sense of reality. They serve as a holding container for many of the unacceptable or confusing feelings we either do not want to own or need to explain away. To avoid the burden of many unpleasant feelings, people project them onto an evil other.

Obviously, this can be very problematic. The more hostile we assume the other is, the greater the danger that our own actions will provoke a hostile reaction from them that "confirms" our sense that they are indeed hostile toward us. The process continues in a downward spiral. At some point one of us may even decide it is necessary to make a preemptive strike against the other. In this way, people demonize their enemies and ultimately create the very hostile world they fear. This has happened to America with Iraq.

Paranoid tendencies become especially problematic and require psychological adjustments whenever people's enemies change. When this happens, people have to construct a new reality sense with a new psychological strategy that lets them manage the feelings that were being managed under the old regime of enemies. Once the war with Nazi Germany was over, there was no plausible place for Americans to project their own internal insecurities for which Hitler had provided such a justifiable target. Americans had to find a new place for them somewhere, and Communism was a sufficient explanation for Americans' own otherwise inexplicable fears. Unfortunately, when J. Edgar Hoover and Senator Joseph McCarthy told America the enemy was "within," Americans began to see Communists infiltrating everything from the State Department to Hollywood to the water supply.[4] The boundary violation Americans felt from the "Red menace" ushered in the McCarthy era. September 11th ushered in the Patriot Act.

For decades, in the post-McCarthy era, Americans saw their enemy as a monolithic Soviet Union, armed with nuclear weapons, but easily findable on a map. After 9/11, America faced the prospect of fighting terrorist organizations that could have been lurking anywhere, that were led by people America's army could not find, who used weapons Americans could only guess at, and who were ready to wreak havoc on America in a sudden surprise attack at any time.

Faced with our fearful, deeply troubling uncertainty, George Bush's construct of the "axis of evil"–however incorrect the idea may have been–provided many Americans with a temporary respite from their confusion and disorientation. The enemy was located on the map in the space occupied by Iran, Iraq, and North Korea. The weapons were the familiar nuclear ones to which Americans had been accustomed during the Cold War, and Americans knew who and where their leaders were. If Americans felt threatened with a loss of control, they at least knew where the battle line was and where to fight back. For the mind, it is often more important to have a firm reality sense than to have a correct one.

This is not without a cost, however. Projection, like other defenses, never fully works because it is based on self-deception and distortions of reality. Ultimately, one pays a price for it. When this happens, the person or nation is ill prepared to cope with the realities they have been avoiding. Chickens do come home to roost. This is the lesson of Iraq. America's distortions of reality have come home to haunt us with a terrible debacle that America will pay for, one way or another, for generations.

The paranoid mind compounds its problems because it avoids confronting reality for as long as it can. It develops a variety of self-defeating and self-deceiving methods for doing so. The mind resists information from the outside world that might challenge its own preferred internal sense of reality formed to make the world seem like the person would like it to be rather than as it really is. In the process, the mind becomes less amenable to self-correction and becomes increasingly rigid. Strategies like "staying the course," the strategy that Bush was able to maintain so long in Iraq despite its continued failures, felt more comfortable than the alternatives because it required no mental flexibility or psychological adjustments.

Gaslighters are experts at exploiting the paranoid dimensions to the mind. At present, millions of Americans struggling with these paranoid mechanisms listen to media carefully designed to make them project hatred onto people who are not the real problem, and dissuade them from listening to anyone with a different point of view from the gaslighter. If people can label the entire independent press a biased "liberal media," then any news that does not come from Fox News, right-wing radio, or the White House can be explained away as biased. People do not even have to consider the alternative viewpoint or any news that does not fit with the less disturbing, rigidly fixed, paranoid reality.

In a paranoid state, people are vulnerable to strongly asserted, confident statements from others who sound superior (and who pander to people's own need to feel superior), especially if those messages tend to support the ongoing paranoid mechanisms in their mind. Sean Hannity's callers tell him he is a "great American," and he says it right back at them.

Authoritarian voices and personalities reflect, and actually command by their demeanor and tone, the self-indulgent way people unconsciously want their own minds to work. People do not want to deal in the doubts and subtleties of nuance when they are trying to hold on to their more comfortable and reassuring fixed "reality" that is already threatened by the external reality they are trying to escape. Nuanced thinking becomes "wishy-washy," and context-based decision making warranted by the complexity of events is characterized as "flip-flopping." Karl Rove's selection of these terms for his assault on Kerry suggests a very keen appreciation of what people wanted to avoid, and he gave them fortification for doing so by denigrating Kerry's attempts to actually struggle with and explain the true complexity of events.

It is also in paranoid times that fundamentalist religious doctrines and political ideologies are most ascendant. We need explanations the most when we are least able to provide them for ourselves and when we feel beleaguered by our own internal psychological state of disarray. Given this loss of mental flexibility and resistance to new external information, many people readily accept any seemingly authoritative explanation for events, if it supports their psychological need for their own more appealing alternative reality. The mind, also, avoids the added stress that a more complex reality-building process requires. Thus, people can go to church on Sunday and listen to a charismatic figure, maybe even one who speaks regularly with the White House. At the same time, they have a comprehensive reality sense handed to them in an ambience of ecstasy.

Any voices that are inconsistent with the paranoid reality are met with contempt and disgust. Contempt and disgust are especially important feelings in paranoid states because with contempt and disgust people turn up their nose at other people (often literally) and do not have to actually see them. Thus, they are quite handy to a paranoid defensive reaction. American right-wing talk radio encourages and models feelings of contempt and disgust to be directed toward anyone who is not a neoconservative. They justify and fortify the listeners' closed and rigid minds, which in turn keeps the unpleasant reality they do not want to face at bay.

Unfortunately, for people to adapt to the world successfully, reality needs to be continuously assessed and reassessed, taxing though that certainly is to a mind already under stress. When people wall off their receptiveness to new information and cling to their fixed perceptions, they stop revising their reality sense to incorporate new information. Instead, over time their perception of the world is increasingly and disproportionately dominated and colored by their own internal emotional states, especially the fears and vulnerability inside the now-closed mind. Paranoia breeds this defensive isolationism. It affects our leaders as well. It is easier to fire generals who tell them they need more troops than it is to readjust one's thinking.

There is another ill effect of paranoia, however, and that is grandiosity. Fear and powerlessness are critical elements of people's retreat into paranoia, and one of the temporary advantages of that retreat into the paranoid's world is that paranoia lets people recreate who they are with an unrealistically grand self-assessment that is in contrast to how they feel about themselves otherwise.

One patient, Charles Alcott, was truly a "poor little rich boy." He had a lifelong history of parental neglect. His father was a successful physician who performed complex cardiovascular surgery at a leading teaching medical hospital in the Midwest. His mother made so many civic contributions to the community that she was rarely home to attend to her young son's needs. Because of the family's preoccupation with career, they decided not to have more children. Charles grew up in a big house with a housekeeper, alone most of the time with his dog as his only companion.

Without any structure, friends, or human contact, Charles was left to devise and live in his own fantasy world. Understandably in the fantasy world that he created, he played a more central role than he did in his real world of neglect. In fact, he was *the* central and most powerful figure in his world, and most of the themes of his fantasy life centered around his dominance of all people in his life, the very opposite of his actual experience. Living in this world was a grandiose compensation for the deep feelings of vulnerability that had driven him into his fantasy world in the first place.

With his high intelligence, Charles could excel at school. He was extremely competitive and his classmates noted his cutthroat demeanor. His personal ambition was to be CEO of a large corporation, and his technical knowledge let him move into a position of prominence very quickly after completing his education. He assumed that the CEO position was his to have. Unfortunately, his arrogance was intolerable to those around him, and he was astonished when he was not only denied the position but asked to leave the company because of the negative effect he had on morale. It was this collapse of his grandiose façade and ambitions that made him depressed and led him to seek treatment. The very fact he needed the treatment was in and of itself a tremendous blow to his self-esteem.

Charles's case illustrates how people can retreat from reality into a grandiose world where they do not have to experience the fears and humiliations of a paranoid world. If people wall themselves off from reality enough, they can at least be legends in their own mind.

Prior to 9/11, Americans had viewed themselves as the exclusive superpower in the world. September 11th was a tremendous blow to Americans' sense of security and adequacy in the world. While still struggling to adjust to 9/11, America was led to war by a small group including Dick Cheney, Paul Wolfowitz, Donald Rumsfeld, and others, and we were encouraged to have the most extraordinarily unrealistic expectations of what we could achieve. We were led to believe that America's military would first "shock and awe" the Iraqis with the power and precision of its bombing. The Iraqi people would respond to this by throwing rose petals at Americans' feet, welcoming us as liberators, and then America would somehow be able to transform Iraq with some purple ink pads into a liberal representative democracy, something for which there was no historical basis.

Given the grandiose dimension to paranoia, truly paranoid people do not necessarily appear scared. More often they come across as superior, even haughty. This same air of grandiosity, of course, has played havoc with America's other relations around the world and portrayed Americans as arrogant know-it-alls. As Mark Twain said, "Sometimes I feel lonely in this lofty solitude."

While Americans have been told they are pursuing lofty ideals by leaders, they have been seen as displaying a contemptuous lofty attitude. America is increasingly alone in the world.

Since we do to some extent create our own reality sense, we have the option of unconsciously disavowing part of reality. When the mind is under pressure or in pain, either physically or mentally, it attends primarily to itself to the relative exclusion of external reality. Thus, the more the mind itself is under pressure, the more its own fears, wishes, and needs shape the view it has of external reality. What I feel inside me is more likely to define how I perceive what is outside me. This is why when people are depressed, the whole world, even one's sense of the past and the future, looks grim.

There are, of course, some practical limits on people's ability to manufacture their own reality. External reality does compete for its share of attention. Knowledge can potentially serve as a partial antidote to paranoia in some circumstances, although it is by no means a *solution* to paranoia. The more people know about external reality, about Iraq for example, the more reality can weigh in on their processing of information about it.

By accidents of geography, history, and personal temperament, America was particularly ill prepared to respond rationally to a threat occurring inside its borders such as 9/11. Unlike European nations, America has always been protected by large bodies of water and friendly neighbors on all sides. Its geographical isolation and educational neglect of geography has left many Americans with comparatively little exposure to the rest of the world. Most Americans were ignorant of the most basic facts about the Middle East at the time America went to war with

Saddam Hussein. Americans had even less sense of the geopolitics of the Middle East and were unable to see through a president who was remarkably uneducated about the world. The lack of any competing reality, or of any curiosity about the unknown, left Americans particularly vulnerable to a paranoia-induced pseudoreality.

The paranoia evoked by 9/11 preempted the rational course of finding out about the enemy—before going to Iraq. If one looks at the basic but critical information most Americans did not have, America's vulnerability to its paranoid reaction to 9/11 is clear.

Americans were told that Saddam Hussein was in league with Al Qaeda. It made no sense. The terrorists are radical Islamic fundamentalists. Radical Islamic fundamentalism was a bigger threat to Saddam Hussein than to America. When bin Laden struck America on its own soil, America responded by diverting troops away from their search for him in order to depose one of his biggest rivals in the Middle East. How Osama bin Laden must have laughed that the American people were led into battle with his enemy, Saddam Hussein, because of what bin Laden did on 9/11! Fighting Saddam Hussein in the name of a war on terror was arguably the most significant uninformed decision America has ever made.

Americans were also told they were in Iraq for idealistic objectives, to spread American-style democracy. This, too, was plausible only because of paranoid mechanisms that are still overactive in the American mind. The hope that America could instill modern democracy in another nation—without the same historical experience of America's own founding fathers or the cultural context of the Enlightenment and where the people who actually

lived in Iraq were focused on other priorities—was grandiose wishful thinking that was tragically unconnected to reality. The
grandiosity was the notion that America could create almost any
reality it wanted.

And, of course, many accepted the notion that Saddam Hussein's brutal rule alone warranted America's intervention in Iraq.
However, if concern for human welfare and abuse by tyrannical
leaders were the actual basis for our action, America would be
doing far more in Africa and Southeast Asia than in Iraq. Its failure to do so has made its invasion of Iraq seem particularly disingenuous and hypocritical to the rest of the world. Writing about
Libyan dictator Muammar el-Qaddafi in an opinion essay in the
New York Times, Libyan novelist Hisham Matar commented, "The
short-sighted paranoia with which the war on terrorism has been
managed has weakened any moral advantage the United States
might once have had."[5]

Tactically, America's reason for toppling Saddam was especially warped in the failure to understand the relationship between Iran and Iraq. Americans did not see through Bush's
preposterous joinder of Iran and Iraq at the hip in an axis of evil
even though the two have been in conflict with each other for
years over border disputes and religious differences. Saddam
Hussein's invasion of Iran in 1980 was a war in which Iran suffered a reported one million casualties, some as a result of poison
gas.[6] The cessation of overt military hostilities in 1988, which
Iran agreed to with the deepest reluctance, did not quell the animosity between the two countries. The prisoner-of-war ex-
changes that followed were not completed until 2003. As a result
of Iraq's use of chemical weapons, the Ayatollah Khomeini decided to pursue the acquisition of nuclear weapons (to which he

had been deeply opposed on religious grounds) as a counter-weight to Iraq's WMD.[7] Paranoia is not restricted to any one nation; in prewar Iraq, it was working as an important barrier to any alliance between Iraq and Iran.

Iran and Iraq were important checks on each other in terms of military and political hegemony in the Middle East. Saddam Hussein's ruling Baathist party was secular, and most of the party members were Sunni. Iran in contrast was dominated by the Shia living under a religious theocracy. Saddam Hussein, by virtue of his dictatorship, kept the majority pro-Iranian Shiites in Iraq from running the country and ensured a hostile relationship between Iran and Iraq. While there was certainly no love lost between the United States and either country, their own enmity kept them from forming any type of coordinated effort against America. This would presumably be the case as long as Saddam Hussein or some other Sunni leader was in power.

Americans were encouraged by Bush, Cheney, Rumsfeld, and Rove to project their fears and rage onto the enemy "axis of evil," and, lacking the relevant geopolitical facts to the contrary, they quickly accepted the notion that America was the exclusive focus of Iran and Iraq. This predictably obscured the regional animosities that made conspiratorial collusion unlikely. It reflected an ego-centric American perspective based on a paranoid mental focus facilitated by political ignorance and exploited by national leaders.

Most Americans were unaware of the long-standing religious and ethnic animosities among the Shiites, Sunnis, and Kurds, and, thus, they failed to anticipate the civil war that ensued after the fall of Saddam. Saddam Hussein's ruthlessness had put a lid on ex-pressions of ethnic hatred, just as Communist totalitarianism did in Eastern Europe for fifty years. The world's recent experience in

Bosnia should have made the possibility of civil war in Iraq obvious. That it did not was not just an error in judgment; it was extreme denial in which wishes overwhelmed reason.

But one cannot simply point the finger at the duplicity of Bush, Cheney, and Rumsfeld. Many Americans let themselves be lulled into passivity about the importance of foreign policy in the 2000 presidential campaign. Al Gore was a foreign-policy expert. He was one of the most respected experts on defense matters in the history of the United States Senate. Gore had served in Vietnam and had been a member of the House Intelligence Committee and the Senate Foreign Relations Committee. Even his most ardent critics would admit that he was a policy wonk.

In contrast, George Bush was widely known for his cheerleading and partying in college and for some time thereafter. He ran an oil business that failed and was part owner of a professional baseball team. He ran a campaign focused almost entirely on domestic issues: taxes, education, and immigration. Fred Barnes, an admiring Bush biographer and editor of the conservative *Weekly Standard*, wrote, "Foreign affairs were tangential to his presidential campaign in 1999 and 2000. . . . Bush's summary of his views was confusing. He endorsed 'idealism without illusions, confidence without conceit, realism in the service of American ideals.' Any candidate could have said the same."[8] Bush provided America with little more than platitudes, but he was seen as a "regular guy" who did not burden people like Gore with complex intellectual matters. Bush did not tax the minds of voters. In fact, he made many Americans feel it was safe to indulge themselves in a form of know-nothingism and mental passivity.

Americans opted for the simplistic approach to the growing complexities of the world around them. They let themselves be lured down a path of passivity and denial about the importance of foreign policy by a sleight of hand Bush and Karl Rove engineered that was typified during the 2000 presidential debates. In the debate, George Bush took the position that since foreign policy was traditionally bipartisan in nature, significant debate in the foreign policy arena was unnecessary. There were no differences between the candidates. Bush said as long as the president relied on "sound principles," he was as capable as someone who had served on the House Intelligence Committee, the Senate Foreign Relations Committee, and the National Security Council. "I think you've got to look at how one has handled responsibility in office," Bush said in the first debate. "Whether or not–it's the same in domestic policy as well–whether or not you have the capacity to convince people to follow. Whether or not one makes decisions based on sound principles or whether or not you rely upon polls or focus groups on how to decide what the course of action is."[9]

This, of course, recast the relevant issue. Knowledge, experience, judgment, and above all the ability to function rationally under pressure were critical issues that were never subjected to national debate. The important issue of which candidate would be more qualified to make decisions about the unforeseen events that would inevitably arise during the course of a presidency–like 9/11–was reduced to vaguely stated principles. Many Americans in effect indulged themselves in George Bush's invitation to simplify the foreign-policy issues, to assume passively that America's basic values and "sound principles" would mean that no American had to worry about the rest of the world–until it was too late.

In a chilling portrayal of the difference between the two men, Bob Shrum, Gore's campaign advisor, describes drafting Gore's acceptance speech at the 2000 Convention:

> *Gore would cut one [line] that has a haunting ring in light of the subsequent events and his own passionate opposition to the Iraq war: "I have news for Saddam Hussein: if I become President, our policy toward you is going to get even tougher. It is time for you to go"–an intentional echo of his most famous line at the 1992 convention. Today, the words about Saddam Hussein sound quintessentially Bush-like. That I penned them so casually says volumes about the fact that the issue was an afterthought at the time. That Gore excised the words reveals both his aversion to bombast about war and peace and a temperament and sense of judgment that would make him the right president post-9/11.*

Facing the effect of what the United States has done in Iraq may well prove to be a national trauma that outstrips even 9/11 in its psychological consequences. That trauma has to be psychologically managed. Right now it will be managed with rationalizations and denial and the psychological maladjustments those things create.

It is an axiom in psychology that paranoids create the very world they fear and project. America's geopolitical standing since Iraq is much less secure. Because the rest of the world saw the Iraq situation in much less threatening terms than Bush, Cheney, and Rice portrayed it, America's motives appeared disingenuous and self-serving. As a result, America has lost its position of respected world power and is, instead, seen as an insensitive power monger.

America has alienated once-friendly people in nations whose

governments one hoped would topple or succumb to more moderate, less anti-Western influences. Immediately after 9/11, there were reports of up to a million people attending vigils of sympathy for America and victims of 9/11 in Tehran. These people were no doubt surprised to be linked in an axis of evil with North Korea and their long-standing enemy, Iraq, as a result of 9/11. Now they are, indeed, America's enemy. Iranian delegates attended the nuclear test conducted by North Korea in mid 2006. Shiites closely aligned with Iran are the dominant party in Iraq. Americans initially were fighting the Shiites' enemy, Sunnis, for them.

America's invasion of Iraq destabilized the Middle East in such a way that nuclear weapons, the very bogeyman Americans intended to fight going to Iraq, can now more easily fall into the wrong hands. The Bush administration has created the very thing they supposedly took America to war to prevent. Such is the inevitable and tragic outcome of the paranoid mind-set.

All empires prior to America have waned. Most have been lost from the kind of poor judgment exercised in Iraq. America's psychological vulnerability and its nuclear capacity make it critical that we understand the psychological mechanisms that underlay the terribly impaired judgment exercised on America's behalf in Iraq. To do that, as a nation we need to develop a more sophisticated understanding of the dangers paranoia creates in international politics. Post-9/11 America is a painful case study for that understanding. It is a process that is still playing out. As the world truly becomes the global village envisioned by Marshall McLuhan, and people move into greater psychological proximity to one another, paranoid pressures can only increase.

Unfortunately, the American mind is struggling with other

psychological battleground states, not just the paranoid state. While 9/11 has been ruthlessly exploited by gaslighters, 9/11 was not created by them. The other battleground states have been created almost from whole cloth by professional gaslighters. They are sexual perplexity and envy. When they are combined with the paranoid pressures created by 9/11 and the subsequent manipulations of it, the gaslighting of America comes into sharp relief, and our national confusion becomes more understandable.

CHAPTER 4
STATES OF CONFUSION: SEXUAL PERPLEXITY

People who have misused their sexual faculty and become bonded to multiple persons will diminish the power of oxytocin to maintain a permanent bond with an individual.[1]

—ERIC KEROACK, M.D., *deputy assistant secretary of population affairs under President George W. Bush, 2006–07*

I n August of 1962, having just turned sixteen, I was visiting relatives in Kennebunk, Maine, as I did most summers. One evening after dinner, wanting to escape from a family event, I took advantage of the newfound freedom my driver's license had given me and drove the four or five miles to Kennebunk Beach.

By the time I arrived, it was well after dark and the beach was deserted. The vastness and the roar of the ocean that had felt soothing and regenerative on so many sunny days took on a powerful and menacing aura in the evening. The only visible landmark was a familiar red house that jutted out into the water. Lounging on the beach during Kennebunk summers, I had frequently wondered about the family that lived there. Years later I learned that it was the Bush family. In fact, it was supposedly here on this same beach that Billy Graham "planted a mustard seed" of faith in young George W. Bush that grew into his powerful religious conversion.

My experience on that beach that evening was a little different. I was halfway down the beach walking in the general direction of the Bush property. Out of the shadows from the north end of the beach I saw the silhouette of a young man, probably in his early twenties, slowly emerge. As he approached me, he inquired if I "had a light," which I did not. We exchanged pleasantries briefly before he said, "Would you care to have sex?" For a sixteen-year-old virginal boy from Dayton, Ohio, in 1962, a "real homosexual" was more frightening than any horror movie. In a bizarre mix of genuine stupidity, bad grammar, and quick thinking, I looked around and said, "Where? With who?" The young man gently said, "Never mind. Be good," and sauntered back in the general direction from which he had come.

The gay man seemed quite relaxed and matter-of-fact about the whole thing. I, on the other hand, was anything but calm, cool, or collected. I panicked and ran, blindly and wildly down the beach in the opposite direction from the young man, as if I were trying to get away from a terrible contagion that was fast on my heels. To this day, I have no memory of when I stopped running, how far I went, or even of driving home. But the utterly irrational, total sense of terror was something that I never forgot.

Sex titillates Americans, but sex also makes many Americans anxious. In fact, it can make them very anxious. They feel uncomfortable and even assaulted when confronted with sexual behavior of any kind. People hate what makes them anxious, and many become indignant about sex for that reason.

Sexual issues are highly explosive and can be very powerful tools for gaslighting, whether they pertain to heterosexual or homosexual sex. While most Americans have handled their sexual anxiety with more personal aplomb than I did that night on Kennebunk Beach, in the last two presidential elections, many Americans have run away from sexual anxiety much like I did. It is arguable that but for sexual fright, George Bush would never have been reelected president.

In politics, sex can be used to associate feelings of disgust with a political candidate that no politician can survive unscathed. Sex can also be used to create anxiety in voters that can divert voters' attention away from other, more important issues. Instead of making their decisions based on important policy issues, voters base their decisions on largely irrelevant, but emotionally perplexing, sexual matters. Yes, sex always gets attention, but if in the marketplace sex sells, in the political world sex repels.

In 2000, the mental image of presidential semen on a blue dress never dry-cleaned created a visceral reaction in many Americans. It hung like a cloud over the 2000 election, and it permitted George Bush to assume the unchallenged role of moral reformer in the race for the White House. Bush promised to "restore honor and dignity to the presidency"[2] even though he admitted to leading a debauched life himself until his fortieth birthday, when his wife reportedly threatened to leave him if he did not stop drinking. Al Gore was left as collateral damage despite a scandal-free reputation and his wife's outspoken stand against violent, sexually aggressive, misogynistic lyrics in music marketed to teenagers, which had earned her the enmity of the record industry.

This emphasis on the private sex life of politicians is an American phenomenon. The Monica Lewinsky scandal shocked Europeans, too, though not because a political figure had a clandestine affair with a younger woman. What Europeans found shocking was America's reaction to the events. The intensity of the sexual disgust and the outrage generated was astonishing to people abroad, for whom such behavior by their elected officials has long been dismissed as irrelevant to civic duties. In France, for instance, it was common knowledge that President François

Mitterrand had had a mistress and an illegitimate child. It was not even noteworthy from a political perspective. The French were upset only when the mistress and child publicly attended Mitterrand's funeral, breaching a long-standing tradition that mistresses do not attend public events.[3]

This difference between European and American attitudes is not explainable by any greater fidelity American presidents have demonstrated over their European counterparts. Presidents Roosevelt, Eisenhower, Kennedy, and Clinton all are now widely believed to have had extramarital sexual relations while president. Putting aside rumors of George H. W. Bush's long-standing infidelity with Jennifer Fitzgerald, dubbed Bush's "White House wife," and Lyndon Johnson's rumored affairs with Alice Glass and others, and assuming no unpublicized sexual infidelity by other presidents, the White House has still been inhabited by a known philanderer nearly half of the last seventy-five years.

Nonetheless, in America, sex creates an emotional political battleground state with powerful implications. When sexuality is in play it creates palpable anxiety, disgust, and a preoccupation that preempts other concerns. Bill Clinton's behavior with Lewinsky did all of that. The image of Clinton and Lewinsky engaged in oral sex made people anxious, and many responded by turning their anxiety to disgust and hatred. The power and saliency of sex turned the Clinton misadventure into a political third rail. The fact that three of Clinton's chief accusers at the time—GOP Congressmen Henry Hyde, Robert Livingston, and Newt Gingrich—have all confessed to having extramarital affairs did little to attenuate the reaction to Clinton.[4] Nor did it make people appreciate that much political gaslighting is conceived in hypocrisy.

To put this reaction to Clinton's sexual escapade with Monica Lewinsky in context, there was no corresponding sense of outrage or disgust when members of the Bush administration exposed CIA agent Valerie Plame, apparently for sheer political revenge. Their actions put at risk our efforts in the war on terror as well as the life of Ms. Plame and other CIA agents. Ironically, Ms. Plame was responsible for U.S. efforts to prevent nuclear proliferation, the concern used to justify our invasion of Iraq in the first place. By exposing her identity, the Bush administration compromised our efforts to prevent nuclear disaster and released information potentially helpful to our enemies. Any distinction between that and treason is very subtle, indeed.

When the leak was first made public, the president promised America that if any members of his administration were involved, they would be taken care of.[5] In doing so, Bush clearly acknowledged the disclosure was reprehensible and illegal. Implicit in all of this was that he, Bush, had no knowledge of how Ms. Plame's identity was revealed. When it was discovered that Karl Rove, Dick Cheney, and Cheney's chief of staff, Lewis "Scooter" Libby, had discussed Plame with reporters, however, Bush stepped forward and said that he had authorized the declassification of her position, so what they had done was not a crime because it did not involve leaking "classified information."[6] When vice presidential aide Scooter Libby was convicted of perjury on the matter, Bush stepped forward to commute the sentence so that Libby would not have to spend any time in jail.

Either Bush had already declassified the information when he told the American public there would be no mercy for anyone leaking the information, or he had not. One way or the other, the president was contradictory about his role in a national security breach that threatened our country's efforts to protect us from nuclear weapons falling into the wrong hands. Had any private citizen done this, he or she would most likely be in prison. This, not oral sex, is what our founding fathers intended with their criteria for impeachment of a president. If deliberately undermining the national security from nuclear attack is not a high crime, it is difficult to understand what is.

But with no sex involved, the reaction differed not just in degree but in nature. Even those who found the Plame action reprehensible never expressed the repugnance that was so much a part of the Lewinsky scandal. Clinton was impeached, not Bush. Such is the power of sex on the American mind.

On October 14, 2006, Republican congressman Mark Foley of Florida was exposed for having written sexual e-mails to congressional pages. That same day, the medical journal *Lancet* published a study concluding that over 650,000 Iraqis, far more than previous American estimates, had died as a result of the U.S. invasion of Iraq.[7] A few days later, then-House Speaker Dennis Hastert was attacked with demands for his resignation because of his failure to exercise appropriate oversight—not over the Iraq war, but over the would-be pedophile.[8] The death toll of Iraqis disappeared from the news, totally preempted by the lurid, but comparatively insignificant story about Representative Foley. Americans were more concerned about the possibility of a pervert scurrying around the Capitol than they were about learning that America's attempt to liberate Iraq from a ruthless dictator who had killed tens of thousands of Kurds had wound up killing many times more Iraqis than the tyrant from whom they were being "rescued." Representative Foley's behavior was, of course, inappropriate and warranted severe sanction, but the deaths of 650,000 people might presumably have been more newsworthy. Instead, news coverage of Foley went on for weeks, and the several hundred thousand lost lives received no further attention.

This was not simply American parochialism at play. When sexuality becomes part of a story, it preempts everything else, even significant matters of life and death. The lurid forms of sexual humiliation used on Iraqi prisoners at Abu Ghraib overshadowed concern for both Americans and Iraqis killed in Iraq. The level of disgust and outrage generated by the pictures of naked Iraqi men being dominated and humiliated by male and female American soldiers at Abu Ghraib exceeded any protest previously expressed, even over the accounts of torture at Guantánamo Bay prison or the ghoulish treatment of the bodies of *our own* dead soldiers by the enemy. With sex, people are catapulted into a new reality that focuses their reaction on the immediate sexual themes to the exclusion of other seemingly more significant issues. This makes sexual material fertile soil for gaslighters.

The use of sexual innuendo and rumor in political campaigns has a long and sordid history. Allegations of Thomas Jefferson's African American slave mistress and child were used against him in whisper campaigns. In the presidential campaign of 1884, Grover Cleveland's alleged illegitimate child inspired one of the more famous political jingles of the nineteenth century: "Momma, Momma, where is Pa? Gone to the White House, ha ha ha."[9]

But the advent of mass media has made America's vulnerability to sexual titillation and sexual fear far greater. For the last two decades, at critical election junctures, the American public has been preoccupied with psychologically perplexing, but irrelevant, issues about sex that have helped shape the course of elections, often trumping important concerns about national policy. In 1988, Senator Gary Hart's sexual liaison with a young woman, Donna Rice, sank his presidential primary candidacy. That same year, images of a convicted rapist, Willie Horton, became the most vividly remembered part of the general election. In the 1992 elections, then-candidate Bill Clinton's liaison with Gennifer Flowers became a pivotal issue in the New Hampshire primary, and his relationship with Monica Lewinsky was the biggest story of his second term as president. In 2004, gay marriage was surpassed only by the Iraq War for news attention.

Sexual innuendo is particularly effective in political campaigns. It can serve many functions. First, as the vignettes above indicate, it can be a powerful tool for character assassination. The psychological mechanisms by which this is done go beyond the apparent rational significance of sexual behavior because of the visceral reaction sex creates in the minds of the public. Ultimately, it became difficult for people to look at Bill Clinton without picturing some aspect of the relationship he had with Monica Lewinsky, whether it was imagery of the presidential semen, the gossip about the shape of the president's penis, or the often unflattering portraits of Ms. Lewinsky. The incessant references to the specifics did not demand much guesswork for the game of Clue. It was oral sex, in the oval office, with the cigar.

While Hillary Clinton was incorrect in attributing the entire episode to the "vast right-wing conspiracy," there is every reason to believe that a vast right-wing conspiracy understood the psychological, political gold mine the Lewinsky matter meant to them and used it on the American public to divert the public's attention from the real issues confronting the nation. For example, Americans seem to have forgotten that during the time the Lewinsky affair was usurping the headlines, President Clinton attacked terrorist organizations in Afghanistan and Sudan. When he did so, he was accused of trying to divert attention from the Lewinsky matter.[10] After 9/11, these same critics alleged that Clinton had been so focused on Lewinsky that he had ignored the terrorist threat entirely and blamed him for 9/11.[11] Subsequent reports from those involved have shown that the incoming Bush administration was far less interested in Al Qaeda than the outgoing Clinton staff had been.

But why are we so vulnerable to these sexually based manipulations? To understand that, one must understand the multiple roles sex plays and the unique problems it creates for the mind. One of the most important things our reality sense has to do is tell us who we are and how we fit into the world. There is nothing more fundamental to that process than our sexual identity, that is, our sense of maleness or femaleness (not whether someone is straight or gay). Gender identity is a critical element that gives definition to people's sense of who they are. This is why one of the strongest needs of childhood is to emulate an adult male or an adult female. Being like mommy or daddy or some similar role model is extremely important. One is a male, or one is a female. This gender identification forms the scaffolding for one's sense of self, on which one can eventually build an adult identity. Without that solid identification with gender–whether male or female–we feel confused and disoriented.

The problem with all this is that as helpful as it might be for people to have a clear gender identity–being unquestionably male or female and unquestionably gay or straight—nature does not provide that kind of absolute clarity for either gender or sexual orientation. Instead, as sex researcher Alfred Kinsey discovered, there are dramatic differences in the way human beings function sexually along these dimensions.[12] Kinsey noticed in his early research with the gall wasp that there was surprising variability to the way gall wasps mated. His research on human sexuality was largely structured around a hypothesis that the same would be true with human beings. It was.

What Kinsey found, relevant to our purposes here, is that what are often assumed to be polar opposites—masculine/feminine, for example, and gay/straight—are by no means that. Instead, most people are a mix of masculine and feminine, gay and straight, although typically one pole or the other along the two dimensions will predominate and dictate how people define themselves. This lack of certainty creates some understandable tension for a mind that requires self-definition to feel secure. It is as if people have to convince themselves they are something they really are not—all male or all female, all straight or all gay.

These ambiguities in sexual identity create three basic challenges for people sexually. First, are they fundamentally adequate in the way they play their sexual role as men or women? The burdens placed on Americans in this regard are staggering. Advertising and Hollywood suggest that if you cannot walk into a bar and become the immediate object of desire for an attractive member of the opposite sex, you are an outcast with limited value.

Americans are on the one hand constantly titillated by sex, but on the other made to feel never fully adequate because of this kind of vicarious experience from TV, movies, and advertising. As a way of life, this is not pleasant, a fact that colors how Americans respond to sexual material in all contexts. For many, the very notion of sex raises threatening questions of personal adequacy. It was this need for exaggerated sexual prowess that President Bush was trying to address for his constituency when he landed "Top Gun" style on the USS *Abraham Lincoln.*

Second, the problem of gender adequacy infects relationships between the sexes by burdening them with questions of superiority and adequacy. Given people's tendency to project and confuse their inner with their outer, trying to stabilize a "balance of power" between men and women is understandably very difficult. When people ask, for example, "Is America ready for a woman president?" they are asking a question about this psychological turf. What they are really asking is, "Can people's need for gender stability now tolerate the ambiguity that people will feel if there is true gender equality?" Are Americans able to be comfortable in a world in which women are assessed on merit rather than the restrictive historical roles used to fortify insecurities in gender roles, for men and, in some cases, women?

It is ironic that in all of Freud's work the only place that envy receives much attention is in the sexual adequacy area, where Freud contended that women want the one thing Freud had that they did not have: to wit, a penis. The suggestion that women envy men sexually more than men envy women, in my clinical experience, is simply wrong. In Texas it was at one time legally justifiable homicide for a man to kill his wife if he caught her in bed with another man. This attitude not only reflects a double standard, it also suggests that men have a very hard time with threats to their sexual adequacy posed by their spouse's infidelity.

Struggles with sexual adequacy affect both sexes, and members of both sexes can sexually envy each other. Attitudes about the relative value of one's gender come in all sizes, shapes, and forms. In reacting to feelings of inadequacy, one can either idealize or denigrate the differences between men and women. Misogynists and man-haters both exist, as do women who feel they cannot live without a man and men who confuse women with their mother. The tensions can run in many different directions.

Whatever progress may have been made in recent years in gender equality, there can be little doubt that America has been heavily dominated by white, heterosexual males. Just because white males have had the upper hand, however, does not mean that they are free from worries about adequacy and competency. Far from it. Paradoxically, there is nothing that makes this clearer than spousal abuse. In my clinical work, I have worked with court-monitored spousal abusers both individually and in couples' treatment. While it goes without saying that it is horrifying for anyone to have to live with a person who inflicts violence on them, the most clinically prominent feature of spousal abuse is the gross and highly defective sexual self-esteem *of the perpetrator.*

In his deepest mental realm, the spousal abuser feels sexually inferior to the woman because she does not appear to him to suffer the same deficit in her sexuality that the man experiences in his. His feelings of inferiority gain such intensity that in the warped mind of the perpetrator, physical violence is necessary to restore a semblance of self-respect. This never works, of course, and as a result the abuser just adds the humiliation of beating someone physically weaker than himself to his feelings of inferiority, exacerbating the downward spiral of the spousal abuser's self-esteem. He then projects blame for his own self-loathing onto the woman and the situation deteriorates further. These escalations in the cycle of violence make domestic violence increasingly dangerous and even deadly.

The difficulty of sexual adequacy can play a significant role in the seemingly puzzling ways many people vote as well. For instance, a man who is eager to find reinforcement for his masculinity experiences a visceral lift from carrying a gun. If someone stepped in to take his gun away, he would feel a loss of potency and feel anxious. In fact, judging by voting patterns, many male voters feel that having a gun is more important than health care and schools for their family. And it is much more immediate and personal than most other issues. The debates over gay marriage and gun control in recent elections presented many men with the prospect, at least symbolically, that one's marital bed could just as well be filled by a gay man at the same time someone is making off with his gun. For someone concerned with genital adequacy and sexual identity, economic issues or foreign policy are simply not as immediately relevant or compelling.

The same masculine inadequacy that arises in cases of spousal abuse is also apparent in hateful homophobic attitudes. Exaggerated heterosexuality is used to support a flagging sense of adequacy about gender identity, even if one is not gay or "latently gay." We see desperate attempts at this strategy in some of the horrible hate crimes against gays. Young men who are uncertain of their male adequacy try to show how "not gay" they are by abusing gays. For boys still developing a sexual identity and the confidence that goes with it, homosexuality can be very frightening.

In fact, the dynamic between heterosexuals and homosexuals is no less problematic than that between men and women. The public's reaction to homosexuality played an important role both in the 2004 elections and in the early years of the Clinton presidency.

Fifteen years after my experience on Kennebunk Beach, I was a young clinical psychologist in North Carolina. In my practice, I was treating several gay men and lesbians. I had been trained in the conventional psychoanalytic theory of the day that homosexuality was a sexual perversion.[13] The readings I remember most clearly were those written by an orthodox psychoanalyst from the then-prestigious Columbia University Center's Psychoanalytic Center, Dr. Charles Socarides.[14] Dr. Socarides, in sophisticated psychoanalytic parlance, explained that homosexuality was a condition caused by a cold and distant father and a domineering mother. The gay male, according to Socarides, was trying to find the powerful father and escape the controlling engulfing mother by contorting the normal desire for the opposite sex into one for the same sex.

Theory can present an illusion of understanding, and if it is endorsed by an established, self-described professional elite of orthodox medical psychoanalysis, it has a seductive allure to the young therapist. As a result, several decades of psychoanalysts were trained in Socarides' explanation for homosexuality. Other schools of treatment held similarly damaging views of homosexuality.

My own anxiety over homosexuality that was driven home so vividly that night in Kennebunk seemed at odds with the explanations that I had read from Socarides. My anxiety seemed to be exactly that: *my* anxiety. It was as if I were going to be caught by a contagion or by a bogeyman that was going to do something terrible beyond words. At the same time, the young men I treated who were conflicted about their homosexual orientation had a very different experience. They were aroused by the homosexual "contagion," not terrified of it. It seemed to me that the pathogenic element in all of them, if any, was my fear, and not the gay man's lust.

At the same time, clinically, I was learning that the sex drive of gay male patients felt like bedrock in their psychological makeup, just as heterosexual libido did in the heterosexual. I did not see patients confusing gay lovers with a powerful and longed-for father. Instead, what I saw most frequently were people at war with their own most basic sex drive. They were constantly hearing that their sexuality was bad and disgusting. Their conflict was the fear of the social and familial consequences of being gay in a culture that was terrified of gayness. Realizing one was gay was like suddenly turning black in an all-white, apartheid society.

Clinically, in working with gay males, what I found was that the more I was able to help the patient identify the trauma that he encountered because of these hostile reactions to his sexual drive, many of which he assumed were justified, the less anxiety and self-loathing he experienced. At the same time, the homosexual desire that had once been inhibited by conflict and riddled with anxiety took on a fuller and richer experience and was largely indistinguishable from the quality of sexual feeling that heterosexuals experienced. Growing up in an oppressive regime where one's core experience—that is, of oneself as a sexual being—meant derision, scorn, and self-loathing in many cases had taken an enormous toll on all aspects of the gay patient.

The problem, however, was not that homosexuality was pathology; the problem was that heterosexuality was so threatened by homosexuality that our heterosexual culture needed to

conquer, destroy, and vilify it. It was as if a "homosexual contagion" was out to get a frightened heterosexual, and the heterosexual had to resort to a fight-or-flight response.

Set in this context, Socarides' work increasingly felt to me like
a terrible assault on the mental stability of gay men and lesbians.
The message gay men were given was not that I, the heterosexual
male, was anxious at the prospect of someone being different
from me and/or possibly wanting to possess me in a way that I
did not want to be possessed. Instead, it was that you, a gay male,
are deviant for feeling the way you do. This "deviancy," of course,
occurred in the deepest layers of their being: their sexuality.

Orthodox psychoanalysis was not the only would-be savior for
gay men and lesbians during this time. There were other schools
of treatment with competing approaches and techniques, all of
which were inflicted on gay men and lesbians. Behaviorists approached homosexuality as a behavior to be "extinguished" by
aversive conditioning. In one treatment approach, gay men were
shown pictures of both men and women. When they were
shown the male pictures they were administered an electric
shock in the hope this would extinguish the sexual response to
the same-sex pictures by the gay male. Not surprisingly, this approach did have the effect of making gays anxious about their
sexuality in general, but it did little to rechannel their sexual drive
in the direction of enjoyable heterosexual sex.

These approaches continue today under different names like
"reparative therapy," in which these presumably "broken" men
can be "repaired." Increasingly, within the mental health community, the treatments were exposed as little more than social prejudice against gay men and lesbians garbed in psychological
accoutrements.

Of course, the mental health field was complicit in all of this since it labeled homosexuality a mental disease. In 1973, many members of the American Psychiatric Association wanted to remove homosexuality from its list of psychiatric diseases, the *Diagnostic and Statistical Manual* (DSM). This was very controversial at the time and the resolution of the controversy was that the APA substituted a new disease–"ego dystonic homosexuality"–for the original disease of plain old "homosexuality." The modifier "ego dystonic" meant that homosexuality was an illness if the gay male was bothered by his homosexuality.

Under the new diagnostic code, every gay who was conflicted about being gay had a psychiatric disease, ego dystonic homosexuality. Those who were not so conflicted did not. This was a political compromise that was intended to let those who did not want to view their sexual orientation as pathological do so, while maintaining a psychopathological rationale for treating homosexuality as a mental disorder. The theory was that this would work well clinically because if one did not see the homosexuality as a problem, they probably would not have entered treatment for it anyway, and they did not have to be stigmatized by a mental health diagnostic code that characterized their regular sex life as a psychiatric impairment. This had the significant side effect of making a mockery of the notion that homosexuality was a disease at all.

The clinical reality was that for the most part after the patient got over the painful issues created by social stigma, the conflicts about the homosexuality were more political than psychological in nature. Those of us in the clinical field were much more likely to encounter an ostensibly heterosexual person who became vastly more comfortable once he accepted that he was gay than we were to find a putatively gay man who was more comfortable once he came to grips with his heterosexuality. And yet the disease nomenclature suggested just the opposite. If mental health professionals only treated recognized diseases, they could treat a man who was living a gay life who wanted to be straight, but we could not justify treating a man living a straight life who was in fact gay.

The psychological research on homosexuality provided no support for the notion that being gay was pathological regardless of how the gay man or lesbian felt about his or her homosexuality. Psychological testing revealed no differences between gay men and heterosexual men. Study after study revealed that gays represented a consistent percentage of the population across all cultures, and the incidence of homosexuality varied little, if any, by virtue of cultural mores, laws, or social customs. There were no symptoms of any psychopathology or neuroticism that correlated with being gay. And, yes, there were even studies suggesting that pedophilia is predominantly a disease that afflicts married heterosexual men, not homosexuals. In the late 1980s, after extensive hearings, the APA eliminated any mention of homosexuality in its list of mental diseases, the latest version of which was the DSM-III-R.

The end of the disease notion of homosexuality, of course, did not end the problem of public attitudes toward gay men and lesbians. Shortly after his election in 1992, President Clinton tried to keep one of his campaign promises to the gay community by supporting the elimination of barriers to gays serving in the military. From a civil rights perspective, the strategy of the gay community was understandable. Immediately after World War II, discrimination against African Americans became much harder to justify after thousands of them had served with distinction during the war. The success of all-black outfits, which were established at the urging of black civil rights leaders, such as the Tuskegee Airmen, provided strong evidence that the prewar attitude that blacks were unfit for combat was simple prejudice. Gays were hoping to repeat that discrimination-smashing precedent.

The strategy backfired because it was based on a faulty understanding of the mental problem homosexuality triggered in the heterosexual. Clinton's efforts on behalf of gays ran into a buzz saw of opposition from the military leadership, who contended that letting gay men and lesbians join the military would create unspecified morale problems. In one sense they were right. Integrating gays into the military might create problems—not from predatory gays, but rather from anxious straights. Some heterosexuals are truly rendered unfit to serve with homosexuals because of the terror they experience when confronted with homosexuality. Homophobia is especially problematic in the foxhole, where men often have to take care of other men and nurture them. If a heterosexual is homophobic, the whole concept of nurturing a male can take on a frightening quality. The presence of homosexuals in the same foxhole could make the anxiety unbearable for some of these heterosexual soldiers.

The "don't ask, don't tell" policy exposed the fact it is not the homosexual who is not fit for duty; instead, it is the heterosexuals' reaction to gays that is problematic. Heterosexual homophobia is by no means an untreatable illness, but it is hard to treat if it is not identified as the true problem. Identifying the homophobic response would also ease the frightening burden of homophobia for heterosexual members of the armed forces. Equally important, desensitizing heterosexuals to their fear could help the military take advantage of the skills that uncloseted gay men and lesbians could provide to the military.

Because America is not doing that, our country is losing talented servicepeople at a time when military ranks are already very thin. The military has already expelled several dozen Farsi interpreters from the military because of its restrictive policies about gays in the military. This comes at a time when intelligence officials say that America's limited number of Farsi interpreters is seriously hampering our war on terror.[15]

As problematic as the gays in the military issue was during the Clinton administration, it was nothing compared to the psychological fallout caused by the Massachusetts Supreme Court's November 2003 decision upholding the right of gays to marry. When San Francisco allowed gays the same right without a court order, they flocked to city hall for marriage licenses. As a result, for several months before the 2004 presidential election, voters were confronted with television news showing same-sex couples kissing as they completed their wedding ceremony. *People participate vicariously in what they see.* It was impossible for heterosexual viewers to experience the picture of gays kissing romantically without imagining, consciously or otherwise, being threatened with a homosexual experience themselves. The visceral experience this created for heterosexuals was of them being kissed passionately on the lips by members of the same sex. The terrifying contagion was going to get them.

For a heterosexual, this can be both repulsive and frightening. The image of gays marrying and the recurring image of gays kissing on national TV was an emotional trauma the immediacy of which simply preempted all other concerns in the minds of a significant segment of the voting population. It was like the trauma I felt that night on Kennebunk Beach. For many, sexual trauma can cut very, very deeply.

Like other political gaslighters, Karl Rove and his various campaign staffs have been accused of making widespread use of sexual perplexity: questioning the sexual orientation of his adversaries, planting rumors that some were pedophiles, and making other specific allegations of a sexual nature.[16] George Bush's 1994 gubernatorial campaign against Ann Richards included a whisper campaign that Governor Richards was gay. As Governor Richards said, "I knew I'd be accused of sleeping with every man in the state, but I didn't realize it would be every woman too."[17] The issue did not have to be true to take effect. For heterosexuals, the physical disgust they *experience* at the *thought* of Ann Richards having sex with another woman was enough to taint her with that association even if it was not true. The connection is made in the mind, the mental experience of her lesbianism is mentally implanted, and the damage is done.

Ann Coulter's characterization of John Edwards as a "faggot" in March 2007, while widely repudiated by conservatives as well as liberals, no matter how loathsome to many, planted the association of John Edwards as gay in many minds.[18] Try not to think of a pink elephant.

However, it was not just the experiential component that made the gay marriage issue so explosive. Psychologically, sanctifying a gay marital bed further blurred the boundaries that separated heterosexuals from homosexuals and made many heterosexuals feel vulnerable to the terrifying contagion. The symbolic protective buffer between "us and them" created by the marital rights discrimination against gays was further eroded by the idea of gay marriage.

In response to all this, amendments banning gay marriage sprung up in seventeen states, especially in states where the presidential race was expected to be very close. There they served as lightning rods drawing affected voters to the polls and to Republican candidates. If Karl Rove had wanted a more effective issue to divert many voters' attention from the Iraq War, the looming federal deficit, or any other policy-related issue, nothing could have been more effective than gay marriage. Any policy or political party that seems to offer a protection from that anxiety will be forgiven many sins if it can deliver on that one promise. By comparison, all other previously important public policy issues become less emotionally immediate and of less importance.

Since one's sexual orientation is never an absolute, many Americans are very frightened by homosexuality because it raises the specter of losing the important mental security of a clearly defined and firm sexual orientation. Clinging to a member of the opposite sex in an exclusive marital club of heterosexuals is a palliative for individuals who are made fearful by the existence of an alternative sexual orientation. Gay marriage smashes that protective buffer and creates considerable perplexity for heterosexuals. This was a dynamic in play throughout the 2004 election. Pictures of gay men and women usurped attention that more rationally could have been devoted to health care, the environment, and national security. While "flip-flopping" may have been on everyone's lips, pictures of men kissing men and women kissing women created a stunningly visceral reaction that left many people silently traumatized.

The gay issue continues to be divisive and with understandable reason. Americans are becoming more certain of their position on homosexuality—but they are dividing into two groups that are moving in opposite directions from each other. Some feel more comfortable with it while others feel more repulsed. In the mass media, movies such as *Brokeback Mountain* and television shows like *Six Feet Under* and *Brothers and Sisters* depict explicit gay sex. This has two very different effects on viewers. Those people whose anxiety is not so intense that it prevents them from watching the shows gradually find that their homophobic anxiety is reduced. Others, in contrast, are repulsed and turn away. Their negative attitudes toward gay men and lesbians are only intensified.

Thus, our country has become more polarized on the issue of homosexuality. Some are made more comfortable by exposure to it, while others are upset, even incensed, feeling that the country's moral decline is only accelerating. The effect of these wedge issues goes way beyond a particular political election. They have a terribly divisive impact on the country because what is at stake psychologically feels so profound that it is hard for people just to say "live and let live." People who feel shocked rather than enlightened by the entertainment industry now target it as part of a liberal and corrupting culture. Many of them even boycotted the Academy Awards presentations, an annual ritual that used to be "as American as apple pie."[19]

The dividing line of political correctness has become clearer and more absolute for many Americans. The problem is that now Americans are fighting over which side of the line is virtuous. In truth, however, this is a war over emotional experiences, not moral values.

For a country that is already in a paranoid state, sexual perplexity, much of it artificially created for political purposes, compounds the difficulty. Paranoia leaves people confused about
what is real and what is not real. Sexual perplexity distracts people from the real political issues that affect their day-to-day lives.
The reality of people's inner world is deliberately stimulated to
overpower their objective assessment of external reality. Thus,
Americans fight the ghosts of largely nonexistent sexual issues
at the polls while ignoring issues of war, health, education, environment, and the economy. These are simply less urgent to the
psyche of a voter assailed by an unconscious psychological desta-
bilization that requires attention and resolution. This is sexual
perplexity.

The third battleground state, envy, is a raw emotion that can
be channeled by a clever political gaslighter into a torrential hatred directed against a political opponent, a group—such as the
poor or liberals—or a foreign country. When these three emotional states—paranoia, sexual perplexity, and envy—are all in play
at the same time, as they have been in America, irrational, self-
destructive, and ineffective policy is almost inevitable.

CHAPTER 5
STATES OF CONFUSION: ENVY

When Envy breeds unkind division:
There comes the ruin, there begins confusion.

—SHAKESPEARE, Henry VI

We have all heard them. A penetrating voice filled with indignant disgust indicts a political rival for immoral or corrupt behavior. A staccato cadence and grainy film lend a dramatic and sinister quality to the ad. Implicit in the message is that we, too, should feel a self-righteous contempt for the candidate. It is both a liberating rationale and a compelling invitation to hate.

We are astonished such negative campaign ads keep working election cycle after election cycle. High-minded politicians tell us they are confident the public is tired of negative campaigning and this time around want to hear something more constructive from their candidates.

And yet the ads continue, and they continue to work. The most famous ad during the 2006 midterm elections targeted Harold Ford, a black Democratic senatorial candidate from Tennessee with a relatively scandal-free reputation. Ford was accused of cavorting with Playboy bunnies, implying that his morality was, at best, loose. No facts supported this assertion except that Ford did attend a party at a football game sponsored by

Playboy magazine. But a seductive blonde looked into the camera with a come-hither gaze and said, "Call me, Harold." Ford lost.

Another ad alleged that Rep. Michael Arcuri (D-NY) called telephone sex operators at taxpayers' expense. Phone bills make it clear that an aide misdialed a telephone number and dialed the correct one a moment later. Arcuri won, but according to *Washington Post* columnist Robert Novak, Washington Republicans complained that his opponent didn't go "negative enough."[1]

In the 2004 presidential election, John Kerry, a decorated war hero, was portrayed as indecisive, cowardly, and unworthy of leading the country in a time of war. A maelstrom of argument ensued, but Kerry's campaign was derailed. Even though he was running against two men who had avoided military combat, Bush and Cheney, he lost.

There are countless other examples. In fact, there are few hard-fought elections in the country that do not prominently feature negative campaign tactics by at least one candidate. There is now little reason to doubt that negative campaigning is a fundamental part of our election process. The question is, if so many find it distasteful, why is it so effective?

Negative campaigning works because it harnesses the enormous blind energy of *envy*. The ads simultaneously loosen people's inhibitions against rage and stimulate an underappreciated, often totally unrecognized latent need people have to hate. The hatred is rooted in envy. To understand the power of negative campaigns one must understand envy.

Like perplexity, envy is one of those psychological words that loses its meaning because of its everyday usage. We talk about envy in such harmless contexts that it sounds innocuous, and we rarely think of it. We may briefly envy our neighbor's new car or promotion, but it rarely holds our attention and is not something that keeps us awake nights. It is a mild feeling that quickly passes, and, if we notice it at all we feel mildly embarrassed at having such a petty feeling and quickly move on to other thoughts.

But envy deserves closer attention. It is one of the least-discussed human emotions. Even in the mental health field, the psychological study of envy has had a curious history that reflects the difficulty people have confronting it. Melanie Klein, a British psychoanalyst (1882–1960), was the first psychoanalytic theorist to write extensively on envy.[2] When she tried to introduce her work in the United States, she was greeted with hostility from her colleagues in the American Psychoanalytic Association and her important work was both denigrated and dismissed. While rigid theoretical orthodoxy was not unusual in the history of the American Psychoanalytic Association, it has been particularly pronounced in the interrelated areas pertaining to self-esteem, envy, and narcissism. It has only been in the last three decades that these important areas have been widely accepted as legitimate areas of psychoanalytic inquiry within the American Psychoanalytic Association.

Yet envy is as fundamental to the mind as hunger is to the body. In fact, envy *is* frustrated psychological hunger. To really see envy firsthand, we can watch a young infant. The infant's first interactions with the world center predominantly around issues of hunger and feeding. When babies are hungry, they feel an emptiness and a craving. They protest, cry, and ultimately scream until their need for milk is met. They then feel satiated . . . for a while.

The paradigm of wanting something, feeling frustrated, and getting angry is one that is established very early on in life and stays with people throughout their lives. If I have a hunger for something that I do not get, I feel a pang, I make a demand, I get angry, and I feel hatred toward the source of my frustration. That hatred can remain inside a person long after the original source of the frustration is gone. And, for reasons we will discuss, it can be redirected toward new objects that have nothing to do with the original source of the deprivation and resentment.

This paradigm and the inevitable accumulation of hatred it creates are core to the feeling of envy. Whether one looks to the evolutionary importance of eating or to the fact that eating was the cause of Adam and Eve's ejection from the Garden of Eden, it is inarguable that what we eat, how we get the food, and who gives it to us are very important, even primal, aspects of human experience.

Greed is the flip side of envy. People try to assuage their envious rage by getting what they want. This is greed. When people acquire something, their greed is temporarily satisfied and the envy abates. But the ongoing paradigmatic response to deprivation is ingrained and plays out over and over again in people's daily lives. The extent of anger it generates will vary according to the individual and to the individual's circumstances, but it is always there.

What could Americans have to be envious of? Despite our national pockets of poverty, most Americans participate heavily in a vast consumer economy their parents never imagined. While Americans are criticized around the world for their crass materialism, this misses the point of the American predicament. The phrase "consumer-driven economy" is a terrible misnomer. Americans are in fact in a *market*-driven economy in which their economic system depends on marketers' ability to convince "consumers" that the consumers want the new products being manufactured. In short, the economic system depends on a whole culture in which people are made to feel there is something they want but do not have, so they will buy it.

Americans are constantly being targeted by greed makers, but they are rarely able to keep up with the desires that are being created. We are stimulated around the clock through every medium in our culture to feel there is something we want but do not have. It is a constant stimulation of the very same impulse people had as infants when it was time to feed. It is a need to nurse gone wild. It is no wonder that Americans walk around in a chronic state of feeling they need more. Our envious craving is the fuel that makes our economy run.

Envy and greed are the feelings the baby has when it craves what is inside the mother, either in the breast or in the bottle. Ultimately, the child's ability to feel satiated and to have his needs met will define his self-esteem. *Envy bears a direct connection to self-esteem.*[3] On its most primitive level, *feeling* full and good is *being* full and good. If hunger is being constantly restimulated, people are in a constant state of agitation and their self-esteem is in a constant state of flux.

Envy is not limited to crass greed for material objects. Other, invisible forms of envy are more insidious. At the core of our reality sense and central to our vulnerability to envy are our feelings about ourselves. One important question that our reality sense must answer is who we are and how we rate in the areas of self-worth, lovability, and the whole host of measures by which we assess ourselves. Being cool, physically attractive, and sexy are all attributes that people are made to feel over and over again they must have in order to feel secure in the world. And, judging just by television and the movies, most people in the world are re-markably more attractive than we are.

People envy those who appear to have those things that they themselves do not have, whether they are material possessions or personal attributes. When they suffer a blow to their self-esteem, they feel painfully deflated. When they suffer that deflation to any significant degree, they harbor latent resentments that can be readily transformed into powerful rage. This makes envy a pow-erful source of latent hatred. Unmet self-esteem wishes lead to frustration and rage. And there are a lot of unmet self-esteem wishes in the American "culture of narcissism."

Envy also extends to people who conspicuously move in dif-ferent circles than others do, who appear more "with it." The in-tense rage directed in some circles at "liberals," for example, reflects a feeling, actively encouraged by hate-filled radio, that some liberals feel superior and have something others do not have. Thus, people are encouraged to resent them. The political consequences are obvious.

Many Americans, as events and issues become more confus-ing, feel envy about the understanding others appear to have but they lack. In today's world, people can be envious of others who appear to understand the world better than they do, who appear more certain of their place in the world, or who appear more confident of their ability to exert control over parts of that world. Not being able to understand the world and the events that are happening evokes powerful surges of envy and inferiority. It gives people a vague sense of there being something wrong with them when they feel confused or uncertain.

This is the source of the latent need to hate that is created by envy. As the world becomes less and less comprehensible—which

Americans are feeling to an ever greater extent—we inevitably develop a particularly aggressive set of feelings toward others who seem to understand this increasingly complex world, or at least act as though they do. This is envy.

This particular form of envy can also introduce a decided anti-intellectualism into the public arena as people channel their envious rage into an arbitrary and defiant know-nothingness. This is apparent in the increasing disdain shown to complex scientific concepts that we can only understand from someone who "knows more" than we do. Evolution, for example, is a truly bizarre concept to a lay person. To picture our own body emerging out of the carcass of a hairy ape, which is what evolution is to millions of people, is unsettling to say the least. If a powerful spokesperson attacks the scientist whose superior intellect makes us feel inferior and offers us a simplistic alternative to the complexity, coupled with a moralistic rationale for hating the scientist, it is a very tempting package to accept psychologically. The defiance it expresses also gives one a self-injected shot of superiority that will often look a great deal like smugness to others. This dynamic is at play in the often arrogant repudiation of scientific warnings about the environment.

To understand envy and its potential intensity, one has to look at it in multiple contexts that go beyond the everyday usage of the word as, for example, when one says they envy a colleague her new promotion. To see the forces of envy at play in broad daylight, simply go to a youth league sporting event and watch the more vocal parents. Many parents try to fulfill their own grandiose needs for self-affirmation through their children. Someone who feels their child is not being given the opportunity to fulfill those

needs will unleash blistering rage on anyone they hold responsible. Most youth coaches will recognize this issue quite quickly.
The mother of a Texas cheerleader was the target of a murder
plot engineered by an envious mother who reasoned that if she
killed one of her daughter's more successful rival's mother, it
would "depress" the successful cheerleader. Her own daughter
would then be able to take her place and the mother would herself experience the satisfaction she enviously assumed her intended victim must have enjoyed.

In a state of envy, one feels that someone else has something
they want and can aggressively reach inside them to take it.
News accounts recently described a woman, seemingly pregnant,
who lured another pregnant woman to her home ostensibly to
talk about their shared experience of pregnancy. Instead, she attempted to kill her. As it turned out, the assailant was feigning a
pregnancy with the help of some costume apparatus and had
been studying how to do a Cesarean delivery on the Internet.
Her plan had been to literally rob the woman of the baby that she
herself wanted, by taking it from the womb and raising it as her
own. In this case, the would-be victim actually prevailed in the
altercation and killed her assailant.[4]

While, obviously, most cases of envy are not this bizarre, envy
often does rear its head in very primitive forms. In Truman
Capote's *In Cold Blood,* one of the most gruesome, powerful, and
seemingly inexplicable scenes was when Perry Smith, the killer,
described his first victim, Mr. Clutter, with the following words: "I
didn't want to harm the man. I thought he was a nice gentleman.
Soft-spoken. I thought so right up to the moment I cut his
throat."[5] This was psychotic envy in its most primitive form.
Perry Smith at that moment experienced a shattering longing to

be the full and complete person that he imagined Clutter experienced himself as being. Perry so longed for that experience he could not tolerate it and, instead, destroyed it by slitting Mr. Clutter's throat. This is envy, when it has overthrown our mind's ability to process it and direct it. It comes out as pure hate. If envy can take this form of murderous rage, it is not hard to understand that milder forms can significantly disrupt rational thinking and behavior.

One can also see envy in a very destructive everyday form in organizational life. A prominent city manager with over twenty years of successful service and the recipient of numerous civic awards was resented by his mayor. The mayor was politically ambitious and saw the admiration and reputation of the city manager standing in his way of getting recognition that he hoped would further his own political career. His envy grew even greater when the city manager, a widower, married an extremely attractive former model. Aware of the tensions and thinking that it might be politically astute to share the attention his wedding would receive with his boss, the city manager asked the mayor to officiate at the wedding. It was a miscalculation. The proximity to the event only intensified the mayor's envy. Four months later on a Friday, the city manager walked into an after-hours council meeting that was called on very short notice and was told, without any reason given or charges levied, that he could resign or be fired immediately. The city manager was several months short of full pension vesting.

The city went for several months without a leader, progress was stopped, and continuity was lost. What had for the entire two decades of the young community's existence been an apolitical administration focusing on effective government became politicized and remained so until the mayor successfully ran for higher office. Over the next eight years after the mayor's self-motivated coup, four city managers came and went, reflecting the destabilizing effect the mayor had on city government. He cost the city great turmoil, but as with many gaslighters, he was never personally held accountable for the damage he had done. Gaslighters are destructive whether they are running a club, a business, or a nation.

Washington life is full of ambition, and frustrated ambition is quickly turned to destructive envy. Ambition for many in Washington is an attempt to fill very deep voids in feelings of self-worth and adequacy. In many political and quasipolitical organizations, there are not enough rewards to go around and the envy begins to drive key events with devastating results for the organizations. When people feel that someone else is receiving the attention or admiration that they crave, many lose their moral values and perspective.

In organizations, people who are actually competent are often the target of envy. In some cases, it is because these people receive the attention and accolades that others desperately hunger for. In other cases, it is the internal resources like self-confidence the achievers have that generate intolerable envy and make some want to destroy the source of their envy. The negative effect of this envy on organizational life cannot be overstated. In one scientific organization, a key scientist who was making critical contributions to his field was overshadowing a CEO who then embarked on a concerted effort to have the scientist removed, wasting badly needed organizational time and financial resources to do it. The organization regressed and became vanity driven, with fawning and self-congratulatory pronouncements that obscured unacknowledged debacles in organizational performance.

In some organizations, the clever and ruthlessly ambitious, if they understand envy well enough, manipulate the envy of others, enlisting them in their own palace intrigues against those who are making the organization successful and adhering to its objectives. After nearly every presidential administration, memoirs and narratives appear that show just how deeply our government is driven by personal needs for power, advancement, appreciation, or simple acquisition. Nancy Pelosi's first weeks as Speaker of the House were briefly diverted from legislation when some mistakenly believed she had demanded a larger airplane for travel between Washington and San Francisco. A firestorm of criticism erupted, criticism aimed at Pelosi's presumed desire to enlarge her sphere but also born of envy (that she should be able to do so). The diversion ended when the sergeant-at-arms of the House explained that he, not she, had requested the larger airplane in his role of ensuring the safety of House members.[6]

Because frustration is so much a part of envy, envy can be extraordinarily powerful. Envy is the energy source that is unleashed by negative campaigning and is a powerful source of energy that drives political activity. When envy is successfully channeled against a political candidate, it represents molten lava of hatred that makes negative campaigning effective. And because it is blind and can be channeled in almost any direction by a clever enough manipulator, it makes America fertile soil for demagoguery. This is why successful politicians have learned that negative attacks must be answered right away no matter how absurd they are. The poisonous messages are being sent to a typically uninformed audience that has a very malleable, often limitless, supply of negative energy that is yearning for an outlet.

Envy is an angry posse that's just been told the bad guys "went that a-way."

The same envious rage one sees in organizations was at play in Congress after the Republican takeover of Congress in 1994. There was enormous, seemingly gratuitous aggression in newly elected members of Congress during this period. Picking up on the ambience created by the very long-frustrated envy the neoconservatives were expressing, Senator Edward M. Kennedy said of the new Republicans, "These people don't want to just beat you. They want to destroy you."[7]

I experienced the same thing quite directly in a personal encounter with Rep. Bill Thomas, who has recently left Congress after a stint as chair of the powerful House Ways and Means Committee. As soon as the '94 election results were in announcing the Republican sweep, the political action committee associated with the American Psychological Association, like many political groups in town, began to court the newly elected Republicans with several fund-raising efforts. Political winds shift. Whatever the merits of the specific giving, I became concerned that we might go too far in the direction of supporting people who had never supported us previously while neglecting our long-standing allies in Congress. Accordingly, I wrote in one of my monthly columns in the *APA Monitor*, the Association newspaper, a cautionary piece saying that reports of President Clinton's political death and certain defeat in the 1996 election were premature and that it was important we not simply turn our back on long-term friends on the Hill (most of them Democrats) simply because of current political fortunes.

A few days later, psychology's political action committee hosted a ten-thousand-dollar fund-raising event for Republican congressman Bill Thomas of California, whom I had never met until that evening. When I introduced myself, I was quite startled by his quick response, "Yeah, you're the one that wrote the articles." Since my work had never been recognized as seminal literature in congressional circles, at first I was simply taken aback and puzzled that he seemed to be saying that he had actually read something I'd written. I only gradually absorbed his following sentence, which helped to clarify my initial bewilderment: "We're going to show people like you that it doesn't pay to make contributions to Democrats."

I had been in advocacy battles since I was seventeen years old, but to capture the body language and tone of Mr. Thomas I had to go back to the fourth-grade playground when an older bully threatened to throw me into the wall and deck me with a hard right if I didn't surrender my basketball to him. Mr. Thomas's demeanor and tone appeared designed to physically menace. There was a gratuitous anger to Mr. Thomas that I had never encountered in any advocacy or political forum, but that was soon to become a calling card of the new players in town. I didn't forget Mr. Thomas's warning. In fact, I followed with astonishment his ascendance to the chairmanship of the full Ways and Means Committee, making him one of the most powerful members of Congress.

While I did not realize it until some time later, Thomas's behavior was part of an orchestrated Republican strategy coordinated by Grover Norquist, Republican strategist, and former majority leader Tom DeLay. It came to be known as the K Street Project, the name referring to the part of the project designed to encourage Washington lobbying firms to hire only Republicans.[8] Those who defended the policy used as a justification their resentment that the

Democrats had done the same thing during their prior forty-year congressional hegemony.

Envy is very difficult for people to acknowledge in themselves because it is an acknowledgment that they feel inferior. To acknowledge my envy I have to first admit that you are better than I am in something or have something I do not have. Even worse, I have to admit this is so important to me that as a result I have ugly covetous feelings toward you. Ultimately, it is humiliating to experience envy.

But if envy goes unrecognized, it can undercut people's personal effectiveness. A twenty-four-year-old graduate student, Jay, came into treatment for anxiety and depression. Jay was unusually bright and had always done well academically until he entered a small graduate program in clinical psychology in a very elite university. He now found himself depressed and very agitated about schoolwork although his grades had been quite good and his work seemed to be well received by his supervisors and course instructors. What soon became apparent was that he was especially uncomfortable in his two closest male relationships in the graduate program. While Jay spent many sessions speculating intellectually about whether this was related to some unconscious homosexual wish on his part, to his therapist it seemed more that Jay's anxiety was most palpable in the sessions when Jay talked about the praise his two fellow students received from the same program supervisor they all three shared.

After allowing some time for a trusting relationship to develop, the therapist gently suggested that possibly Jay wished that the comments his classmates had received were directed to Jay. Jay canceled his next three sessions before simply saying that he would not be back despite the therapist's suggestion that he come in to discuss his reaction. Jay successfully finished graduate school, but his career was clearly less distinguished than most of his classmates and not commensurate to his considerable ability. The anxiety his unconscious envy caused had a paralyzing effect on his ability to function comfortably and so limited his occupational growth and progress.

Feeling deprived in a context in which someone else appears to be getting what a person covets for himself is the cornerstone of envy. By envying someone, people tell themselves they are not as good as someone else, and so envy eats away at their self-esteem and makes them resentful of what others have. In turn, this makes it hard for them to form solid and enduring relationships. What they admire and what initially attracts them to the other person becomes the source of envy that ultimately makes the relationship intolerable. For people suffering from clinically pathological envy, like Jay, oftentimes the envy even permeates the relationship with the therapist so that the patient begins to envy the therapist for his or her very ability to help the patient. It is as if the patient chokes on his own envy and is unable to make continued use of the relationship. Envy, born out of one's self-esteem problems, by its very existence makes those self-esteem problems worse and creates an increasing reservoir of pent-up resentment and rage that is difficult for most people to address and acknowledge directly. Thus, a pool of latent envy is present in highly variable degrees in many people. And it clamors for expression.

Historically, many of the biggest political manipulators have been driven by intense envy. Hitler himself resonated deeply with the German feelings of shame and inferiority between the two world wars and was able to use his own understanding of envy to manipulate and maneuver German throngs. He understood envy because he lived with it and was driven by it himself. The German public mirrored his own envy-filled inner world so powerfully that he could use them to wreak havoc on the rest of the world.

But there is another unusual characteristic of envy that has to be appreciated in order to understand the role it plays in politics, especially in negative campaigning. Why is it that envious rage can be seemingly targeted to just about anyone? Why can a war hero be made out to seem like a coward by someone who appears to have evaded significant military service?

Envy's target is remarkably nonspecific. A very young infant will accept feeding from any source. Envy is so critical to a child's survival that to to some extent it supersedes the infant's attachment to its own particular mother. If the infant cannot alert the world at large to its hunger, it is in trouble. Since it is the infant's first communication to the world, the target for that communication is not well differentiated. Thus, the object of the rage born of envy is very transferable. If one is frustrated, the anger can be directed just about anywhere. Envy, formed from an accumulation of frustrations, can be channeled or discharged in almost any direction.

Since it is humiliating to experience envy, people will do anything to disguise their envy, even to themselves. Converting it to self-righteous feelings of superiority is one particularly effective way to avoid that feeling. People can obscure their envious feelings from themselves as well as others if they can convert their envy into a moralistic position that the other is evil, and they are virtuous. Thus, people are particularly vulnerable to a gaslighter who gives them a moralistic justification for discharging the primitive feelings of hate that the negative political ad, for example, seems to justify and even encourage.

In effect, people substitute feelings of self-righteousness for feelings of envy and inferiority. It is as if they hate because they are superior, not because they feel inferior. They will, for example, often blame their feelings of animosity on the target of their envy. We see this play out in our daily lives when we notice the resentments and character slurs that often follow our successful colleagues on their trail of success. A classmate is a "brownnoser," a successful businessman is "cutthroat," or a politician is "ruthless." Some certainly are, but often they are the victims of disguised envy.

People are understandably grateful to anyone who can help them channel their envy into a more palatable outlet and facilitate this transition. Because of this, envy readily converts to an important energy source to tap for fundamentalist religions and ideologically inclined groups of all kinds. It is also the raw material of demagoguery.

Rush Limbaugh, long one of the most influential of the political-radio commentators, was a powerful factor in turning "liberal" into "the l-word." He made his listeners feel that liberals, the poor, or the government are the reasons for their discontent. He instinctively understands how to unleash latent envy with attacks such as these: "The poor in this country are the biggest piglets at the mother pig and her nipples. The poor feed off the largesse of this government and give nothing back."[9] Limbaugh encourages the audience to project their own cravings and sense of deprivation onto his adversary, the liberals, and then depicts the liberals as caving in to their cravings while his frustrated audience is not being so self-indulgent. Thus, it becomes perfectly acceptable for his audience to indulge their pent-up venom at what they can tell themselves is the liberal's self-indulgence, not their own. The projection makes the target appear to be doing what the listener really wants to do himself, namely, indulge himself in an emotional bath of aggressive, greedy feelings.

"You are morally *superior* to those liberal compassion fascists. . . . You have a real job; they just beg for a living."[10] If you are morally superior, your hatred is understandable. They are cheating you. Go ahead and hate, it makes perfect sense given what is being done to you. Your frustration is not a function of envy and greed; it is a function of injustice. This, of course, makes it a lot easier to justify.

"Some of them—many of them perhaps—are just plain diabolical and dishonest to the core."[11] In other words, they are not worthy of your Christian orientation to other people.

Ann Coulter, conservative author of several best sellers, is expert at playing on envy. In *Slander: Liberal Lies About the American Right*, she opines, "Liberals can't just come out and say they want to take more of our money, kill babies, and discriminate on the basis of race."[12] Here Coulter facilitates the kind of projection of hatred that is at play in such situations. You do not need to have concrete evidence of the other's evil nature. It is their cowardice that keeps you from actually seeing it. But rest assured, your hatred is fully justified. They simply won't own up to the justification. That, in fact, is part of what makes them so worthy of your hate.

Coulter writes, "The environment is only the left's most transparent expression of their contempt for the middle class."[13] It's not that you envy and hate them; they hate you as evidenced by the uncomfortable feelings you have.

This makes disagreements about values especially hateful and driven by disguised feelings of envious rage directed not at the original sources of the frustration but at the targets that Limbaugh and Coulter want them to hate: liberals, the poor, and the government. Envy is the pool of resentments that can be readily tapped by a hate-filled voice.

One price America is paying for this palliative is a divided country rapidly regressing into a hateful posture toward Islam. In some instances, even Christian soldiers march onward with their moral certitude supported by an underlying state of envious rage. Coulter says, "Liberals hate America. ... They hate all religions except Islam (post 9/11). Even Islamic terrorists don't hate America like liberals do. They don't have the energy. If they had that much energy, they'd have indoor plumbing by now."[14] Coulter is thus able to allow her audience to release the anger on both domestic opponents and foreign terrorists in one fell swoop by ascribing to them moral failings ranging from treason to laziness.

Just as people burdened with envy are grateful for anyone who can help obscure the true nature of their envy by converting it to self-righteous feelings of moral superiority, they resent anyone who interferes with that process of self-justification. Just try to preach "understanding" to a group that is psychologically in need of a target to hate and using their moral superiority to justify it. You will not be well received. Or, for that matter, try to be a news organization that presents objective and badly needed news about our country's shortcomings when one of its competitors is taking the opposite tack, encouraging Americans to indulge themselves with blind, rabid nationalism.

When one of the battleground states of mind is at issue, reality will often bend to accommodate the person's need for comfort—whether it is envy, sexual concerns, or paranoia. Freud described this tension over whether reality should succumb to short-term emotional convenience or to the person's long-term best interest as a conflict between the mind's wish to pursue pleasure, the pleasure principle, and the mind's tendency to acknowledge reality, the reality principle. For Freud, the single most pivotal aspect of the developing mind was its ability to acknowledge painful reality. In confronting reality and the demands it makes, the mind matures and maximizes its ability to function effectively. Developmental maturity for Freud consisted of tolerating anxiety and uncertainty without resorting to temporarily expedient, but ultimately self-defeating, distortions in reality.

Society can hinder or help the way Americans respond to this dilemma so deeply rooted in our mental makeup. If leaders and institutions support Americans' efforts to struggle with complex reality, it helps us. If, however, they pander to Americans' more regressed minds and give us rationalizations for venting our envy, America's energies are wasted in the service of irrelevancies. The American mind is not exercised, but, instead, falls into the same state of disrepair that one's body does if it pursues hedonistic pleasures without proper diet and exercise. A mind that is preoccupied with artificial targets for envy is a mind diverted from the real challenges it must face.

Most people think of envy, narcissism, and even anger as base emotions, and they certainly do oftentimes lead to base behavior. But that is simply because they are the energy source that makes people do much of what they do. Politically, there is no more reason that the existence of envy in the human psyche should lead to stupid and self-destructive public policy than that atomic energy must inevitably be used to blow us all up. It is frustration, aggression, and personal dissatisfaction that motivate us to do much of what we do. The energy sources are eerily the same. The question is how mature our deployment of those energies is.

Envy, and the rage associated with it, are not necessarily evil, but their power points to the extraordinary importance of good leadership, leadership that directs people's attention to pressing issues in a way that inspires people to confront challenges. This is what Roosevelt did in World War II, what Kennedy did with the space program, and what Johnson did with the War on Poverty.

Envy is an energy source the management of which often determines public policy. The spoils will go to the side that harnesses envy more effectively. In the Clinton administration, health care reform was inevitably going to be a contest between reformers and the health insurance industry. Either the administration would harness the rage the public felt against the insurance industry more effectively, or the health insurance industry would harness the rage people felt about big government more effectively. It turned out to be the latter.

Envy can also play a role in the success and failure of any politician. The beauty of Camelot that forms the Kennedy legacy was certainly a real component of JFK's thousand days in office. However, a person's death will attenuate much of the envy that is directed at them during their lifetime. What is largely forgotten now about JFK was the deep hatred that was also directed to him during his administration. I was seventeen at the time of his death and remember being furious, but not surprised, when a high school teacher in Dayton, Ohio, gave a huge grin as news of his death was announced. What can be summed up as JFK's charisma was for some people an infuriating statement of what he had that they did not have–and many hated him for it.

Ronald Reagan had a genius for using what other people envied in him to his advantage. He appeared to be sharing it with them. His self-deprecating humor, his apparent comfort with himself, and his seemingly genuine romantic and loving marriage all supplemented his remarkable good looks and charm to create a package that because of his style everyone who saw him felt that they could readily have through vicarious participation with him. His sense of humor suggested that he wanted them to have it and to have at him as well, all in good fun. Ironically, Reagan was in fact a very private man, but he was able to craft the role of a very likeable public figure extremely well.[15] The more he had in Americans' eyes, the more they felt they had. This is why despite the fact that Reagan was very much an ideologue, he generated very little hatred.

Ironically, the last two decades in American politics have been dominated by two political families who could not be more different along the spectrum of envy. George H. W. Bush's style was so inoffensive, if at the same time so uninspiring, that he could probably talk about anything without generating envy even though he was personally wealthy and born into privilege. His personality felt like a pabulum in which one could dissolve almost anything from fascism to unilateral disarmament. Envy was absolutely no problem for the first President Bush.

It was, however, a big problem for Bill Clinton and an even bigger one for Hillary Rodham Clinton. While the Lewinsky scandal serves as a catchall rationalization for the intense hatred to which Clinton was subjected, it does not really explain it. The envious hatred for Clinton predated the Lewinsky scandal. The

Clintons were dogged by animosity and attack from President Clinton's first day in office–from Whitewater to Travelgate–by a series of attempts to create a scandal from whole cloth.[16] And this was not ideology based. Clinton was first and foremost a political centrist who came from very humble origins. What Clinton had inside him appealed to many people. But for others it stimulated an ugly envy in them. While George H. W. Bush and Clinton have a well-publicized friendship now, Bush was reportedly stunned that he had lost the presidency to someone who he felt was of such inferior status.

While the Democratic candidate in 2000, Al Gore, did not stimulate much envy as a politician, he appeared to feel he had to "do something" to be likeable. He frequently seemed not to realize that for voters to like him and support him they merely had to feel they knew him. I think this may be why he said recently on a television interview that he was beginning to think that he is "not very good at politics." Most people who know Gore personally find him very likeable and comfortable, as did I in my very brief encounters with him. Tragically, he often seemed to feel he had to be something more than that, especially in public forums, and, as a result, the public rarely saw his congeniality, spontaneity, and sincerity. Instead, they experienced him as "wooden" because he was taut with effort and lacked the fluid grace and engaging personality people who saw him in person found to be quite charismatic. Contrary to the popular myth, I strongly suspect having a beer with Al Gore would be a lot more enjoyable than with George W. Bush. And if family values was really an issue, the Gores, unlike a majority of Washington politicians, have a real marriage. My friends who worked in the Clinton White House saw Gore as extremely competent and focused during times of crisis. Few people in American history have had the breadth of understanding about defense matters, and his grasp of the environmental issues is unsurpassed. But because Americans now vote on how they "feel," we failed to elect a man who was so well suited for the crisis confronting our country that he may well have become one of our greatest presidents. Instead, we elected our Nero. "For want of a shoe . . ."

George W. Bush, on the other hand, provided a welcome reprieve for many from the agitation they felt during the Clinton years. While Bush is widely criticized for the politics of divisiveness orchestrated by Karl Rove, his personality style does not generate much envy. In fact, a major factor in his election was that, in wake of the intensity of the Clinton years, his rambling style and inarticulate speech allayed a lot of anxiety. When he said "the internets" during the second debate, the result was an increase in his support.[17] What voter could feel inferior to a candidate who could not name the new president of Pakistan and advocated "good relations with the Grecians"?[18]

Like Gore, John Kerry did not offer the lovability of Ronald Reagan; people simply could not develop strong personal feelings toward either one. When it came to presidential performance, America twice opted literally to let the cheerleader carry the ball over two experienced players. They voted on the basis of comfort, a standard that is broadly accepted in America today.

Envy was obviously not the only factor at play in recent presidential politics in all of this; however, it has been one of the most underrecognized and least-appreciated factors.

The battleground states of sex, envy, and paranoia can have a cumulative effect, and when they do, the result is politically explosive.

If one considers the power of the three battleground psychological states, one can see that anyone who understands these forces and is inclined to manipulate them can create great confusion and great evil. However, it is also important to notice that these forces in and of themselves are not necessarily evil. Paranoid mechanisms are what enable us to understand one another. Sexuality is the means by which we love and create our children. And envy creates our motivation to work and be productive. If Americans have the wisdom to select leaders who want to harness these forces to make us a better country, there is an enormous opportunity the battleground states provide. They are a battleground, however, and political adversaries have to fight over them if they want to prevail.

At the present time, these forces have been almost the exclusive province of those who have used them to divide America, start a disastrous and needless war, stifle social progress, and steal both our national treasury and our national resources. They are the gaslighters.

CHAPTER 6

THE GASLIGHTERS:
ARCHITECTS OF FALSE REALITIES

When devils will the darkest sins put on,
They do suggest at first with heavenly shows.

—SHAKESPEARE, Othello

Paranoia, sexual perplexity, and envy are emotional states that can fluctuate dramatically and tax the mind's already limited ability to maintain a stable reality sense during times of crisis. They make people ready targets for gaslighters.

Historically, the study of these deeper dimensions of the mind, psychoanalysis, and the art of manipulating them, public relations, are closely intertwined. Ironically, both come from the family of Sigmund Freud.

Freud, more than anyone, advanced our insight into the nonrational, unconscious aspects of the mind. Whatever absurd caricatures may have evolved about some of his theories, biological studies of the brain are giving Freud the last laugh on many of them. In particular, Freud's model of the mind, with its unconscious level of activity and its emphasis on defending itself from conflict by distorting reality, is increasingly borne out by technologically advanced studies of the brain, some of which can actually measure the brain's resistance to political information that is inconsistent with the person's preexisting political point of view.[1]

It was Freud's nephew, American Edward Bernays, who became known as the Father of Public Relations.[2] While some contend that Bernays's accolade was more a product of his skill at creating his own grand public image than it was his performance in the trenches of advertising and public relations, his work clearly did show how readily the mind could be manipulated to form new constructs of reality when in the hands of a clever manipulator.

Despite operating with tools that were very limited by today's high-tech standards, Bernays was extraordinary in his skill. He designed a campaign that successfully gave cigarette smoking a feminine and even healthy image for women, who until that time had avoided the tobacco habit. Retained by the United Fruit Company to protect its interests in Guatemala from government takeover, he engineered a successful campaign to convince the American public that it was critical to their national interests to overthrow the Guatemalan government. Bernays is said to have chafed at suggestions that his skills had not always been employed to the betterment of humankind and embarked on a series of campaigns that were designed to alter that image.

The current state of political gaslighting began serendipitously with the 1960 Kennedy–Nixon debates. Prior to that, television had been seen almost exclusively as a mirroring witness to political events. The Kennedy–Nixon debates showed that television was a more psychologically powerful political tool than most had anticipated. The new medium challenged and even overrode policy issues that had previously been assumed to shape voters' behavior.

In these early days, the primary lesson politicians learned was that Richard Nixon's jowls, perspiration, and gray suit on gray background contrasted very poorly with John Kennedy's hand-some, chiseled face and cool appearance. Politicians realized these factors operated on the viewing psyche more deeply and more powerfully than the content or intellectual merit of any debate.

But TV did much more than that. It exponentially increased the effectiveness of the applied psychological disciplines of marketing, public relations, and advertising. TV has done nothing less than create a new set of criteria by which people select their president. TV afforded voters direct real-time access to the presidential candidates, enabling them to vote on the basis of very subjective emotional states people experience when watching the candidates close-up. Objective assessments of personal accomplishments, policy issues, and party affiliations–the primary bases of voters' decisions prior to television–were replaced by what voters *feel* when they observe the candidate on TV. JFK was cool and made us *feel* cool, while Richard Nixon was hot and made us *feel* sweaty and uncomfortable. For a critical number of voters, this overcame Nixon's eight years of experience in the White House and his extensive foreign policy experience, neither of which Kennedy could claim. One can only wonder, for example, if Nikita Khrushchev would have been as willing to test Richard Nixon as he was to test the unproven John F. Kennedy in the Cuban Missile Crisis. Americans were lucky . . . that time.

This, of course, does not mean that Americans were necessarily wrong to select John Kennedy. But it does raise very serious questions about whether TV does not lure people into a much simpler analysis of candidates by picking the one who makes them "feel better" over one who, for example, feels "wooden." The image people get of a candidate from TV operates on a much deeper emotional level than do attributes such as experience, position on issues, and character. Ultimately, many Americans are now selecting presidents on the basis of how the candidates make them feel in their body when they observe them on TV. This is a strikingly different criterion.

During the three decades after the debates, it became increasingly apparent that television held even more power than originally thought. Television was a probe into the deepest recesses of the voters' minds, influencing and shaping the voters' experiences in such a way that it could create totally new issues and emotional responses that had nothing to do with the reality of the extant political issues. While there are disagreements as to what Marshall McLuhan actually meant in his famous dictum that the "medium is the message," he may not have gotten it quite right. He correctly understood the significance of the shift to the new communication, but he missed its actual mechanism. The medium was not the message; it was simply bypassing the conscious, rational part of the mind and delivering the message to a deeper and more powerful stratum, which greatly expanded the potential power of the spokesperson.

The recognition of the power of TV in politics itself became a Trojan horse, bringing in a whole new cadre of political advisors: public relations and marketing consultants. These people understood TV and orchestrated its use. Nothing could have been more logical to them than to take advantage of the expertise they had acquired over the previous decades and apply it to political campaigns.

Marketers were measured by their ability to create a "product" that had very little to do with the product they had been hired to sell. They did not extol the virtues of a cereal. They created the fun fantasy experience for children of talking to three cute little cartoon figures named Snap, Crackle, and Pop or Tony the Tiger as they downed their morning cereal. To sell cigarettes, they created a rugged, romantic, and eroticized experience of being a no-nonsense, John Wayne–like cowboy.

In television marketing in particular, rational evaluation became a thing of the past. Emotional experience replaced relevance and reality in marketing. Salesmen no longer celebrated the alleged virtues of their product; instead, they tried to make you *feel* good about it. Creating a pleasurable fantasy was found to be more persuasive than extolling a virtuous product, whether that product was toothpaste or a political candidate.

In the Kennedy–Nixon debates, the creation of the fantasy was accidental, but advantageous for Kennedy: he was young, energetic looking, and virile. The baby boom was beginning to influence the country, shifting the center of gravity from the supposed wisdom and experience of the Eisenhower generation to the energy and vigor of the New Frontier. Nixon was trapped in the middle.

Marketers learned to address the mind on the more primitive level that becomes apparent in psychoanalytic treatment. Neither rational nor logical, it is "associative" or what some call "symbolic." When ideas or things are associated with one another in the mind at this level, there is a spillover of qualities attributed from one to the other. This is what makes symbolic marketing so effective.

In addition, from a mental health perspective, marketing seductively disconnects the mind from reality and actively encourages it to engage in fantasy. The mind is encouraged to let that fantasy predominate over reality in making decisions.

This combination of loose symbolic thinking permeated with

fantasy is the essence of psychological regression. It undercuts the rational functioning of the human mind. In small doses or when the subject is a breakfast cereal, this is not of great concern. But when it occurs on a grand scale, in regard to geopolitics and important national issues, regression extinguishes the reasoned discussion and debate that enables a democracy to make good decisions.

The political world was intrigued and excited about the new political opportunities television, in particular, ushered in. In the same way that sex can be symbolically associated with an automobile, so can envy, feelings of persecution, and other feelings be symbolically associated with political candidates, political parties, and political issues. Ironically, it was a liberal, Lyndon Johnson, who fired the first shot in the new style of campaigning. The advertising firm Doyle Dane Bernbach created an ad for Johnson attacking his opponent Barry Goldwater in which a young girl was pulling petals from a daisy as a voice in the background counted down from ten. When it reached zero, the picture of the girl dissolved into a mushroom cloud.[3] Bill Moyers, who was in charge of television advertising for the campaign, ordered that the ad be run only once, but that was sufficient to create a huge outcry. In an era when the threat of nuclear war seemed imminent, the ad struck deeply at viewers' needs for security.

"In the modern presidency," Richard Nixon wrote in his memoirs, "concern for image must rank with concern for substance."[4] Nixon's emphasis on what seems so apparent to us today indicates the extent of the sea change he lived through in his political career.

Sensitized to the importance of the new media, Nixon retained a very young television producer, Roger Ailes, for his 1968 campaign. While Ailes today is well known in media circles and inside the Beltway in Washington, he is surprisingly unknown outside those spheres. A pubic relations prodigy who moved from an equipment manager to producer of the Mike Douglas show by the age of twenty-five, Ailes met Richard Nixon on the set of that show and worked for him in his campaign efforts. Ailes established his political bona fides in 1984 with the Reagan-Mondale debates, when he was given credit for reversing Reagan's lackluster performance in the first debate.

It was in 1988, however, when working for George H. W. Bush, that Ailes oversaw the perfection of the most primitive and deadly weapon in the political gaslighter's arsenal: the sexual assault ad. Ailes's work was abetted by the talent of Bush's director of political strategy, Lee Atwater, who developed the now-famous Willie Horton ad. That ad depicted a large African American man convicted of and imprisoned for murder and dismemberment in Massachusetts. Furloughed on a weekend pass in 1987, while Dukakis was governor, Horton assaulted a man and raped his fiancée in Maryland. Overtly, the incident was presented as an example of Dukakis's soft-on-crime liberalism, but the ad's effect was supercharged by the racial and sexual undertones involved. Roger Ailes is alleged to have said, "The only question is whether we show Willie Horton with a knife in his hand or without it."[5]

The formula for the sexual assault ad is to create perplexity and make sure that one's own candidate appears to offer the solution. The Willie Horton message addressed a deep, frightening, and unconscious layer of the American psyche. Instead of creating a consumer fantasy associating breakfast cereals or automobiles with pleasure, the vision created by the Willie Horton ad was of a powerful, potent black male forcibly having sex with a white woman.

"Women particularly were affected by the ad," said Dukakis

campaign manager Susan Estrich. "The symbolism was very powerful.... You can't find a stronger metaphor, intended or not, for racial hatred in this country than a black man raping a white woman.... I talked to people afterward.... Women said they couldn't help it, but it scared the living daylights out of them."[6]

The Willie Horton ad effectively assaulted the mind with menacing images of sexual inferiority and bondage. As with the idea of homosexuals kissing, viewers could not escape mental images of interracial rape. Inevitably associated with that fearsome image was Michael Dukakis. Although the ad was ostensibly about Dukakis's stand on crime, its real power lay in connecting Dukakis with a feeling of sexual disgust and an aura of personal impotence that made him seem unable to protect people.

The Horton ads took marketing's amoral approach, its disregard for any actual reality, and added a psychological scalpel to penetrate the mind with a subliminal message. It hit heavily on sexuality, paranoia over personal boundaries, and the envy born of sexual inferiority attributed by some to race. It was the psychological trifecta for political advertising. The psychological crisis it created effectively preempted any interest in the real issues facing the nation. Instead, the affected voters were preoccupied with resolving the artificially created emotional crisis that was more compelling.

The incident could not have worked better for the Bush campaign. Bush was seen as decidedly lacking in strength, power, virility, and/or sexiness. He had been dogged at the outset with what even a *Newsweek* cover story called "the wimp factor."[7] However, after the Horton ad, Dukakis in a televised debate failed to respond directly to Bernard Shaw's unusually blunt

question–"Governor, if Kitty Dukakis were raped and murdered, would you favor an irrevocable death penalty for the
killer?"–by saying that he would not, and he referred to statistics
about crime and the war against drugs. He seemed not to have
noticed that his wife was being instanced in the question, thus
making the mental image in voters' minds all the more
repugnant–himself lecturing bystanders while his wife is being
raped and murdered next to him. Vice President Bush responded by saying that the election was all about "values" and
that he "would support the death penalty for certain crimes."[8]
Later trying to recoup, Dukakis posed in an army tank with an
ill-fitting helmet. Following a series of ads (created by Roger
Ailes) using this failed attempt at alpha-male iconography, it
was Dukakis who had to fight the wimp label, and the race was
essentially over.

Assigned to Atwater's team during the 1988 campaign was a
young political novice by the name of George W. Bush, the candidate's son. "W" was naturally drawn to the Atwater "magic," and
when he ran for governor of Texas, he made sure that he had his
equivalent of the Ailes/Atwater team in Karl Rove. In the 2004
campaign, Karl Rove had his Willie Horton handed to him in the
form of gay marriage. Ironically, this issue, like the Willie Horton
incident, came courtesy of the Massachusetts legal system and
addressed the same deep strata of the mind. After Massachusetts's
highest court affirmed a ruling in February 2004 asserting that homosexual couples should be allow to marry, for weeks voters were
confronted with news pieces showing same-sex couples kissing
after their wedding ceremony. It was essentially impossible for
many heterosexual viewers to experience the picture without having the involuntary experience of imagining kissing someone of

the same sex. For people who were shaky to begin with about their sexual adequacy, this was especially terrifying and prompted a spontaneous uprising in support of constitutional amendments to prohibit gay marriage and build a protective fortification against letting gays share the marital bed. In February 2004, Bush called for a ban on gay marriage.[9]

The American mind is increasingly assaulted with a confusing and conflicting drumbeat of messages that challenge any mind's capacity to integrate a coherent reality. As we have shown, a person's reality sense is the result of a complicated and inevitably idiosyncratic process. The mind's sensory overload alone creates a fertile loam of perplexity in which gaslighting can take hold.

Gaslighting can occur in many different settings. While the mental health community has commented on gaslighting primarily in the context of marital and family relationships, gaslighting permeates our culture. With the increase in employee protections from arbitrary and discriminatory treatment in the workplace, there are now more cases of gaslighting in employment settings from false accusations and other forms of deception. Since employers are much more restricted legally in their ability to arbitrarily fire employees, many CEOs and employers use their power in deceptive ways to achieve what would be otherwise illegal or politically costly job discrimination. The case of Dr. Young illustrates the degree of deception that takes place with a highly skilled gaslighter.

Dr. Young was a distinguished scientist who had recently taken a prestigious position with a scientific association in which he reported directly to the CEO, a man with a lengthy history of gaslighting. The CEO had hired Dr. Young to placate a dissatisfied segment of the membership and had anticipated that Dr. Young would be willing to function as an organizational figurehead, as many of the CEO's high-profile appointments had.

The staff that Dr. Young inherited had been without leadership for some time and had grown unruly and angry at the neglect they felt from the CEO. When Dr. Young assumed his new position, his all-female staff took out their resentments on Dr. Young for now having to work under direction. The women decided that since the staff was all women, and Dr. Young was a male, the environment constituted a hostile work environment within the meaning of the Equal Employment Opportunity Commission. The women told the CEO that they would file a complaint if he did not remove Dr. Young.

While the case against Dr. Young was nonexistent, there were two things that made the situation very problematic for the CEO. First, the CEO was already actually covering up cases of sexual harassment by senior officials who were now beholden to the CEO for the "protection" he afforded them. If the women filed the complaint Dr. Young would be fine, but the CEO would be in serious trouble for the obvious cover-ups. Second, Dr. Young was less of a malleable token spokesperson than the CEO had anticipated and had been more faithful to his role as representative of one of the major constituencies in the organization. He opposed the CEO's own self-serving plan to undo some recent organizational changes that had been popular with the rank and file. Like many gaslighters, the CEO was extremely unforgiving toward anyone who disagreed with him. While the CEO showed no emotion when Dr. Young expressed his opposition to the CEO's reversal of organizational policies, from that point forward Dr. Young's fate was sealed.

The CEO decided to kill two birds with one stone. Through

complicated maneuvering, the CEO denied Dr. Young any opportunity to speak in his own defense to the association board of directors and advised the board that Dr. Young was a serious risk to the association because of the allegations of sexual harassment. He forced Dr. Young's resignation.

Dr. Young returned to academia, but in the association's next election, he ran for president, which would have made him the CEO's boss. Dr. Young came in second, but custom dictated that he would probably become the association president in the next election cycle. The CEO knew he had to move quickly, and he devised a plan to derail Dr. Young's candidacy. He advised his board of directors that if they let Dr. Young run in the next election, the aggrieved women might sue the association. On the other hand, he said, if they did not let Dr. Young run, Dr. Young might sue. The CEO recommended that the association file a motion for declaratory judgment with the courts, ostensibly to ask the courts to advise the association which course to take so they could avoid legal risk. The CEO presented this to the governance of the association as a necessary way to protect the association and be fair to all parties.

The CEO, like many successful gaslighters, had an ability to stay five steps ahead of his unsuspecting governing body. The CEO anticipated that Dr. Young would not have the resources to participate in the legal action and fight the legal battle necessary to stay on the ballot. If he did, however, the CEO could use the publicity from the trial to smear Dr. Young's good name and substantially reduce the likelihood he would be elected. Dr. Young hired an attorney, spent almost one hundred thousand dollars of his own money, and was seemingly vindicated when the court ordered that he had a right to be on the ballot.

The CEO had prepared for this contingency, however. When the presidential ballots were mailed out, the association newspaper carried a story indicating that a "harasser" was required to be permitted to run for president of the organization. The article mentioned Dr. Young by name and described the allegations.

The association was a very liberal organization with a long record of strong support for women's rights. The notion of someone standing accused, as the story was written, made it appear that the association had been forced to let a sexual harasser run for association president. Dr. Young was defeated. Even after the election, Dr. Young had no means to even express his side of the story. In addition, the CEO was a master at whisper campaigns, as are many gaslighters, and the truth was concealed by a storm of fake rumor and innuendo.

The psychological toll on Dr. Young was heavy. He and his wife, who had led lives of complete probity with many honors, were left to contend with the confounding experience of having this horrible cloud hang over them, never knowing who would believe what and never really being able to address the matter directly. Dr. Young stood accused of violating the values that much of his life's work had supported. His wife, knowing her husband was the victim of false accusations, was also forced to bear the unspoken assumption by others that she was living with a sexual harasser even though she knew it to be untrue. The CEO, meanwhile, was commended for managing a "delicate matter" with sensitivity and compassion, and despite many serious but obscured organizational debacles, he was viewed as a kindly and caring person.

Dr. Young's story illustrates that there are often two sets of victims to gaslighting. There are, first, the specific targets of the assault and, second, the audience whose reality is toyed with. Individuals who are the target of the gaslighters, like Dr. Young, can suffer very painful psychological effects. They become anxious, depressed, confused, and demoralized. For them, gaslighting can lead to personal disintegration, self-destruction, and even suicide. With apologies to conspiracy theorists, former presidential aide Vincent Foster's suicide note, decrying what he felt were the intentional and unchallenged distortions of some media critics–people who he said "lie with impunity"–suggests the psychological effect of gaslighting was a more likely cause of his death than the untethered speculations that abounded in its wake.

For the second set of victims, the deceived audience, gaslighting can also be confusing, distressing, and destructive. People often resort to some very ineffective and irrational coping mechanisms when their reality sense becomes confused. In those times, they simply create, or let others create for them, an alternative reality that at least temporarily fills the void in their own reality sense. They become sheep. In the case of Dr. Young, the association became increasingly dysfunctional under the CEO's manipulative style. Elected leaders, initially confused and suspicious, became adept at avoiding any leadership responsibility and ultimately ignored or rationalized the CEO's successful termination of many of the successful aspects of the organization that were threatening to him personally. Gradually, the association became detached from real issues and heavily preoccupied with members fawning over one another and commending themselves for avoiding conflicts and "working together." When the association was confronted by real external crises that required professional talent, it was ill prepared and suffered a series of debacles.

Ironically, to avoid the unpleasant conflict with the gaslighter on whom they have become dependent, these participant-observer victims of gaslighting repudiate the very parts of the mind that create their vital reality sense. Compliance with a "reality" that is not firmly rooted in significant part in one's own independent mental processes leads to a psychological atrophy in their all-important reality sense. This causes a global reduction in effective psychological functioning. Each time a person accepts a gaslighter's reality, he or she weakens the independent functioning of their own mind and becomes more and more vulnerable to the gaslighter. The victim will become increasingly disoriented and his or her mental functioning and behavior will tend to revert to childlike patterns. This psychological reaction occurred in post-9/11 America when Americans' inability to detect political manipulation caused them to fall out of synch with the rest of the world by blindly accepting the Bush reality.

When gaslighting operates in a large organization, the organizational objectives will be undermined, leading to waste and a terrible loss of productivity. But when it is done to an electorate in a nation armed with nuclear weapons, grappling with the paranoia-inducing reality that it has lost its island fortress security, the potential outcomes are truly terrifying.

While gaslighters themselves come in many different sizes and shapes, in my experience, it is helpful in political contexts to divide them into two prototypes of gaslighters: the authoritarian and the paradoxical. The authoritarian gaslighters typically stay out of the public eye and are manipulative and psychologically coercive in the development and implementation of their political strategies. They are the powers behind the scenes that exert enormous control, often without leaving their fingerprints on any of their work.

Their personality profiles show some striking similarities to one another. Childhood abandonment, family secrets, and social ostracism are frequent parts of their history. Many have a social history of not being well liked and a preoccupation with sexual and sadistic pranks from an early age. While many use moral concerns to advance their goals, a startling number have histories of addiction disorders and sexual impropriety. Underneath their bland façade, they typically have fantasies of enormous grandiosity in which they vanquish the many people in their lives by whom they have felt slighted.

Paradoxical gaslighters, in contrast to the authoritarian, are prototypically beguiling, clever, and deceptive. They are also decidedly asexual and, most importantly, rarely evoke envy in others. For example, they may be quite small in stature or bumbling in speech. This causes them to be underestimated by their adversaries and provides a protective camouflage when their victims cry out in outrage about their behavior. Whether it is his slight physical stature, his unsexy appearance, or his difficulty articulating a complete sentence, he does not appear to be someone who would be able or inclined to do something as sadistic or diabolical as gaslighting. This can make him difficult to expose.

Karl Rove has been one of the most widely criticized and successful authoritarian political gaslighters. Journalist Joshua Green, writing in *The Atlantic Monthly* says,

> It is frequently said of [Rove], in hushed tones when political folks are doing the talking, that he leaves a trail of damage in his wake—a reference to the substantial number of people who have been hurt, politically and personally, through their encounters with him. Rove's

reputation for winning is eclipsed only by his reputation for
ruthlessness, and examples abound of his apparent willingness to cross
moral and ethical lines.[10]

Rove grew up as a self-described nerd. It was not until he was a young adult that he learned the man he had identified as his father was in fact not his father. Rove was actually the product of an earlier marriage, but the biological father left the family. When the mother's second marriage ended in divorce, she committed suicide. He has never earned a college degree but dropped in and out of formal education to pursue campaign and political activities. In 1970, Rove obtained a letterhead from the campaign office of Democrat Alan Dixon, then running for Illinois state treasurer, and sent one thousand invitations to a Dixon fundraiser on the letterhead promising "free beer, free food, girls and a good time for nothing." He later dismissed the incident as a teenage prank.[11]

The "pranks" continued into adulthood. Rove was an understudy to Donald Segretti, whose tactics against George McGovern in the 1972 presidential campaign came to light during Watergate and made the name Segretti synonymous with "dirty tricks." When Segretti was sentenced to a six-month prison term, Rove was promoted.

Rove's professional history includes numerous examples of political espionage, two of which reportedly caused George Herbert Walker Bush to fire Rove from his campaigns on two separate occasions. The first in 1980 was for leaking information to the press, and the second in 1992 presidential campaign was for allegedly leaking information to make a costaffer look bad.[12]

This pattern followed him to the White House. Rove was presumed by many to have been involved in the disclosure that Valerie Plame was a CIA agent, a retaliation against her husband's opposition to Bush's factual misrepresentation about weapons of mass destruction in Iraq.[13]

Joshua Green described his investigation of what it was like to be targeted for gaslighting by Karl Rove with an illustration from the 1994 Alabama supreme court race when one of Rove's clients, Harold See, ran against George Wallace's son-in-law, Mark Kennedy:

> *One of Rove's signature tactics is to attack an opponent on the very front that seems unassailable. Kennedy was no exception. . . . Some of Kennedy's campaign commercials touted his volunteer work [with abused children], including one that showed him holding hands with children. "We were trying to counter the positives from that ad," a former Rove staffer told me, explaining that some within the See camp initiated a whisper campaign that Kennedy was a pedophile. . . . "What Rove does," says Joe Perkins, "is try to make something so bad for a family that the candidate will not subject the family to the hardship. Mark is not your typical Alabama macho, beer-drinkin', tobacco-chewin', pickup-drivin' kind of guy. He is a small, well-groomed, well-educated family man, and what they tried to do was make him look like a homosexual pedophile. That was really, really hard to take."[14]*

Mark Kennedy narrowly won the election, but after serving out the term, he decided not to run again.

In an article for the *New York Times Magazine* that ran on October 17, 2004, Ron Suskind described a conversation he had with an unidentified senior Bush advisor some speculate was Karl Rove:

> *The aide said that guys like me were "in what we call the reality-based community," which he defined as people who "believe that solutions emerge from your judicious study of discernible reality." I nodded and murmured something about enlightenment principles and empiricism. He cut me off. "That's not the way the world really works anymore," he continued. "We're an empire now, and when we act, we create our own reality. And while you're studying that reality—judiciously as you will—we'll act again, creating other new realities, which you can study, too, and that's how things will sort out. We're history's actors . . . and you, all of you, will be left to just study what we do."* [15]

If this is accurate, it is the language of a frighteningly grandiose man. It is also the language of a gaslighter who focuses on being able to rewrite reality for other people who are left helplessly to reap the whirlwind of the machinations of the gaslighter.

One of Karl Rove's favorite stories from American history suggests that the possible scope of his grandiosity is the election of 1896. Industrialist and Republican Party strategist Mark Hanna and Republican presidential candidate William McKinley recognized that America's population was changing as a result of its rapid industrialization, and they wanted to make the Republican Party the most attractive home for the new voters. Hanna raised a then-staggering sum of money and McKinley swept through the election, inaugurating a Republican period of domination of the White House that lasted, with the single exception of

Woodrow Wilson, until 1932. Rove has openly speculated whether it would be possible to do the same today.[16]

Rove's gaslighting genius is his ability to paint the reality he needs to suit his purpose relatively unconstrained by the actual reality around him. He operates as if he has a blank slate on which he simply writes the reality he wants. When things are playing particularly poorly on the front pages for the administration with both Iraq and the White House leak investigations, Supreme Court nominations are rushed onto the front page and the hemorrhaging in presidential approval ratings is momentarily stopped. In mid 2006, after being treated with long months of indifference, Osama bin Laden was prominently featured as part of Bush's effort to refocus attention away from Iraq. But when Pakistan announced an embarrassing and problematic "hands-off bin Laden" policy, bin Laden promptly disappeared once again from the White House stage.[17]

Symbols have been a significant tool for Rove. Under Rove, White House pictures of Bush take the traditional photo op to new levels of psychological manipulation. While a few, like the "mission accomplished" photo, have come back to haunt Bush, other photos depict Bush with halos and other suggestive religious symbols that reinforce Bush's connection to his Christian base.[18] Good symbols are manufactured and negative ones kept at bay. Remains of American troops returning from Iraq are not to be photographed out of "respect for the families."

Rove is at his most skillful during elections. During the 2004 election, John Kerry obviously believed that his military service would take away any advantage Bush might have had as a wartime president. Instead, he was aggressively "Swiftboated" by one attack ad after another contending that because of his military service and subsequent antiwar views, he was unfit to lead. Rove simply rewrote reality and declared Kerry a cowardly turncoat. Rove himself was, like many from that era, a draft dodger, and he was supporting a president and vice president who also actively avoided combat. The fact he was able to do this to one of the few members of a privileged America who actually volunteered to serve and clearly did so with distinction could only have reinforced his grandiosity.

Karl Rove is one of the more successful gaslighters, but he is by no means unique. Authoritarian gaslighters play behind-the-scenes roles in many parts of our society. Ms. Moore, for example, was by all outward appearances a career bureaucrat. In fact, however, she was a prime example of an authoritarian gaslighter. People like Ms. Moore all too often gravitate to petty positions of authority where they can exert power over others, oftentimes with confusing bureaucratic maneuverings. She had worked her way up in a state agency until she became the staff director of a licensing board for a mental health profession. Outwardly quiet and professional, she had long harbored resentments at the faceless anonymity of her life. Like many gaslighters, she compensated for these hurt feelings by developing grandiose fantasies of herself as a powerful moral force punishing mental health professionals for mistreatment of patients. Ms. Moore projected her feelings of being slighted into her professional work, seeing disrespectful mental health professionals in almost every complaint that came before her. Under her well-developed ability to manage the professionals serving on the board, the board's decisions quickly became extremely punitive toward any therapist about whom a patient complained. When news of these decisions were published by the state licensing board, the affected professionals suffered all the effects of other gaslight victims whose reality is denied and who are not in a position to correct the misperceptions created. Their career opportunities were sharply limited because the licensing board decision served as a "scarlet A" for all professional credentialing matters.

George W. Bush, in contrast to Rove and Ms. Moore, is a typical paradoxical gaslighter, different from Karl Rove. In 1988, he worked closely with one of the other politically successful gaslighters, Lee Atwater. While Bush does not have the creative capacity or the organizational skill to do what Atwater did, he was no fool about appreciating its potential political value. He appears to have known and appreciated from the beginning what he had in Karl Rove. As demonic as Rove can appear, Bush is ostensibly his opposite. He appears harmlessly inept and even dull. Bush inspires many to feel that "what you see is what you get." This, of course, makes him the perfect foil to present things to the public quite differently from how they are. His sales ability is a critical component to building a convincing case for the reality that Karl Rove creates.

George Bush and Karl Rove were an effective gaslighting team because of the complementary skills they have. Rove is the creative genius who manufactures the reality, and Bush is the non-threatening, affable salesman. Bush does not have Rove's creativity, psychological sophistication, or knowledge of American politics, but Rove does not have Bush's disarming charm.

Any suggestion that gaslighting has been unique to Rove and Bush is simply wrong. Paradoxical gaslighters are destructive players in many organizations from the White House to youth sports and everything in between.

A CEO of an academic Washington professional society, Dr. Frank was most noteworthy for his small stature and soft-spoken, ostensibly self-effacing interpersonal style. This made people trust him and see him as both humble and interested in them. The style, however, masked an extremely grandiose and isolated man who had never had close relationships and only used the appearance of closeness, as many gaslighters do, for the advancement of his own grandiose objectives. Unbeknownst to those who had not followed his career and personal life quite closely, Dr. Frank had a pattern of allegedly abandoning responsibilities, from his children to his duties as chair of an academic department, where he was typically absent pursuing financial opportunities that his status with the university afforded him. As his power grew in national circles, those who worked closely with him began to note a highly manipulative and deceptive component to his behavior, but they were fearful of confronting him because of the personal power and cunning with which he exercised it.

Like many gaslighters, Dr. Frank's career was a trail of former colleagues who complained of being victims of dirty tricks and character assassination that had had very disruptive impacts on their own careers. The only expression of this that broke through Dr. Frank's almost total masking of his attitude was his office wall, which he decorated with magician's paraphernalia. Some argued that these symbolized Dr. Frank's manipulativeness and ongoing pattern of deception.

When he became the organization's CEO, his techniques mirrored those of many gaslighters in organizational settings. He swiftly turned on anyone that he viewed as a potential rival and forced competent personnel out of the organization. He also did what he could to collect information on other staff and key people in the governance that could potentially be used against them. His time was heavily spent on organizational politics, schmoozing with key people whom he had to flatter and placate to maintain his position. Gaslighters are notorious for "suffering fools" well because for the gaslighter, all relationships are merely opportunities for manipulation. The typical boredom that sets in for many people in suffering fools is less of a problem for the gaslighter. For the gaslighter, people are very fungible anyway, although his or her seductive charm rarely betrays that fact.

It went largely unnoticed that Dr. Frank never developed any proactive agenda for the organization and never moved out into the real world to advance organizational objectives himself. He turned a deaf ear on any new ideas that might complicate his efforts to control events or take away from the time he needed to maintain his newfound sinecure.

Throughout Dr. Frank's tenure, as long as the outside world did not intrude on the organization, things could proceed without ostensible problems. But when real-world events required competent staff skill or creativity, it was lacking. The debacles these created were either hidden or diffused with the well-developed manipulative skills Dr. Frank, like most successful gaslighters, possessed in abundance. When Dr. Frank left the organization he was widely feted for having provided years of service and for being well liked. The absence of any leadership and talent left the organization rudderless and directionless.

People are especially vulnerable to gaslighting because most people do not think that someone would be trying to manipulate their reality in this way. If they did, the uncertainty that would create would itself be very perplexing. People could never have a reliable sense of what is real and what is not real in the political world. Eventually if people become convinced that they cannot tell what is real from what is false, many will give up, feel vaguely demoralized, and simply become passive and compliant. The truth quickly becomes a casualty of gaslighting.

People who see through gaslighters like Dr. Frank feel a deep antipathy toward them. Those who do not, however, are puzzled by how anyone could be so mean-spirited as to speak critically of such a "harmless," "gentle," or "kindly" soul. Because of this, ultimately, paradoxical gaslighters become highly divisive figures who must vanguish anyone who sees through them in order to preserve their façade.

The problem of gaslighting is now endemic to the American political processes and Americans cannot "vote it out of office" in any single election simply by dispatching a particular political party. To say gaslighting was started by the Bushes, Lee Atwater, Karl Rove, Fox News, or any other extant person or group is not simply wrong, it also misses an important point. Gaslighting comes directly from blending modern communications, marketing, and advertising techniques with long-standing methods of propaganda. They were simply waiting to be discovered by those with sufficient ambition and psychological makeup to use them.

Once the genie is unleashed, no one can put him back in the bottle. The same gaslighting tactics employed by the Bush clan were already well under way in the 2008 presidential campaign as early as January of 2007, without George Bush or Karl Rove. In the 2000 election, George W. Bush hired a Texas public relations firm to help him win the South Carolina GOP primary against Senator John McCain. One of the tactics they used was to spread the word that John McCain had fathered a black child. In fact, McCain and his wife had adopted and raised a little girl of South Asian heritage. Nonetheless, the Bush firm's depiction of it appealed to the still-extensive racism in parts of South Carolina. In part because of that whisper campaign, Bush overtook McCain in South Carolina at a critical point in the primaries and secured the nomination.[19] Of course, it created bad blood between Bush and McCain, especially with McCain.

But that's not the significant part of the story. What is significant in terms of American political trends is the announcement in early January 2007 that John McCain had hired to represent him in his efforts to secure the 2008 Republican presidential nomination the very same PR firm that in 2000 had smeared him.[20] A few weeks after this announcement, South Carolina newspaper *The State* posted an article reporting two mailings attacking McCain GOP rival Mitt Romney for his Mormon faith. One of them, an e-mail, said, "Those dark suspicions you hide deep inside yourself about Mormonism are trying to tell you something. Trust your instincts! The light of truth will burn through the smoke and mirrors of Mitt Romney's movie star looks and crafty words." The newspaper reported that the e-mail included a copy of an article saying that Romney's ancestors practiced polygamy. The e-mail was signed "Martin W."[21]

But in today's world of political gaslighting, the situation gets more confusing. Who actually sent the e-mail? Was it McCain? Or was it someone who wanted it to look like it came from McCain?

This style of making it look like the other is slinging mud has now become a mainstay in American politics. *The State,* for example, points out that McCain's South Carolina campaign director in a prior campaign for a different candidate "sent party loyalists a copy of an article from *The State* that accused his candidate's rival of accepting a bribe. He admitted he made the email appear to have come from an opponent's campaign."[22]

One of Karl Rove's reported tricks is to make it appear he has himself been "victimized" by an opponent's dirty trick to make his opponent look bad. In the 1986 Texas governor's race, for example, Rove discovered that his office was bugged on the very day his candidate was to have a debate in which his candidate was not expected to do very well. The alleged bugging raised the suspicion that the opponent had been caught in skullduggery. It also deflected attention away from the debate.[23]

Joshua Green describes another race in Karl Rove's successful attempt to turn the Alabama Supreme Court from a Democratic stronghold to a Republican probusiness court:

> *A typical instance occurred in the hard-fought 1996 race for a seat on the Alabama Supreme Court between Rove's client, Harold See, then a University of Alabama law professor, and the Democratic incumbent, Kenneth Ingram. According to someone who worked for him, Rove, dissatisfied with the campaign's progress, had flyers printed up–absent any trace of who was behind them–viciously attacking See and his family.*
>
> *The ploy left Rove's opponent at a loss. Ingram's staff realized that it would be fruitless to try to persuade the public that the See campaign was attacking its own candidate in order "to create a backlash against the Democrat," as Joe Perkins, who worked for Ingram, put it to me. Presumably the public would believe that Democrats were spreading terrible rumors about See and his family. "They just beat you down to your knees," Ingram said of being on the receiving end of Rove's attacks. See won the race.*[24]

In fact, Rove's modus operandi has caused some to speculate whether he set up Dan Rather in the Bush military record error that toppled Rather from CBS. Whether this is true or not, the fact that Karl Rove's name would quickly come to mind is both noteworthy and understandable.[25]

Gaslighting will not end with Bush and Rove because the forces benefiting from the gaslighting have realized that their goals are larger than a single candidate and demand commitment beyond a single term of office. Grover Norquist, director of an organization he created, Americans for Tax Reform, has become a power player among conservative Republicans. He holds a weekly meeting for conservatives of all stripes to coordinate tactics. The Bush administration sends a representative and Vice President Cheney sends a personal representative. Norquist has a variety of aims, but whenever one of his objectives is officially adopted by a party or a president, he starts a timeline. His welfare reform timeline started in 1980, under Reagan, and ended in 1996, under Clinton. Others are incomplete.[26]

Bush and Rove are just the tip of the iceberg. There have always been people willing to exercise the kind of machinations Americans have seen in recent years. Prior to this the means have been lacking. The structure is now in place. As we shall see in the next chapter, the American political process today is a gaslighter's paradise. By creating a television network to advance, amplify, and reinforce an artificially created reality, the gaslighters can operate 24/7.

CHAPTER 7
FOX NEWS: SPEAKING POWER TO TRUTH

She knows what you need, but I know what you want.

—BOB DYLAN

The CEO of Fox News is Roger Ailes—the same Roger Ailes of Willie Horton fame. The owner of Fox News is archconservative Rupert Murdoch, a media mogul whose communications empire reaches four and a half billion people worldwide. Between the two of them, they have created a new tripartite media creature that is part infotainment, part news channel, and part instrument of political gaslighting. The three components combined have created a powerful new force in American politics shaping how many Americans form their political reality: Fox News.

The most dangerous aspect of American politics began with the 1988 presidential campaign of George H. W. Bush when a few strategically placed neoconservatives recognized that with the right set of circumstances they could manipulate and even create people's reality sense to an extent never before dreamed possible. The tail could now wag the dog.

Symbols, manufactured feeling states, repetition, and associational reasoning are the four primary tools of Fox News. They have put Fox News on the cutting edge of transforming the news into a massive system of subliminal communications that are very much at odds with what their listeners understand to be taking place as they listen to their nightly news. It is gaslighting, pure and simple.

Advertising succeeds on the basis of repetition. Assert the reality you want over and over again. Be absolute and never tentative. Tentativeness encourages independent thinking. The more people think independently, the less malleable they are. If there is a gap between your position and common sense, simply rewire the connection with "associational logic" that obscures the gap. Associational logic, described more fully below, creates the illusion of logical connections where there are none. This is where the unique talents of Roger Ailes come into play.

After leaving the Bush campaign in the late 1980s, Ailes participated in efforts on behalf of the tobacco industry to thwart the success of antismoking and antitobacco measures.[1] Understandably, advertising for tobacco products took on unique difficulties after the increasingly devastating research on the health hazards of smoking with the imposition of health warnings, increased sales taxes, state regulations, and consumer lawsuits. For the tobacco industry, these created a public relations nightmare.

I was working in Washington during this period. One of my tasks was to establish a public relations and marketing program to promote psychology and mental health services. In this time of great upheaval in the public relations programs of tobacco, many tobacco marketers applied for our open positions, and, as a result, I unexpectedly wound up meeting with a number of tobacco public relations workers. They were by far the most unusual public relations thinkers I encountered.

When I asked them to describe their work, they went into great detail on many of the messages they had developed for tobacco. Most strikingly, there were no protobacco themes in the ads. Instead, there were carefully constructed, but nonsensical, messages that amounted to intellectual gibberish for anyone who really tried to follow the content. There was so little coherence to the message that even after listening to a few examples, I was unable to repeat them. These were marketing initiatives that were seemingly apropos of nothing. The closest thing to this I had ever seen were TV advertisements during the 1984 Olympics that simply said "Saudi Arabia." Nothing more. My naive explanation at the time was that they were from a very wealthy oil sheik who did not understand marketing in the United States and had failed to provide any advertising message.

The joke was on me. I frequently had to confess to the tobacco experts that I could not understand the message of these ads. They laughed and said, "That's our goal. We don't want you to come away with a message; even if we had a positive one, it would run afoul of government regulations banning tobacco advertising. What we want is for you to hear the word 'tobacco' and/or 'smoking.' A message with any content would only dilute that experience." The gleeful expression on these invariably attractive and bright young professionals was eerie.

Other tobacco ads were public service ads that were ostensibly antismoking. I assumed it was simply an attempt to undo part of the negative image that the companies had generated by associating themselves with worthwhile causes. But it was still striking that a company would spend money on ads that seemingly told people not to use their product.

In fact, it was far more cynical than that. The apparent motive was but a front for a more sinister one that was predicated on an understanding of how the mind really works, rather than how we might think it works. The mind works symbolically, not logically.

Symbols, mental representations we have in our mind, create images of emotionally laden experiences that we associate with those symbols. These can be very powerful. Because we see ourselves primarily as thinking people, acting on the basis of logic, we can very easily overlook the impact that these symbols are having on us. They operate almost exclusively on a feeling level; that is, they create a visceral experience that we have in our body but not necessarily in our conscious, rational thoughts. Because of this, symbols motivate us through unarticulated feeling states in ways we often do not understand. The conscious thoughts that we have then tend to arise only in response to these primitive feeling states, not in response to logic.

For example, one tobacco advertising campaign told people, "Think, Don't Smoke."[2] In the workings of the mind, the *operative* language of that ad is "smoke." Smoke is the symbolic object. The negation "don't" is like an inert substance. We cannot think of not smoking without thinking of smoking. The concept of smoking becomes an image that takes the form and plays the highly active role of a symbol in the mind. Once there's an image about smoking in people's heads, they are just as likely to light up a cigarette as they are to become more resistant to lighting one up.

That visceral experience in this case is of smoking a cigarette. The image this creates is not merely a verbal thought. It is, instead, an emotional experience. As one has that experience, all of the carefully conditioned prior associations to cigarette smoking come into play, including the Marlboro Man, "You've come a long way, baby," Humphrey Bogart, and other implanted associations connected with being "cool" or of being soothed by a cigarette.

Once it has that status as a symbol, the image functions as an emotional implant. That implant is much more powerful than any verbal content that might come attached to the symbol–such as, in this case, to "think." The verbal content in which the symbol is ensconced is comparatively inert and of limited, if any, importance. Paradoxically, then, one can plant the idea of smoking by telling someone *not* to do it. The content of the message is anti-smoking, but it can be a powerful and effective form of suggestion to encourage people to smoke.

Recently, the federal antidrug programs discovered this same thing: their campaign against drugs was creating more users than it was reducing the number of users. A study by the U.S. Government Accountability Office found that the more kids viewed the antidrug advertising, the more likely they were to use drugs. The GAO stated: "[G]reater exposure to the campaign was associated with weaker anti-drug norms and increases in the perceptions that others use marijuana."[3] The tobacco industry knew what they were doing in telling people "not" to smoke.

Given the way the mind works, for the viewer the relevant issue is not whether Fox News is actually fair and balanced; the issue is whether the symbolic language of fair and balanced is associated psychologically in their minds with Fox News. In that light, it is easy to see why viewers, asked what they like about Fox News, frequently respond, "It's fair and balanced." The words are repeated to them with such numbing regularity that even people who hate Fox News find it difficult not to link the two. Symbols in this way can be implanted in the viewer's mind and become the determinative emotional experience characterizing the associated person,

place, or thing. For the mind, symbols can far outstrip more lan-
guid policy discussions in importance.

The source of the ideas being implanted is an important factor in
the impact the ideas have on people. This is one of the critical
reasons it is important to Fox News that it be seen as *the* fair and
balanced network. Television personalities are powerful to begin
with. If they are also respectable journalists or newscasters, not
propagandists, the power is amplified.

This problem of suggestion about what is real and what is not
real from someone powerful has been dramatically seen in the
mental health field in what was known as the "repressed memory" dispute. The repressed memory dispute concerned childhood incest and sexual abuse. In Freud's early years of practice,
many of his patients reported memories of being sexually abused
as children by their father or some other caregiver. Freud initially
thought most of these were actual childhood memories, but he
later concluded that many were childhood fantasies born out of
Oedipal wishes, the presumed love relationship between the
child and the opposite-sex parent.

In relatively unquestioning acceptance of what was for Freud
simply a shift in emphasis, many therapists told patients who reported having been molested as a child that they had confused a
childhood wish with reality. This assertion came from a therapist
on whom the patient was dependent and who was ostensibly an
expert on such matters. People who actually had been victimized
by incest were told that they were just imagining it because of
their own lascivious longings, not because of the very experience
they in truth found so traumatic. They were told that their basic

reality sense was incorrect and that their mind was deluded, just as Ingrid Bergman's character was in the movie *Gaslight*.

Eventually, many people in the mental health community began to realize that some of their patients experienced real childhood sexual abuse. In response, the pendulum swung the other way. Soon some therapists began to see sexual abuse behind every rock and tree. In some cases, psychologists interpreted faint bodily sensations reported by patients as evidence of childhood sexual abuse. Of course, bodily states can come from many different sources, some real (generated in external reality) and some fantasized (generated from internal experiences). Regardless, they are hardly presumptive evidence of sexual abuse.

What is intriguing for our purposes here, however, is that the therapist's suggestion of incest so readily took hold as reality in the minds of the patients. When patients were advised that these highly subjective psychological states were evidence of incest, they began to have "memories" of such encounters. Naturally, when they confronted the family "perpetrator" about these events that allegedly happened decades earlier, it created considerable uproar. Often the damage to the patient's family was irreparable.[4]

But why were these suggestions so quickly and convincingly accepted? First and foremost, the mind needs a reality sense. If the trusted therapist's suggestion helps to organize a series of still unexplained, vague, or inchoate bodily experiences, it can start to feel very compelling. As we have noted, the wall between internal reality and external reality is much more porous than people appreciate.

If we doubt this, we can look at our dreams. Whatever chaos we experience in our dreams, on a moment-by-moment basis we are having a sense of a very real "external reality" *without* any external reality. Dreams are visual images, like one's presumed external reality, but they are manufactured completely within the internal recesses of the person's mind. When the therapist raises the possibility of incest, the patient has a fantasy of incest even if it is just part of the process of determining whether in fact it actually happened. That fantasy imagery can take on a life of its own and in the mind become as much a reality as any other life experience. Because of this, it is not as hard to create mental images in someone's mind as one might expect it to be. Once the image is there, it is surprisingly close to being experienced as a reality. Our reality sense is formed in our mind, not in external reality.

Symbolic experiences make all people especially vulnerable to the kind of suggestion implanted in these patients. A symbol's distinguishing characteristic is that it creates or invokes "feeling states," psychological experiences strong enough to require psychological attention. That is why symbols are so powerful. To varying degrees, these feeling states can make people uncomfortable, and, when that happens, naturally they seek relief in the form of explanation, reassurance, or rationalization.

Many people will do anything to get away from such uncomfortable feelings and are eager for anyone's help in doing so. Any person or system of thought that can help them escape the subjectivity and uncertainty of the problem will gain adherents. Gaslighters exploit existing feeling states or they can create their own with symbols. A common mood state Fox News engenders is reminiscent of the movie *Network*'s famous line, "We're mad as hell and we're not going to take it anymore." Sarcasm and even contempt often seem to drip from the screen with Fox News, intense feelings that prime viewers for aggressive and negative positions. It is hard to picture Sean Hannity reporting on a situation that requires maintaining our national collective calm—the Cuban Missile Crisis, for example, or the assassination of President Kennedy. Since 9/11 in particular, Americans have had an abundance of disquieting feeling states, but they have had precious little constructive help in managing them.

Symbols and vague visceral feeling states are integral components of any attempt to build a reality sense. So is repetition. Words create symbols and take on symbolic value *if they are repeated often enough.* This is why political ads are repeated over and over and over again long after we assume the market is "saturated." If one understands this vulnerability, it opens endless political possibilities to a skilled political architect.

Late-night liberal comedy shows like *The Daily Show* and *The Colbert Report* demonstrate with great hilarity the fact that White House media supporters all use identical language in supporting a political point of view. While the ostensible joke is that these people are all like puppets articulating a canned message from the White House, there is much more than that at play. If the same language is used, the words can be transformed from language into symbols. University of California at Berkeley linguist George Lakoff writes:

> *When a word or phrase is repeated over and over for a long period of time, the neural circuits that compute its meaning are activated repeatedly in the brain. As the neurons in those circuits fire, the synapses connecting the neurons in the circuits get stronger and the circuits may eventually become permanent, which happens when you learn the meaning of any word in your fixed vocabulary. Learning a*

word physically changes your brain, and the meaning of that word
becomes physically instantiated in your brain.[5]

Repeating over and over does not simply persuade someone that what is being said is true; it actually *makes* it true in the inner workings of the mind. The target audience may not even be aware that they have adopted the particular point of view in question, but a space that was once filled with uncertainty is now filled with an idea. Further, it is an idea shared by a very self-confident and powerful other person. If that idea is repeated over and over, it begins to play a symbolic role in the mind.

Building a secure reality sense in confusing times is difficult. The state of perplexity is a frightening one. Fox's message appeals to people who unconsciously want someone to weave them a comprehensive "reality" that reduces their perplexity caused by confusing events. If a strong and attractive person with an aura of confidence repeats the same message over and over again, and if that message is packaged in content that offers a solution to the perplexity, many will succumb to the message and accept uncritically the "reality" that is offered by the messenger.

The spokespeople for Fox News speak with a certainty that a perplexed mind craves as much as a drowning man craves air. Listening to Bill O'Reilly or Sean Hannity is hearing power. Their power, for some, bulldozes reality and dethrones independent thinking. "If you accept my reality, you can resolve your perplexity and bask in the reassurance that comes from my power." For many Americans, that is an offer they cannot refuse.

Symbols, primitive emotional states, and repetition are not the only vulnerable aspects of the mind. Associational thinking also plays a key role in current political gaslighting. Sometimes it is very humbling to recognize the true nature of our mind. It is made out of symbols that are connected to one another by associations of emotional connections. What we think of as logical connections play a much more limited role in mental functioning. This has tremendous implications not just for advertising, but also for political reality formation. Gaslighters can build emotional connections between symbols without their target audience really even knowing that it is being done. In 2000, the Republican Party spent over two and a half million dollars running an advertisement attacking the Gore prescription plan that had the word *rats* written across it but that flashed with such speed that it was invisible to the naked eye.[6] With today's technology, people can literally build a connection in the mind between rats and an opponent's policy position.

These same associational connections once established can also create a pseudologic in which *associations* create the illusion of *logical* connections used to support policies and positions that simply have no logic behind them. The fact that two items are in some way associated in the mind serves as a substitute for the formal logical connections that people associate with cause and effect and rational thought. The mind is tricked just as our eyes are tricked in a shell game. For an undiscerning audience, this can be very effective. People frequently do not appreciate, or even notice, the role that highly subjective emotional states play in formulating what they take to be rational and logically constructed "thoughts." Psychologist William James said, "People often think they are thinking when in fact they are just rearranging their prejudices."

If these associational forms of "logic" lead to a pleasant emotional state such as a simplistic and self-gratifying conclusion about a difficult and complex problem, people are even less likely to challenge the faulty reasoning behind it. If one's mind is saturated with images that are the psychological equivalent of a trademark that brands Fox News as fair and balanced, it will for many people completely override any assessment of whether Fox News is actually fair and balanced.

Similarly, if people focus on and reject one unacceptable solution to the country's predicament in Iraq, without noting there is no other acceptable alternative, they can feel satisfaction at dismissing a "bad option." After all, the country must succeed in Iraq; America cannot "cut and run." By assuming they can simply reject this bad alternative, the advocates of war create a more comfortable emotional state in which people do not have to accept the inevitability of the pain that comes from seeing they are really faced with a horrible dilemma—a bloodbath if America leaves on the one hand, or a bloodbath if America stays on the other. While logic dictates one must choose between two undesirable options, discarding one that is clearly bad creates the illusion of being logical and the satisfied feeling state that comes with it.

If someone brings this problem up for public discussion, one can still avoid facing the painful reality by labeling the comments "defeatism" that "emboldens our enemies." The anger with which this is said fortifies the resistance the listener has to experiencing the perplexity of being in a no-win situation given the painful dilemma reality holds. Not surprisingly, it is a very easy task to encourage people in this state to rationalize these feelings into a conclusion that the media is captured by the bogeyman-liberals and is not "fair and balanced."

Thus, America, in the service of temporary emotional comfort, continues down self-defeating paths to avoid undesirable dilemmas it cannot escape and can only make worse by ignoring them. In doing so, it obscures latent conflicts and lets gaslighters use delay and procrastination to their advantage.

Given the new technology and the increasingly sophisticated understanding of the mind, political gaslighting is no longer limited to election time. Now people can work to shape the reality they want other people to have on an around-the-clock basis if they have the media resources and the political expertise. Ailes had the political expertise; Murdoch had the media resources.

No private citizen in history has had the logistical capacity to influence the world's view of reality that Rupert Murdoch has. Like Ailes, Rupert Murdoch is well known in publishing circles, but less so to the viewing audience of Fox News. To them, he is anything but a household name. He started his media enterprise in his native Australia, migrated to Great Britain, and finally moved to the United States where he took up U.S. citizenship. He is unabashedly an archconservative and a great admirer of Ronald Reagan.[7]

Murdoch reportedly owns 175 newspapers, 100 cable TV channels, 40 television stations, a movie studio, and 40 different book imprints. His personal fortune is estimated at more than $6 billion. Murdoch's publishing empire has the potential to reach about three-fourths of the world's population. In the United States alone, his media reach 280 million Americans.[8]

Murdoch's influence has led to a sea change in the news marketplace. *News as information has been replaced by news as stimulation.* Part of Murdoch's genius lay in his appreciation of the fact that media, especially news media, can be packaged in ways that

are much more appealing to people than they have been traditionally. These changes are reflected in the new terminology of
"infotainment" and "soft news." Given the unique extent of Murdoch's control over mass media around the world, it is not surprising that he has been blamed for the now well-documented
changes that have taken place in the news over the last twenty-
five years.[9]

Hard news is defined as news that people need in order to understand current matters of state. Soft news is "more sensational,
more personality-centered, less time-bound, more practical, and
more incident-based than other news." It is "what will interest an
audience rather than what the audience needs to know."[10] Both are
called news, yet they are very different creatures. On the day that
the verdict in the trial of Lewis "Scooter" Libby was announced,
that judgment was the top story on Foxnews.com, as it was on the
other major news sources, and it received generous attention and
commentary from conservatives Robert Novak, Brit Hume, and
Rich Lowry.[11] Much of it was critical of the jury's decision and of
the prosecution itself. What is significant for our purposes here,
however, is that the other top stories on Fox were TEXAS PROBES
JUVIE INMATE ABUSE, SAUDI RAPE VICTIM FACES 90 LASHES, and NOT
GUILTY PLEA from a man who was accused of killing and dismem-
bering his wife. Its "Top Video" was RUFF RESCUE, about a dog rescued from icy water. On MSNBC, by contrast, the Libby story was
followed by DOZENS OF IRAQI PILGRIMS MASSACRED, and SUMATRA
QUAKE KILLS SCORES, while the top video was DOW SURGES TO
BEST DAILY GAIN OF YEAR.[12] The Fox stories reflect a preference for
the sensational over the traditional criteria for the news. It is no
longer what people need to know; it is simply what will appeal to
their more primitive need for stimulation.

Fairly or not, Murdoch has been blamed for the increasing tilt toward stimulation in the media that has led to the extensive coverage of high-profile crimes and other stimulating events that are of limited news value. If stimulation is more important in attracting a larger number of viewers, stimulation becomes the new criterion for "newsworthiness," replacing the public's need to know.

Fox News, in its battle with traditional television news media, fights on a very uneven playing field, not unlike the one that parents confront each evening in fighting with their children over whether to do their homework or play video games. The video games are more stimulating and have the joy of an escapist fantasy. Homework is, well, homework, and it is decidedly less stimulating. It is not surprising that Fox News has gained market share in media news.[13]

Many have lamented the debilitating effect this emphasis on stimulation over newsworthy content has on the minds of the viewers, who come away with less of the information they need to pass judgment on critical issues confronting the country. Former PBS anchor Robert McNeil says that the trends "toward the sensational, the hype, the hyperactive, the tabloid values tends to drive out the serious."[14] Others note that the emphasis on the sensational gives people incorrect information on important matters like crime. In the 1990s, when there was a dramatic increase of crime coverage in the media, for example, the public thought that crime had increased, when in fact it had decreased.[15] Politically, people who watch Fox News have a different view of reality when it comes to Iraq. Fox viewers were substantially more likely to believe there was a connection between 9/11 and Saddam Hussein than the viewers of all other networks.[16] And, of course, when

George W. Bush repeatedly used the words, *Iraq, Saddam Hussein,* and *9/11* in proximity to one another, the "associational logic" was created, substituting for real logic.

Marketing research results document the effectiveness of this transition to soft news in building viewership. Some critics contend that this is only a short-term effect of soft news and in the long term, people will actually lose interest in the news itself.[17] Regardless, that is not the full extent of the problem. What is particularly problematic, research indicates, is that the distinction between hard news and soft news is dividing America.

From a marketing perspective, news outlets that emphasize exclusively soft news and news outlets that emphasize exclusively hard news do better than new stations that try to walk a middle ground between the two. The implication is that America is heading down two divergent tracks of reality formation. One audience listens to hard news and the other listens to soft news. They will arrive at very different realities.[18] One can already see this happening with Fox News.

Obviously, those who watch Fox News prefer the experience they have watching Fox than the one they have watching other news channels. Why? Listening to Fox News is quite simply a different emotional experience from listening to traditional newscasts on other networks. Fox News provides stimulation. The sound and visual effects of Fox News are almost carnival-like, with multiple crawlers and a seemingly constant state of news crises created by "Fox News Alerts." The Fox News visual landscape conjures images of a Salvador Dali painting or a Fellini movie ensconced in American-style pop culture. Comedian Stephen Colbert's *Colbert Report* on Comedy Central, with its American flags, soaring eagles, and other patriotic symbols all vying for attention, mocks the Fox News emphasis on such visual symbols.

Unfortunately, as absurd as it may seem in caricature, these mechanisms are shaping reality in America and overriding rational policy deliberations. They create a mood or feeling state that makes us easy prey for ideas handed to us in dramatic, stimulating, and repetitive fashion. The set colors make other networks seem drab by contrast. And their spokespeople are anything but subdued. Bill O'Reilly and Sean Hannity, for example, provide a powerful presence that is very stimulating. Whether one likes them or not, the drama of the performance is unquestionably more intense than the experience one has watching another news network anchor.

Fox News also makes its listeners feel special. Its reports leave viewers feeling that they have been told the real scoop, and by virtue of that, they are special. Bill O'Reilly tells his viewers that he is "telling it like it is," and they feel he is doing just that. As a result his viewers feel that because of him they will not fall for what the less-informed fall for; they know what's "really going on," and they are grateful to O'Reilly for it. They cannot get that same experience elsewhere. For people suffering from the self-esteem deficits caused by confusion and uncertainty, the disdain and superiority O'Reilly exudes can provide a temporary but welcome relief. He is for them a balm of relief from the narcissistic burden of envy and pervasive perplexity.

O'Reilly uses this special relationship to pontificate on some matters that appear well beyond his expertise and in some areas can do considerable damage even when he may intend none. Child rearing is one such area. In January 2007, O'Reilly suddenly launched into what was for me as a psychologist one of the most startling presentations I have ever seen on TV. He gave a brief commentary on how fathers should raise sons. He said that fathers should be like "knights" for their sons. The father should tell the son that the world is a very scary and dangerous place and that the son must stick very close to his knight and do exactly what the knight tells him to do if he wants to be safe. The knight will even on occasion serve as the little boy's "avenger." In this way the father-knight will keep the boy safe from all evil.[19]

After saying this, without much explanation or elaboration, O'Reilly appeared satisfied that he had conveyed his message, and the show broke for commercial. I should emphasize that I did not feel O'Reilly necessarily meant any harm by his comments or that there was any underhanded objective. The problem I have with it is that with apparently little awareness or malevolent intent, O'Reilly prescribed for America a recipe for raising a little fascist boy, one who is so frightened of moving away from a powerful authority figure that he will do whatever the authoritarian personality tells him to do. In the musical classic *The Sound of Music*, the young Nazi, Rolfe, who struggled between his loving feelings for one of the von Trapp daughters and his own fearful need to comply with the dictates of Nazism, personified the personality that O'Reilly's prescription would encourage. For people struggling to maintain control of their own emotional conflicts, having an external authoritarian force self-control and compliance through fear and promises of protection will always have its appeal. This, of course, is also the allure of a "strong" president protecting America from terrorists.

In addition to the powerful allure of its O'Reillys and Hannitys, Fox News gives its viewers the visceral experience one gets when experiencing righteous indignation—the "harrumph" response. This component to indignation for many is a pick-me-up for flagging self-esteem and an outlet for envious rage masked as contempt and disdain. *I* am superior to *them.*

Above all, Fox gives the viewer a huge emotional catharsis through rage. It is difficult to watch Fox News without feeling tremendous animosity about what one hears. From a psychological perspective, this is an emotional feast of epic proportions in comparison to any of the other news networks. The problem with this relief, however, is that the viewer ultimately becomes dependent on it, putting the viewer at the mercy of the messenger. And when that happens, news can be a vehicle for manipulation.

With such an attractive emotional package for many people, Fox News can deliver whatever partisan message it wants. When Murdoch first bought Fox Network, some of its staff reported that they were frequently ordered from on high to espouse particular points of view and ordered literally to create stories that suited Murdoch's political objectives. Murdoch hated Senator Edward M. Kennedy, so stories about Chappaquiddick became mandatory for Fox reporters even though there was nothing new to report. Former Fox News employees reported, for example, that they were assigned to create a news story about the response to Ronald Reagan's birthday—though there was very little response to it to report. The list of such episodes goes on and on.[20]

But the long-term psychological effect on the viewer of Fox News goes beyond the individual political messages. Fox encourages a self-indulgence that has a regressive impact on people and encourages them to accept psychologically simple, emotionally cathartic solutions to problems, solutions that are oftentimes less reality based than they should be. The notion that "they hate us for our freedom" as an explanation for America's current problematic relationship with much of the Islamic world does not bode well for America's ability to work out a modus vivendi with its world neighbors. A more reality-based explanation is more complex and taxing.

In obvious response to Fox News, MSNBC has tried to create the same type of ambience and emotional experience with Keith Olbermann's lengthy commentary, often directed at President Bush. His ratings have improved. On the whole, however, liberal attempts to emulate the conservative Fox News approach have been unsuccessful, as evidenced by the difficulties of Air America Radio. A few liberal writers of the genre such as Maureen Dowd and Al Franken have experienced some success, but there seems to be a limited appetite for what they offer. The only real exception has been in the comedy area where the satirists Jon Stewart and Stephen Colbert have been highly successful. The emotional payoff for their viewers, however, is the ironic humor that underlies most of what they do. This is quite different from the emotional ambience people experience with the relatively humorless Bill O'Reilly and Sean Hannity.

But it is not just that Fox News provides people with more pleasurable stimulation than other networks. Fox also benefits from the fact that the traditional or hard news is by its very nature heavily weighted toward the "bad" news, something that is not the least bit pleasurable.

People's aversion to hard news manifests itself in several ways. One is the public clamor that news stations report the "good news," not just the bad, in effect asking to hear about the sheep that did not get lost that day. Another is the prevalent complaint that the traditional news casts America in a negative light. These requests for the news to be more "positive" are a straightforward statement of the difficulty people have integrating the news into a reality sense that they can tolerate. Instead, people are made to feel perplexed about the plight of their country by listening to the news.

But, of course, that is exactly what the news media's job is if it is to help people be effective citizens in a democracy. The democracy works only if there is ongoing criticism and self-critique. In a pluralistic society, a central task of a news organization is to bring troubling facts of the day to the public awareness so that the people, operating through their other political institutions, can assimilate and address those problems. In today's world, addressing those problems is mentally taxing, indeed. Former CNN correspondent Bob Franken says, "We historically are not supposed to be popular, and it's almost our role to be the bearer of bad news."[21] For many, the traditional presentation of the news is an ongoing assault on their reality sense. They hear and see wave after wave of problematic information—much of which is negative, threatening, and complex—and have to integrate it into their reality sense.

The phrase *liberal news media* symbolizes the discomfort that some people feel listening to the news. One can avoid that burden if he or she shoots the messenger and, instead, listens to a newscast that offers simple, psychologically reassuring, and/or cathartic political solutions. Doing so reinforces a new dimension of psychological management to the news and effectively means Americans are flying blind, devoid of real facts necessary

to make informed and competent decisions. Fox News's definition of the liberal news media includes ABC, NBC, CBS, PBS,
and CNN—in short, all of its major competitors.

The total control Murdoch and Ailes have over Fox News content, given their backgrounds, should raise the obvious question
of bias. Despite the protests of groups like MoveOn.org, it is surprising how few questions have actually been raised about this in
mainstream media. Bias, of course, can and does infect any media
outlet. However, the question of bias might seem especially compelling in the case of Fox News. This is particularly true when
Fox is compared with its competition—an imperfect but established and diverse press corps with a professional standard of fair
and balanced reporting, personified by American icons such as
Walter Lippmann, Edward R. Murrow, Walter Cronkite, Peter
Jennings, and many others who are identified exclusively with
news media and not with partisan politics.

And yet many Americans choose Fox over any other cable network for their news. And, if you ask, many of them will say verbatim the reason they choose Fox is because Fox is "fair and
balanced." Not that Fox is less "biased" or more "objective" or
other words of similar meaning. They will use the exact words,
"fair and balanced."

At the 1996 press conference that was held to announce that
Roger Ailes was to be the CEO to build the new Fox Cable
News network, Ailes himself raised and dismissed any significance
that might be attributed to his political background. He said
that his political days were long behind him and that in the last
several years he had been working exclusively in the media with
MSNBC.[22] In fact, Ailes's tenure at MSNBC was two years, and be-

fore that he was executive producer of Rush Limbaugh's television program, which he had created. He had been working almost exclusively for Republican interests, the tobacco industry, and other large corporate clients as a consultant for the twenty years before that. After asserting his objectivity, Ailes then fired what was the opening salvo against his competitors, saying he was coming to Fox News to "restore objectivity" to the news industry.[23]

This tendency to seize the offensive by accusing the adversary first of one's own vulnerabilities has become a common feature of political gaslighting. Effective gaslighters anticipate their own vulnerabilities and preempt any anticipated assault before it can do them any damage. Oftentimes, they turn it to their advantage. George Bush's assault on John Kerry's military record, startling to many for its boldness, was a clear example.

Fox has continued to address its potential credibility problem with an aggressive two-pronged approach, asserting its own virtues and denigrating its adversaries in a manner unprecedented in major American television news. From its inception in 1996, Fox simply asserted that it was "fair and balanced." This self-ascribed characteristic became a Fox banner that psychologically served as a combination of symbolic talisman and mantra, repeated again and again, creating a reassuring mental state in the viewer. Few would now doubt its effectiveness. But *why* is it so effective?

Fox's appreciation of the significance of its banner "fair and balanced" took on comic, but telling, proportions when it tried to restrict use of the phrase. In its lawsuit against comedian Al Franken, who wrote a book entitled *Lies and the Lying Liars Who Tell Them: A Fair and Balanced Look at the Right,* Fox contended that Franken's use of the phrase "fair and balanced" might confuse viewers or readers who associated the phrase with Fox as a trademark infringement and sought an injunction against distribution of the book. This seemed preposterous to many people who see the phrase *fair and balanced* as everyday adjectives. But, as the lawsuit made clear, Fox's psychological intent for the phrase is that of a trademark. If they truly could have a monopoly on the concept of fair and balanced, Fox would become the only media game in town.

Understandably, it would be a lot easier for gaslighters to communicate their messages if they could neutralize the credibility of any other news source that might challenge the reality they are presenting—that is, the free and independent press. The phrase *fair and balanced* is not just a defensive shield to avoid being attacked, but also a tremendous offensive sword designed to undercut the credibility of any entity that seeks to define reality in any way other than the way Fox News wants it defined. Getting the exclusive attention of the target audience makes gaslighting much, much easier.

Armed with the symbolic protection of its Fair and Balanced implant, Ailes and Fox News have added to the psychological lessons of political marketing that entered politics after the Kennedy-Nixon debates and applied them to an around-the-clock cable news network. It generates psychologically sophisticated political indoctrination twenty-four hours a day, seven days a week.

For millions of Americans, Fox News and their church are the two most powerful external influences helping their minds create a reality sense. If media has changed in America, so, too, has religion. The potential effect on reality formation of changes from either the media or the pulpit is significant, but when the two occur at the same time, it can be extraordinary.

CHAPTER 8
THE RELIGIOUS RIGHT: FAITH-BASED REALITY

Religion is regarded by the common people as true, by the wise as false, and by the rulers as useful.

—SENECA

Forty-three percent of Americans now consider themselves to be born-again in the Christian faith.[1] This does not just mean Americans believe different things about religion. It means that Americans are walking about in very different realities and are using very different criteria for determining what is real and what is not.

For most Americans who grew up prior to 1980, religion was a staid, moderating influence in American life. It was an institution that lent a predictable element to their social order, and was at most only marginally connected to the political world. It was very much an anchor for the established social order.

Yes, Americans had heard of small pockets of people who spoke in tongues and handled snakes. Like charismatic tent revivalists, these groups were primarily considered to be a backwater phenomenon, an endangered species that was dying out. They were dismissed with the same cultural prejudice directed at much of the American South at the time, where most of them lived.

That has changed. For the growing number of Americans that

now embrace fundamental Christian and Pentecostal beliefs, religious faith is a radical psychological experience. It establishes its own reality, logic, emotional priorities, and set of criteria for determining what is politically relevant. This has made the religious right especially fertile ground for the gaslighters.

Many of the religious right thought they were doing God's work in helping elect George Bush to the presidency. In the 2004 presidential election, George Bush used fundamentalist and Pentecostal churches to disseminate campaign literature and to get out the vote in an organizational structure very similar to the sales and distribution model of Amway soap.

The politicization of religion is not limited to the fundamentalists and Pentecostals. In 2004, the Sunday before the election, many Catholics received "Guidelines for Catholic Voters" explaining that there were five and only five "non-negotiable issues" for good Catholics to consider in voting. They were abortion, euthanasia, stem-cell research, human cloning, and homosexual union.[2] These, of course, all favored George W. Bush.

Since the 2004 election, very direct assaults have been made on the separation of church and state. In Virginia in 2007, a bill (HJ 724) was introduced into the state legislature to amend the Statute for Religious Freedom by limiting its guarantee of the separation of church and state. The statute had been written by Thomas Jefferson.[3]

For those who are not part of this resurgence of religious fundamentalism, it feels both alarming and perplexing. Religion has long been singled out, especially by parts of the mental health community, for its alleged refusal to see reality as it is and its desire instead to substitute an overly simplistic comforting fantasy of unwarranted and unsupportable conclusions. Freud, for example, dismissed religion as an illusion: "It would be very nice if there were a God who created the world and was a benevolent providence, and if there were a moral order in the universe and an after-life; but it is a very striking fact that all this is exactly as we are bound to wish it to be."[4]

But if one looks at what the mind has to do to create a reality that leaves people comfortable, the expansion of religion, or more precisely fundamentalist religion, is not so surprising. For many minds facing a confusing world in which they are buffeted about by envy, sexual perplexity, and paranoia, religion has much to offer.

Religious fundamentalism plays three psychological roles, all of which reinforce one another to make fundamentalist religion very appealing for millions. First, it fills in important gaps in our reality sense, and in doing so it eases the perplexity that the mind feels from uncertainty. Second, religion provides support for the mind as it struggles with the three battleground emotional states—envy, sexual perplexity, and paranoia. Finally, and least apparent to those who are not part of Pentecostal or fundamentalist religion, it provides an ecstatic experience that is a powerful antidote to the fears and stresses of modernity.

Most religions provide a comprehensive explanation of the world that answers many perplexing questions that can disrupt people psychologically. Why are we here? Is there anyone looking after us as we walk through "the valley of the shadow of death"? What happens to us when we die? These are questions that have enormous implications for how people view life and how they feel. People can only feel certain about these parts of their reality through acts of faith. There is no empirical evidence.

Given how important a coherent sense of reality is, from a psychological perspective, the answers religion provides are very important to many people's feelings of personal security.

While there is no doubt religion has provided great solace and comfort to millions, critics of religion have long decried the number of wars fought in the name of religion. And religions have been associated with tremendous acts of unspeakable violence. But if people *need* a comprehensive view of reality, and if religion alone addresses many of the things that are uncertain, it is not surprising people fight to defend their religion. Those are the parts of people's reality that are most easily threatened and, from a psychological perspective, the most perplexing. To paraphrase the great twentieth-century philosopher, Bertrand Russell, men are only willing to die for things they are unsure of.

To say people go to war over religion is really incorrect and misses the point. People go to war because of the vulnerabilities and limitations of their mind. Religion is simply one of the vessels that can make these shortcomings more apparent because of the subjectivity and uncertainty of its subject matter. If an important part of one's reality sense is called into question, as when people's religious beliefs are challenged, it is not just an arid dispute about an empty ideological issue. It goes to their basic sense of anchorage in the world. The infirmities of the mind, however, are the enemy—not religion. Most Americans supported the war in Iraq to support the illusion that they had found the enemy in the form of Saddam Hussein. Of course, they had not, but for a while they had the comforting illusion that they had. It was a costly illusion. Whether it is in religion or politics, it is the mind's inability to tolerate uncertainty that is the real problem.

Answering perplexing questions with psychologically soothing answers that may not have any support in reality is made easier by a religious context. It is a given that nothing under the umbrella of religion can be proven by independent objective reality. In fact, believing without evidence to support the belief is rewarded in religion; it is evidence of faith, the most esteemed value in a religious culture. Religion has always been dependent upon the leap of faith. St. Paul even defined religion as "the evidence of things unseen." As a result, the burden of proof for the tenets of religion is lower than for ideas that are more of this world. Furthermore, once under the tent of gospel reality, there is an abundance of religious institutional reinforcement to help overcome the very same doubt that actually keeps many others from entering the tent in the first place.

Religion also provides enormous support for minds struggling with the three battleground states discussed throughout this book—paranoia, envy, and sexual perplexity. And it supports them from multiple perspectives. Jesus's love is potentially an important antidote to the self-esteem problems and feelings of unworthiness that lead to envious rage. An everlasting life after death puts the issue of envy onto a whole new plane, making a lack of material goods and other insults suffered on Earth less relevant. Religion can reduce envy by promising future rewards for one's forbearance and deprivation in this world. It promises that the meek shall inherit the Earth (presumably from the current ruling elite). And today's wealthy will be heavily handicapped in the future. Mark 10:25 reads: "Sooner can a camel walk through the eye of a needle, than a rich man enter the gates of heaven." There is no need to envy those with more. You will get yours later, and, if it helps you feel better, be assured that they will "get theirs," too.

But if envy should still break through, there is a stick that supplements the carrot. Strongly worded religious punishments provide an authoritarian control to buttress one's own self-control and willingness to accept God's love in lieu of being consumed with envy. It was envy of God's knowledge that caused Adam and Eve's expulsion from the Garden of Eden, and, despite God and Jesus's love, the punishment for deviating from the path of righteousness is eternal hellfire.

When it comes to concerns with sexually perplexing matters, religion answers every question one could possibly have about sex. Nothing is left to doubt or uncertainty. The most salient contemporary religious concerns involve sexuality and reproduction: abortion, stem-cell research, homosexuality, premarital sex, and abstinence. Sex is to take place only in the context of marriage, primarily for the purpose of propagation and not pleasure, and it is to be exclusively between a man and a woman. When Joycelyn Elders, President Clinton's first surgeon general, said in response to a question that masturbation should possibly be encouraged as a way to avoid riskier sexual behavior, the religious furor was such that Clinton asked for her resignation.

Religions differ on some issues, but as a general principle the more fundamentalist the religion, the less control the woman has in decisions about sex and pregnancy and the more judgmental the attitudes are about extramarital sex. However, while one may be inhibited sexually by the prohibitive nature of religious control of sexuality, fundamentalist religions leave little unexplained to a mind uncertain about how to manage the complexities of human sexuality.

Clinically, what I have seen, especially with many forms of Catholicism, is that these rules about sex create massive guilt, particularly in young people who have grown up in a state of reverence toward the Catholic Church and adopted its teachings wholesale. Oftentimes the young adults that I work with in therapy try to harness the awe they feel in early adolescent religious experience to stem the tide of sexual longing. This can lead to a choice of careers as priests or nuns, for example. It can also lead to terrible emotional conflicts and suffering because the teachings are such punitive attempts to deny the development of healthy sexuality, which is so fundamental to human adjustment. The rules are simply out of synch with human sexuality and the broader function it plays in intimate relationships beyond procreation. It is not surprising that attempts at celibacy often prove so problematic, as recent scandals in the Catholic Church have shown.

The mechanisms of paranoia also play a significant role in religion. They facilitate the notion that one has a direct connection with God. Prayers are heard by a God who is all-knowing and can read our mind and all other minds simultaneously. And they make plausible the notion that though we walk through the valley of the shadow of death, God is there comforting and protecting us.

Freud contended that the entire religious worldview was a projection of a longed-for wish for the father. In her *History of God*, Karen Armstrong describes Freud's view.

> *The idea of God was not a lie but a device of the unconscious which needed to be decoded by psychology. A personal god was nothing more than an exalted father-figure: desire for such a deity sprang from infantile yearnings for a powerful, protective father, for justice and fairness and for life to go on forever. God is simply a projection of these*

*desires, feared and worshipped by human beings out of an abiding
sense of helplessness. Religion belonged to the infancy of the human
race; it had been a necessary stage in the transition from childhood to
maturity. It had promoted ethical values which were essential to
society. Now that humanity has come of age, however, it should be left
behind.*[5]

But Freud's analysis of religion was incomplete by his own admission. There was a significant part of the religious experience
that Freud never personally experienced and about which he
professed ignorance. He referred to it as "the oceanic experience" that others have used to describe the subjective religious
experience. For many it is the most important part of religion and
it dwarfs in importance the other contributions religion makes to
the human mind. It is most commonly called ecstasy.

*If one wants to understand the changes in the role of religion in
American political life, they have to understand both the psychology
and the theology of religious ecstasy.* It more than anything else is
what has given energy to the religious right and to the political
activism of fundamentalist and Pentecostal churches in America.
It put George W. Bush in the White House, and even his failures
have not diminished these churches' political zeal for their political causes. If anything, these foibles have only intensified it, making the religious right a force that will be a significant part of the
American political process for the foreseeable future.

Critics of the 2004 GOP convention attacked the orchestrated
stage show they felt was clearly designed to create the misleading
impression that the Republican Party was a party of inclusion
with strong ties to ethnically diverse groups in America. What
was more striking, however, from a psychological perspective

were the shots panning the audience in the dimly lit convention hall. This was neither a diverse group of Americans nor the staid business set typically associated with the Republican Party. Instead, it was a group of people who were obviously in an exalted state, some crying, literally waving the flag, most of them seemingly caught up in the spiritual glow of the moment. These people were in an intense state of spiritual ecstasy. (Engraved in the convention podium was the unmistakable sign of the cross.)

The psychology of ecstasy is a critical missing piece in understanding both fundamentalist and Pentecostal religious sects and the infusion of energy they have brought to the political arena. America's first great psychologist, William James, felt that the neglect of these experiences was a serious shortcoming in efforts to understand the mind and the forces that influence and motivate people. He emphasized its importance in his seminal book *The Varieties of Religious Experience.*

Some have compared religious ecstasy to a drug high, and one of the synthetic street drugs, MDMA, a mix of amphetamines and hallucinogens, is actually called "ecstasy." The experience of ecstasy is similar to the excited feeling many people feel at crowded, highly charged sporting events when tension builds and the game is on the line. Others have compared it to the more tranquil experience that one feels after exercise, when endorphins have kicked in and caused a soothing and pleasurable wave to rush over the body. Obviously, these comparisons can be used to dismiss or denigrate this religious experience. Doing so, however, blinds one to the fact that ecstasy is a major component of religious life, especially fundamentalist religious life.

Most Americans have some understanding of the intellectual beliefs of fundamentalist religions, having been brought up in religions that include many of the teachings of fundamentalist and Pentecostal believers and having read the same Bible. But for most Americans who are not part of this fundamentalist or Pentecostal movement, their religious education took place during their prepubescence when the sense of awe critical to the ecstatic experience was less developed than it is in adolescence.[6] They did not experience the religious ecstasy that is the most important experiential part of fundamentalist religion.

Talking about Pentecostal religion to someone who does not understand the feelings associated with religious ecstasy is very much like trying to tell a prepubescent child about sex. Even if they understand the mechanics of the activity, the prepubescent child responds with a very peculiar look of shock followed by a decidedly negative "Yuck." Pentecostal religions often meet with the same kind of disdain when their ecstatic experiences are viewed by outsiders. Rarely is there much understanding or appreciation of this experience of ecstasy outside of those who actually experience it for themselves.

It is important to recognize, however, that ecstasy as an emotional experience is not limited to religious contexts. Sales distributorships like Amway draw on this same form of ecstatic experience to keep their sales force narrowly focused on their sales objectives. The Bush campaign was heavily supported by Amway interests and made extensive use of the Amway communication technology throughout the 2004 campaign.[7] Bush's phrase "compassionate conservatism" appears to have come from a book by Amway founder Rich DeVos's *Compassionate Capitalism*. George Bush successfully harnessed this ecstatic feeling to fuel his Amway-like distribution system to secure and get out the votes. "Bush girls" excitedly and enthusiastically participated in canvassing and getting out the vote in key states like Ohio, Pennsylvania, and Florida. George Bush would not have carried Ohio but for this ecstatic state among his supporters inculcated with many of the same Amway-type techniques that have long been employed by the Amway company.

The subject of ecstasy permeates Christian religion, especially the rapidly increasing Pentecostal mind-set that has spread across America. The ecstatic experience is nothing less than what is referred to in Christianity as the Holy Spirit. Today, people who do not belong to fundamentalist groups scratch their head in wonderment at the power of the religious right to control people's political judgment. But religious ecstasy creates a mind that, in many important ways, functions and feels quite differently from the mind of someone who does not have a powerful religious experience shaping their mind and their experience of the world. Ecstasy is the experience that biblical Abraham had when he took his son Isaac to the mountain to sacrifice him on the altar to show his devotion to God. As a frightened young Isaac lay upon the altar and his "father's hand was trembling with the beauty of the word,"[8] a heavenly angel intervened and told Abraham that God did not require Abraham to finish the deed. Isaac was spared and replaced on the altar by an unfortunate goat. But it is a chilling statement about the power of religious ecstasy. This same ecstatic state that is driving American Christian fundamentalists is also shaping Islamic fundamentalism and other fundamentalist surges in different parts of the world threatened by the rapid changes of modernity. As these changes grow, each side will feel increased pressure to fight a holy war caused by the kind of rampant projection already underway in the world.

Much of the mainstream public media attention given the

fundamentalists and Pentecostals has focused on the sensational charismatic political theologians, such as Pat Robertson and the late Jerry Falwell–or on the Elmer Gantrys, those who have so spectacularly fallen from grace such as Jim and Tammy Faye Bakker, Jimmy Swaggart, and Ted Haggard. While these people are certainly vulnerable to charges of hypocrisy, their highly publicized scandals have been used by many to justify their simply dismissing the ecstatic religious experience as little more than con-artistry. This, however, does little to help explain what ecstasy is like for the millions of everyday born-again Christians who are not fallen angels. There is a real ecstatic experience that is the subject of much religious teaching that cannot simply be dismissed as hucksterism.

The less notorious Pentecostals emphasize the significance of the *feeling states* associated with their religious experience. That feeling is both the "power" and the "glory" of religious thought. Religious ecstasy is described in the Bible as an internal psychological experience. Jesus said, "The kingdom of God does not come with observation; nor will they say, 'See here!' or 'See there!' For indeed, the kingdom of God is within you." (Luke 17:20–21, New King James or NKJ)

In their work, Pentecostals explain the significance and nature of the ecstatic experience in Pentecostal language. The Reverend J. Rodman Williams of Regent University in Norfolk, Virginia, for example, sees the church coming to a new understanding of itself through what he calls "Pentecostal reality." Rev. Williams emphasizes the experiential aspect of the Holy Spirit:

> By "the Pentecostal reality" is meant the coming of God's Holy
> Spirit in power to the believing individual and community.
> *[Emphasis in original]*

The faithful have experienced a coming of the Holy Spirit wherein God's presence and power has pervaded their lives. It may not have been quite like "wind" and "fire," but they do confess, in joy and humility, that they know what it means to be "filled with the Holy Spirit." There has been a breakthrough of God's Spirit into their total existence—body, soul, and spirit—reaching into the conscious and subconscious depths, and setting loose powers hitherto unknown.[9]

This is not flowery, empty rhetoric. The Holy Spirit is an all-consuming experience of rapturous joy. Williams places great emphasis on a total surrender of oneself to that emotionally ecstatic state. "What many have found to be quite important is the need for total yieldedness to God's possession."[10]

The priority given to the Holy Spirit in the Pentecostal faith is absolute. The Holy Spirit is inviolable, and respecting the Holy Spirit is even more important than respecting God or Jesus. As Jesus said, "Whoever blasphemes against the Father will be forgiven, and whoever blasphemes against the son will be forgiven, but whoever blasphemes against the Holy Spirit will not be forgiven, either on earth or in heaven." (Gospel of Thomas verse 44, New Testament Apocrypha; also see Mark 3:20–35, KJV)

This clear priority that respect for the Holy Spirit is more important than respect for God or Jesus is an extraordinary set of priorities given the central role of Christ and God in the Christian faith. But it reflects the enormous emphasis on the feelings, not just the content, of beliefs in the Pentecostal tradition.

But, as most true believers will attest, this Holy Spirit is also elusive. It can come and go. Fear of losing it is omnipresent and explains much religious fervor. Jesus said, "Ye shall seek me, and shall not find me." (John 7:34, KJV) Maintaining the ecstatic experience is a critical component of all religious practices. These practices help keep one in the fold, whether the fold is a Dominionist congregation, Amway, or the Republican Party.

Of the Ten Commandments, for example, the first four are devoted to exercises to help maintain the ecstatic religious experience: Be attentive to God. Do not be seduced into idolatry. Do not use your belief in God in the service of vanity. Renew your contact with the Holy Spirit on a regular basis, observe the Sabbath. In the Ten Commandments, Christians are schooled in these things even before they are admonished about killing, stealing, and adultery.

The Ten Commandments is really a list of the pitfalls that can keep one from being able to experience this ultimate feeling state, the Holy Spirit, or ecstasy. The first commandment tells the worshipper to worship but one God. A mind is, indeed, more quickly and effectively indoctrinated if there is no competing reality. If there is competition for one's attention to God, people's experience of God will be diluted, and they will be less able to achieve the experience of the Holy Spirit. To experience the Holy Spirit, they must have an experience of absolute thralldom. When people are enthralled by something, they are captivated by it; it intensely and exclusively occupies their mind whether they want it to or not. This is the first rule of Christian, Muslim, and Jewish religions: believe wholeheartedly in God. If the goal is to give one the experience of the Holy Spirit, this is sound advice. It also, however, discourages flexible and independent thought.

The second commandment is more psychologically sophisticated than generally appreciated. Do not make graven images. Killing, stealing, and committing adultery all take a backseat to not making any graven images. This is popularly interpreted as a caution against worshipping false gods. While that is correct, it misses the psychological significance and more fundamental psychological principle behind it. The point of the second commandment is that religious beliefs are an inner emotional experience, and if one starts objectifying that experience with symbols, pictures, and the like, the purely experiential aspect of the Holy Spirit will be lost. The symbol stands as a barrier between the believer and the true experience that makes him a believer.

Interestingly, the Islamic world was trying to articulate this exact point in its vehement reaction to the publication of cartoons depicting Mohammed with a terrorist rocket in his turban in the Danish newspaper *Jyllands-Posten* on September 30, 2005. Creating an image of Mohammed, regardless of whether the message was respectful, is a violation of the religious principle that lies behind the second commandment, a principle that is shared by fundamental and Pentecostal Christians, Jews, and followers of Islam alike. The Koran says, "Those who paint pictures would be punished on the Day of *Resurrection* and it would be said to them: Breathe *soul* into what you have created." (Sahin Muslim vol. 3, no. 5268)

One cannot miss the similar emphasis on the importance of the actual experiential end of the religious process. When the hadith says, "Breathe soul into what you have created," it could be Rev. Williams writing.

But the reliance on the ecstatic experience raises some psychological issues that are especially problematic regardless of the particular religion. The emphasis on fortification of the ecstatic experience through religious practice, more often than not, is only partially successful. The mind is constantly threatened with a loss of the religious attitude. The mind projects blame for its own wobbly ability to maintain the religious exuberance onto an external enemy. It is not that my faith is faltering; it is that infidels or liberals hate my religion and are out to destroy it. Thus, it is the projection of one's own religious struggles that then intensify the religious hatreds that exist in the world. The danger of loss of faith is externalized so "true believers" have a sense they must fight to preserve it.

The Islamic world's fierce reaction to the violation of the stricture against representation suggests why wars are fought to preserve and pursue this ecstatic experience. If the experience of the Holy Spirit is at stake, believers don't back down. This fear of losing the Holy Spirit and the ecstatic feeling that defines it is a source of constant danger and leads to a fear of persecution even from within its own ranks, which is not without historical foundation. This fear of persecution connected to loss of the Holy Spirit is shared by Christian and Islamic fundamentalists alike. Williams writes:

> *However, if he turns joyfully to his church to testify to what has happened, quite often there is antagonism and opposition–as if the Pentecostal reality were a foreign foe. Thus frequently is repeated, though at a different point, the situation of Martin Luther. His experience of "free grace" was likewise strange to many in the church of his day, and as a result Luther found himself, while praising God for this momentous rediscovery, being ostracized by his own people.* Truth, re-opened and re-lived, does not set well with tradition long established. *[Emphasis in original]*[11]

The ironic and potentially hopeful political note in all this it is that the American religious right, Jews, and the followers of Islam have much in common, if they can ever find and use that common ground to bridge the current gap in their understanding of one another. Religious fundamentalism all over the world is fueled by the frightening dimension that change and modernity create for the limited human mind. To build bridges of understanding in this regard requires great leadership, like what the world has seen in South Africa with its reconciliation efforts. Unfortunately, it is very much in contrast to the paranoid exploitations of divisive leaders like Bush, Mahmoud Ahmadinejad, and Kim Jong Il.

For millions of Americans, there is an increasing tendency to listen to God's will through charismatic preachers, who are by definition assumed to have a special understanding of the divine that is not known to the layperson. In the Roman Catholic Church, the Bible is interpreted for parishioners by priests through catechisms. Reading the Bible itself is actually discouraged. In mainstream Protestantism, reading the Bible is encouraged, but there is still an obvious longing for religious authority that expresses itself in an attraction to fundamentalist and evangelical experts. From a psychological perspective, one practical impact of the empowerment of the priest or minister is an increasing shift of the shaping of reality from the individual to the pulpit. What the religious leader teaches about the life hereafter and other religious concerns can make the preacher seem equally indispensable to defining how one ought to understand the secular world as well, especially as it becomes increasingly confusing.

Delegating reality testing to another is debilitating and facilitates gaslighting. People who begin to accept another's version of reality in some areas start to defer in other areas as well. Because of its potential for encouraging people to forfeit independent thinking, religion can also cause psychological regression.

The psychological regression that can occur in a religious context can be dramatic and even alter the very standard for logical thinking. Faith by definition demands a transition to belief without knowledge and typically includes a surrender of self to a higher power. Both are integral components to religious ecstasy. This creates an environment in which *loose thinking* is indulged and even encouraged. As Cardinal Bellarmine, the pious, scholarly, sixteenth-century Jesuit said in response to the Copernican revolution, "It is just as wrong to say the earth goes around the sun, as it is to say Jesus did not have a virgin birth."[12]

Similarly, today, many fundamentalist Christians support Israel, not because of the Holocaust or any position on geopolitics or because of their admiration for Judaism. Instead, their support is based on the scriptural prophecy in the Book of Revelations that Jesus will not return until Jews are firmly ensconced in Israel. After this, those Jews who do not die in the Battle of Armageddon are expected to convert to Christianity.

Information preached to believers by clergy in religious settings is far less likely to be assessed with critical rigor by someone pursuing a state of ecstasy and in the process of surrendering themselves to the Holy Spirit. In some cases, the speaker's message is much less important than the fact that the audience is being offered the opportunity for a religious ecstatic state, which they crave.

For the first time in our country's history, when a president speaks of rallying his base, it is not an ethnic, economic, or racially derived base; it is religious. And it is predominantly a fundamentalist and Pentecostal religious base that forms what is called the religious right.

Fundamentalist and Pentecostal groups, unlike the major religious groups of the midtwentieth century, are anything but apolitical, as the growth of the term *religious right* makes abundantly clear. They have been closely identified with the conservative wing of the Republican Party, and George W. Bush has been the closest thing this country has had to an elected spiritual leader in the White House.

This has not occurred by chance. George W. Bush played an active role in his father's 1988 election, courting the then-emerging religious right and building a political alliance that was critical to his victories in 2000 and 2004. Bush's public relations imagery has been carefully cultivated to communicate subliminally with Christians. Photos of Bush with halos and other religious symbols are prevalent and hardly attributable to chance. Words that are meaningful specifically to born-again Christians punctuate his speeches, largely unrecognized by those who are not members of the religious groups that he is cultivating and courting. When Yasser Arafat died, and Bush was asked for his reaction, he quickly said, "I pray for his soul." What his death would mean to the tragic conflict between Israel and the Palestinians was not mentioned.

The mantle of Christianity has become a political asset to the Bush administration. Throughout his tenure, Bush has communicated with the religious right through regular monthly telephone calls with evangelical leaders to discuss issues of mutual concern. Those discussions include matters relevant both to Caesar's realm and to God's.

The importance the religious right plays to any Republican

presidential candidate is now well established. As would-be successors lined up in early 2007 for the Republican nomination, they were almost invariably assessed in terms of their potential support from the religious right and social conservatives. Sam Brownback, Rudolph Giuliani, and John McCain all had their prospects assessed in terms of their relationship with the religious right. McCain tried to mend fences with the religious right with a commencement-day address to Jerry Falwell's Liberty University. Newt Gingrich wrote a book about his religious views[13] that was endorsed by Sean Hannity, who said the book had "personally" deepened his own religious convictions. Asked about a law passed in New Hampshire legalizing civil unions for gays giving them all the "rights, responsibilities, and obligations of married couples," Rudy Giuliani reversed a long-held stand in favor of civil unions for gays. Though in 1998 he had signed into law a groundbreaking domestic partnership act, in 2007 he rejected the New Hampshire law because "the law states that same-sex unions are the equivalent of marriage."[14]

Since religious issues are oftentimes irrelevant to the economic agenda of a political party, the political party can afford to support the things a religious group wants without sacrificing any of the party's own important objectives. In return, the religious group supports the party on matters not consequential to its religious agenda. If a party is interested in promoting the interests of the oil or pharmaceutical industry, for instance, opposing gay marriage is a low-cost means of bringing the religious group into the fold. A collusion, conscious or not, is established between a party that supports the religious leaders and the church leaders that endorse the political party for its adherence to its Christian values. For most churchgoers, the "truth" is preached to them by a very small group of religious leaders who are courted by the neoconservatives.

In the process, the religious group supports the party's economic objectives. Because religious thought permits looser forms of logical connections, the economic theories of conservative-interest groups when they become associated with religious concepts take on a quasireligious aura. In effect, the "invisible hand" of Adam Smith begins to feel like God's will rather than an economic system that like all others has its strengths and weaknesses, requiring assessment on an issue-by-issue basis. If it, too, is God's handiwork, it is not to be questioned. It is accepted as an article of faith. It is in the midst of this faith-based reality that millions of Americans continue to blindly give their hard-earned dollars to an insurance industry and a pharmaceutical industry that charges them billions of dollars to avoid relying on an "inefficient" government solution to problems like health care and drug distribution.

This religious thralldom ties many of these same people to an economic system that denies them health care security, threatens their Social Security, saddles their children with debt, and ruins their environment, possibly in a cataclysmic fashion. These are all justified by an invisible hand of greed that is confounded with God's love and goodness. The effect on the electorate is that they are misled by a church that tells them their political interest is served by a party that in fact has little to do with the interests of the rank-and-file churchgoer in America.

Pundits were incredulous in recent elections when millions of Americans seem to have voted against their own economic interests. In truth, however, the electorate was not casting a vote; it was reflecting the decision that had been handed to them by a team composed of politicians and clergy operating to support one another. The electorate was in effect voting to maintain their defense against perplexity by reliance on faith-based reality.

Gaslighting permeates the relationships that neoconservatives have formed with religious groups, however. George W. Bush's Office of Faith-Based and Community Initiatives was a prominent part of his appeal to the Christian Right. By supporting faith-based charitable initiatives, Bush could play upon the mind's ability to split and convince people that things could really be done for the poor in his neoconservative administration with its emphasis on tax breaks and war. Despite all the fanfare and even the controversy that such a program was a violation of the principle of separation of church and state, the program itself was really never developed and was used as little more than a 2002 midterm election campaign technique. This was acknowledged by David Kuo, the second-in-command of the initiative:

I realized I had passed through to the other side. I wasn't just a Christian trying to serve God in politics. Now I was a Christian in politics looking for ways to recruit other Christians into politics so that we would have their votes. I couldn't figure out if I was suddenly playing for a different team or if I was an Amway business owner suddenly let into some elite multilevel marketing club.[15]

According to Kuo, the religious leaders themselves were pandered to for their political support but bought off with vanity political prizes.

There were just so many ways to make them happy. In addition to myriad White House events, phone calls, and meetings, they could be

given passes to be in the crowd greeting the president when he arrived
on Air Force One or tickets for a speech he was giving in their
hometown. Little trinkets like cufflinks or pens or pad of paper were
passed out like business cards. The White House used them all,
knowing the Christian leaders could give them to their congregation or
donors or friends to show just how influential they were. Making po-
litically active Christians personally happy meant having to worry far
less about the Christian political agenda.[16]

Ironically, what kept the Christian Right from fully appreciating the extent to which they had been duped was the fact that
the press made the Office of Faith-Based and Community Initiatives seem real to the religious right by airing so many complaints that the program violated the principle of separation of
church and state. If "the liberal media" was complaining about
the program, it presumably did exist.[17]

Kuo described his exit interview with then-White House
Chief of Staff Andrew Card after deciding to leave his White
House position.

I told him everything I thought. The president had made great
promises, but they hadn't been delivered on. Worse than that, the
White House hadn't tried. Worse than that, we had used people of
faith to further our political agenda and hadn't given them anything
in return.[18]

Kuo then quotes himself verbatim in the interview, "And finally, sir, this thought. I don't know if you are aware of this, but
your staff frequently refers to the faith-based initiative as the
'f *#$ing faith-based initiative.' That doesn't help."[19]

Whereas Jesus threw the money changers out of the Temple, today's Christian leaders played "let's make a deal." No Americans, Christians or otherwise, won. Only the gaslighters and the money changers behind them profited.

CHAPTER 9
THE ASSAULT ON PROFESSIONALISM

First . . . we . . . kill all the lawyers.

−SHAKESPEARE, Henry VI

n the movie *Gaslight,* the manipulative husband fired the elderly maid and carefully controlled his wife's social environment. He did not want any threats to his control of his wife's
reality. Politically, that same thing is happening today in America
in the form of a de facto war on professionalism.

However one interprets Dick the Butcher's scheme in Shakespeare's *Henry VI, Part II,* "The first thing we do, let's kill all the
lawyers," it is clear that he sees these professionals as impeding
his own nefarious objectives. In contemporary America, it is not
just lawyers who are under attack. Most of our other traditional
professions are also under siege. If one kills all the lawyers, dis-
credits the mainstream press, substitutes religious beliefs for scientific and medical judgment, and eliminates the teaching of
subjects necessary for effective citizenship, there will be few
Americans capable of espousing and defending the values of a
liberal democracy.

Collectively and individually, the major professions that have
traditionally fortified our natural defenses against gaslighting–
reporters, lawyers, doctors, scientists, and teachers–are all under

unprecedented attack and have suffered significant reductions in their professional autonomy. They are being increasingly replaced by the needs and dictates of corporate America, fundamentalist religious leaders, and media-based ideologues. Some of this is intentional, some of it is not. None of it, however, is having a salutary effect on the American mind.

The mind does not develop in a vacuum. It is honed from many directions. Teachers help develop mental reasoning abilities, as they teach history and civics and other subjects we need to participate constructively in a democratic society. Religious leaders help clarify moral and ethical values and maintain morale. Lawyers help search for the truth in areas of disagreement and injustice. Scientists explore the unknown and provide more understanding of the world. Journalists extend our horizons into areas we cannot go ourselves and help organize and prioritize information.

At the cornerstone of each of these occupations is the concept of professionalism. Professionals operate independently, with special expertise, and they are expected to adhere to higher standards of professional ethics than the traditional world of commerce, where the moral standard is "let the buyer beware." Professionalism demands that the best interests of others–patient, client, student, or parishioner–be given priority over the professional's own narrow self-interests. Professionalism also provides a model for effective mental functioning, with its emphasis on objectivity, thoughtful reflection, and integrity.

Ideally, these professions support the mental functioning required to exercise sound judgment. They serve as brakes on the primitive mind that lives deep in all people and makes them vulnerable to perplexity and the ill effects of a prematurely established reality sense based in irrational fantasy. At the same time, they help harness and manage the essential, but potentially problematic, emotional tasks related to envy, sexuality, and paranoia. Without such a model for rational functioning, people are left to their own bottomless pit of fantasies, suspicions, and superstitions that will quickly emerge from the depths of the mind to fill vacuums in their understanding of reality. With professionalism, magical explanations are increasingly replaced by more reality-based explanations.

Unfortunately, in recent years, all of these institutional supports for effective mental functioning have been themselves under increasing assault, making them less able to provide the historically constructive and helpful role they were designed to perform. To the extent these groups are compromised in their ability to do their work, the support they provide for our reality sense is lost. This is altering how Americans determine what is real and what is not real.

THE PRESS

In January 2005, American broadcast news was represented by highly respected journalistic icons. Tom Brokaw, Peter Jennings, and Dan Rather held down the network anchor positions, and Ted Koppel of *Nightline* was a tremendously admired and respected journalistic figure. By January 2006, all were gone. Koppel encountered political opposition from his commercially oriented upper management at ABC. Brokaw retired. Jennings died very suddenly from cancer. Rather was severed from CBS over an error in a *60 Minutes* piece concerning George W. Bush's military service.

The national news anchor role had personified the independent press for almost six decades in America. At critical moments of national crises, they or their predecessors had always played a central role in helping to stabilize a tilting ship of state. Edward R. Murrow served as a critical reality beacon during the McCarthy era. His role in exposing Senator Joseph McCarthy's smear tactics was dramatized in the recent film *Good Night, and Good Luck*. During the days following the assassination of John F. Kennedy, Walter Cronkite provided a sorely needed sense of continuity for many Americans. He so symbolized stability and professionalism that an entire nation was reassured. One father figure had been lost, but there were others there to help carry on. In 1968, after Cronkite expressed doubt about the conduct of the Vietnam War, President Lyndon Johnson moaned, "If I've lost Cronkite, I've lost middle America."[1]

In the late 1960s, the major networks reportedly considered removing several of the venerable anchors for a more youthful image. They decided not to do so. When Watergate arose, they were very glad they had not. America was rocked to its foundation by a corrupt presidency that was brought down largely by the media, especially the work of the *Washington Post*. Night after night, Americans heard the unfolding news about Watergate from a trusted and well-respected media icon under the auspices of the three major news networks. When the national reality was changing, having a stable and respected messenger was especially important. September 11th, of course, was no exception.

The simultaneous departure of a generation of network anchors is only a small part of the challenges confronting the free press in America. The free press is under a withering assault from three directions.

First, there has been a persistent attempt to convince the American people that the independent press has a liberal bias and that the only journalism that presents an accurate view of the world are Fox News and a few conservative outlets that spew forth a remarkable torrent of invective. America has never had such a campaign to discredit the news media as it has at the present time, emblematized by the phrase *liberal news media*.

Conservatives have funded several groups to do the legwork of attacking this supposed liberal bias in the media, notably the Media Research Center. On its Web site, the group describes itself thus:

> *Leaders of America's conservative movement have long believed that within the national news media a strident liberal bias existed that influenced the public's understanding of critical issues. On October 1, 1987, a group of young determined conservatives set out to not only prove—through sound scientific research—that liberal bias in the media does exist and undermines traditional American values, but also to neutralize its impact on the American political scene. What they launched that fall is the now acclaimed Media Research Center.*[2]

But numerous studies have shown that the idea of a liberal bias is a fiction—that television news is more likely to employ conservatives as guest commentators than liberals and that a majority of newspapers endorsed George Bush for president in both 2000 and 2004, for instance.[3] In fact, even conservatives will admit there is no such thing as a liberal bias across the board. Political journalist Joe Conason writes,

> *Back in 1995, the witty and sometimes candid conservative commentator Bill Kristol confessed that his movement had little reason to complain. "I admit it," Kristol told* The New Yorker. *"The liberal*

media were never that powerful, and the whole thing was often used
as an excuse by conservatives for conservative failures." Rush
Limbaugh made a similar point.... "There's been a massive change in
media in this country over the last fifteen years," he said. "Now it's
2002 and the traditional liberal media monopoly doesn't exist
anymore."[4]

Nonetheless, *liberal news media* is still used as a magic wand that effectively makes disquieting news, news that does not fit in to the desired reality of a political viewpoint, disappear. The recurring message from the new, neoconservative media is that if news is perplexing, psychologically demanding, or inconsistent with short-term American business interests, people do not have to accept it. They never have to assess or confront the actual issue. Global warming is just one case in point. People simply assault the truth by name-calling directed at the messenger. They hold on to a magical talisman, *liberal news media,* and put their heads in the sand. As comedian Stephen Colbert said at the 2006 White House Correspondents' Association Dinner, "Who's *Britannica* to tell me the Panama Canal was built in 1914? If I want to say it was built in 1941, that's my right as an American."[5]

One of the things the professions subject to these attacks have in common is that they are surprisingly ineffective in defending themselves. It is as if their status as professionals has left them assuming that their authority would never be challenged, and so they are unprepared to fight for their autonomy. For example, when managed health care driven by corporate economic interests seized control of the medical community, it was striking how ineffective the medical interests were in fighting off the incursions to their professional autonomy. The once powerful AMA was a pitiful giant in the managed health care takeover of medical care.

In the case of the media, given the history of American journalism and the importance of the First Amendment in this country, one of the most disturbing aspects of the Dan Rather CBS episode is that it did not evoke much protest from the independent media. How can one confidently report the news that really needs to be reported if one mistake in an otherwise correct story leads to professional execution? However serious one may find Rather's mistake, there are few such summary executions at Fox News, where many contend misleading information is common.

NBC's David Gregory was a leading member of the media trying to hold the Bush administration accountable in the Iraq War. After he was accused of partisanship by White House Press Secretary Tony Snow, one can only wonder what kind of chilling effect it had on his personal sense of freedom to function independently.[6] If a media giant like Rather can be toppled for one error in verification of a document, how cautious must one be?

What is especially telling about the Rather incident is the way his replacement, Katie Couric, has been subjected to concerted right-wing accusations of liberal political bias led by the Media Research Center. The fact this was done so early in her tenure at CBS is reminiscent of the Swiftboating of John Kerry, also done early in the 2004 presidential campaign so that no one would have a chance to form an independent first impression of him. Before Couric even got to build a track record of her own as a news program anchor, she was assailed for bias, so that no matter how good a job she does, she will be hard-pressed to overcome the impression created by adversaries of the traditional independent media.[7] And she will be constantly pressured to "prove" she does not have a liberal bias.

The so-called liberal media let America down badly in Iraq, as did most of the nation's other major institutions and leaders. Difficult questions were not posed, and there was an aura of fear that to challenge going to war was to be unpatriotic. No one, for instance, questioned how Iraq's armaments could grow as quickly as the administration alleged. On February 4, 2001, Secretary of State Colin Powell said that Saddam Hussein "has not developed any significant capability with respect to weapons of mass destruction. He is unable to project conventional power against his neighbors."[8] On July 29, then-National Security Advisor Condoleezza Rice said, "We are able to keep arms from [Hussein]. His military forces have not been rebuilt."[9] After 9/11, President Bush described Iraq as having large stockpiles of "the most lethal weapons ever developed."[10]

In early February 2003, the BBC reported on a leaked top-secret intelligence memo that concluded that there were no current links between Saddam's regime and the Al Qaeda network.[11] Though it was widely reported around the world—India, Australia, Scotland, and China—it received only passing, and spotty, attention in the American media. None of the network news programs reported it, nor National Public Radio, nor public television, nor the *New York Times*.

Certainly, very courageous young reporters risked their lives to provide a firsthand view of how the war really looked in the months that followed President Bush's triumphant "Mission Accomplished" performance, overcoming rose-colored reports from the administration. Ironically, however, only Hurricane Katrina helped forestall the freefall decline in the press's responsibility to challenge official government statements. The media defied the White House's own self-congratulatory messages that they were doing a "heckuva job" in responding to Katrina by picturing the reality of what New Orleans and its people stranded on their roofs really looked like. In doing so, for the first time, many began to conclude that the Bush administration, whether it was evil or not, was certainly incompetent. As with 9/11, it took a violation of America's psychological borders, an invasion that laid waste to American soil, before minds were sufficiently disturbed to be open to a new reality sense.

In addition to the omnipresent charges of bias, the traditional media are also vulnerable to the susceptibility of our minds to different forms of seduction. Increasingly news networks substitute stimulating quasinews—infotainment—for the more tedious traditional news. Hard news is replaced by soft news.

A critical variable for a nation's mental health is the nature of gratification and stimulation its people seek and how they seek it. Rome succumbed to its bread and circuses because of the psychological debilitation it created. Infotainment is the American bread and circus. To the extent it slides unrecognized into the place once occupied by professional journalism, infotainment is another serious threat to the effective functioning of the traditional independent press and, ultimately, to the American mind. Infotainment shifts the focus of the news from information to stimulation, particularly a passive form of stimulation that operates on much more primitive aspects of the mind. Passive stimulation does not require one to focus or stimulate their mind through their own effort.

Today, television news as infotainment has become a twenty-four-hour-a-day source of stimulation. Television programs are

three-ring circuses with multiple "crawlers" and stage sets of daz-
zling colors. In contrast, public television, created to inform the
public about the state of our nation and its government, has been
partially privatized, and its budget is constantly threatened.

This transition to emphasizing stimulation over content is infiltrating almost all mass communication that Americans receive.
Newspapers like *USA Today* and magazines like *People* provide
glitzy color photos and headlines introducing stories that are
barely longer than the headlines. Political communications have
been amplified many times over through very intense and stimulating television advertising. Religious communication has increasingly become more concerned with ecstatic states than
traditional religious teachings.

Stimulation per se is not necessarily bad. People need to feel
alive and vital, and stimulation is what creates that feeling. But
how people obtain their stimulation carries enormous psychological implications for the mind. Stimulation can come from
outside us or from within. People can grab it in coarse quantities
with sex, drugs, or alcohol. Gambling can "jack" them up and
provide an easy thrill. Shocking acts of violence in movies can
stimulate people, as can explicit sexual scenes. Intense angry
voices on talk radio can serve the same function.

The mind that relies too heavily on these things for its stimulation is functioning passively, instead of practicing the more
mentally taxing forms of self-stimulation that come from thinking, study, discussion, and independent reflection, the exercises
that maintain and strengthen the rational faculties of the mind.
Depending on the relative balance between active and passive
forms of stimulation, the mind will either stay toned and condi-

tioned, or it will atrophy and become increasingly dependent on the source of passive stimulation.

Our ability to form an effective and independent reality sense requires a capacity for delaying stimulation long enough to exercise the mind. Ideally, listeners should become involved intellectually and delay making premature conclusions, like Americans did in Iraq. The media can facilitate that by giving useful information in a noninflammatory fashion that does not interfere with Americans obtaining a clear view of the facts, the first step they need to have effective reality formation. Infotainment's appeal is that it provides passive stimulation, requiring less mental effort from the listener in order to feel stimulated. Passive stimulation is the very opposite of thought and reflection. When this passive stimulation provided by infotainment blurs with the news, it disrupts the mind's ability to process the news independently.

Regardless of how one evaluates individual newscasters, it is very difficult to deny that there is a difference in the quality of stimulation watching a Sean Hannity or a Bill O'Reilly broadcast and one by Walter Cronkite or Peter Jennings. Cronkite and Jennings spoke in even, calm tones. They avoided strongly provocative language. Hannity and O'Reilly speak with powerful and angry voices. This is not a tone or a tenor you hear on any of the other news stations, with the possible exception of MSNBC's Keith Olbermann, who was installed as a response to Fox News.

The effect these changes have on the mind is profound. Increasingly, stimulation comes from without, not from within. That promotes a shift from an active to a passive mind in these important areas. A passive mind is also much more suggestible than an active one, and it can be readily beguiled by any stranger with psychological candy, like the gaslighter.

A third important aspect of the changing role of media is the effect of market segmentation. The proliferation of media outlets made possible by technological advances is creating such a highly segmented market that America is rapidly approaching the point where groups are more and more able to "dial-a-reality" by selecting the news network that meets their psychological wishes rather than one that prides itself on high journalistic values.

Mental dysfunction and vulnerability are no longer corrected by the news; instead, they are indulged and even cultivated. If it is less taxing for me to assume that the terrorist threat can be addressed by the Iraq War, I can dial up a television news network that will give me information that makes me feel much better than the frustration and worry I feel watching news programs that take pride in presenting the complexities of many issues. And, of course, if I can blame others for any residual discomfort, be they "liberals" or "Muslims," life is much simpler.

The good news and the bad news is that everyone can choose with remarkable specificity what they want to see and hear. Those who watch only Fox News and listen to Rush Limbaugh receive one view of the war. Those who watch what Fox News adherents refer to as the liberal press–ABC, NBC, CBS, CNN, or PBS–see another view. I do not mean by this just that they have different viewpoints; I mean that they have literally different realities. Despite long denying any particular bias in the news, Rupert Murdoch has now allegedly admitted that he wanted Fox News to encourage America to go to war in Iraq.[12] Its viewers at this time of uncertainty were no doubt comforted by a strong and compelling voice "making things clear" at a time when other media outlets were at best noncommittal about policy, as one might argue the objective media should be.

The Annenberg Public Policy Center compared audiences in 2004 for Michael Moore's decidedly anti-Bush film *Fahrenheit 9/11* with those of Rush Limbaugh. Of five thousand adults polled, approximately equal numbers had either seen the movie or listened to Rush Limbaugh, about 8 percent for each. However, only twelve of the respondents, less than one-quarter of 1 percent, had done both.[13] Kathleen Hall Jamieson, who directed the survey, said, "One-sided partisan communication tends to attract an audience of believers and reinforces their beliefs rather than change their minds."[14] Those who liked the film overwhelmingly believed that the war in Iraq was a mistake and that terrorism was more likely than before 9/11. Those who liked Rush Limbaugh, in almost equally overwhelming numbers, believed that the war was worth it and that America was safer in 2004 than in 2000. Of course, Moore's film eventually disappeared from daily consciousness, while Limbaugh continues to opine for thirteen and half million listeners three hours a day, five days a week.

In short, the politicized tabloid-news style of Rupert Murdoch has gained ascendancy and the traditional news media is in eclipse. The American mind does not have the supportive structure of the media that it once did. That has been replaced by a regressive force pandering to our wishes for passive entertainment and simplistic solutions. The news is no longer the news. It is gaslighting. Reality is created by another person or group often with nefarious objectives.

SCIENCE

If the free press is under assault, so, too, are other critical professional institutions that have traditionally helped support the independent functioning of the mind as it struggles to establish a viable reality sense. Until the last decade, most Americans felt that the principles of the Enlightenment of three centuries ago had gained a permanent foothold in the mental processes of advanced societies like that of the United States. People trusted in the careful, objective research of scientists not only to provide us facts, but to use these facts to establish reality. If wishes led us down one path, but science another, then science generally triumphed.

Many Americans no longer feel that constraint. For instance, conservative columnist Dennis Prager, writing on a much-admired conservative Web site called RealClearPolitics, posed the question "why liberals were more exercised about global warming than conservatives." Among his many fascinating answers (for instance, "liberals are more prone to hysteria") was "The Left believes in experts.... For liberals, 'expert' has come to mean far more than greater knowledge in a given area. It now means ... that non-experts should defer to experts not only on matters of knowledge, but on matters of policy, as well."[15] In other words, while one might listen to experts, one should not act on the basis of their expertise.

In comedian Stephen Colbert's satirical portrayal of right-wing talk show hosts, he uses the word "truthiness" to mock pundits who base their decisions on what they want the facts to be as opposed to what the facts are. In this context, the joke is not very far off. Ultimately, people are encouraged to decide what is real by relying on primitive feelings that have little connection to external reality. People are given a rationale for rejecting what science tells them is true.

The Bush administration has actively supported this attitude of defiant know-nothingism. In 2002, a National Cancer Institute statement reporting no link between abortion and breast cancer was changed by the administration to say that evidence of a link was inconclusive.[16] The administration cut language about global warming from a 2003 Environmental Protection Agency report. In March 2007, the House Committee on Oversight and Government Reform produced documents showing that in nearly two hundred instances, the former chief of staff of the White House Council on Environmental Quality, Philip Cooney, edited reports on global warming "to play up uncertainty of a human role in global warming or to play down evidence of such a role."[17] Mr. Cooney, however, is not a scientist. He had previously worked for the American Petroleum Institute, the lobbying arm of the oil industry. After leaving the White House in 2005, he went to work for Exxon Mobil.[18]

However, the Bush administration is only following the lead of American business. This defiant attitude that one can reject science if it clashes with our emotional comfort is ruthlessly exploited by corporate economic interests. Speaking to the House Committee on Oversight, Research Director for the Center for Media & Democracy Sheldon Rampton testified, "A few years ago, the *New York Times* obtained some leaked documents from the American Petroleum Institute, in which the Institute detailed its plans to spend $600,000 to develop a team of pro-industry climate scientists who would dispute the link between greenhouse gas emissions and global warming." Rampton concluded his testimony by saying, "the manipulation of science for public relations or political advantage inevitably has a corrupting effect on science itself. It undermines the integrity and objectivity of scientific research. It creates confusion in the minds of policymakers and the general public."[19]

Another hallowed tradition going by the wayside is the separation of science and religion. Most Americans believe that since the Scientific Revolution and the Enlightenment, the religious mentality that confined Galileo to house arrest for his final years surely has been overtaken by "rational" forces of observation and science, and that religion and scientific disciplines can coexist in the human mind. There are millions of Americans, however, who have now been cut loose from this tradition. For many, the mind has simply been too taxed to tolerate the perplexity such a juxtapositioning causes. In contemporary America, this regressive phenomenon is most pronounced and frightening in the growing repudiation of the mutual accommodation that evolved between science and religion over the last century. To the extent that religion encroaches on scientific enterprises, as it now appears to be doing, the role that science can play in facilitating rational reality-based thinking is under the same type of assault as the other learned professions. For the decades leading up to the new millennium in America, the often fluctuating truce between science and religion had been an easy one. The church was largely concerned with moral ethical issues, and science was left to unravel the mysteries of the physical universe. That is no longer the case.

RELIGION

In the 1960s and 1970s, one of the most salient activities of many American churches was doing the legwork of integration. In many small communities across the South in particular, communities that adjusted peacefully to the social demands of racial integration often did so with enormous help from churches. In Chapel Hill, North Carolina, for example, in 1967, the Church of Reconciliation was formed by Presbyterian groups to address the need for religious input into the process of racial integration.[20] (To appreciate the era in which this started, it might be helpful to note that at that time, the University of North Carolina had never given an African American an athletic scholarship.)

In Catholicism, this same religious social concern was captured in a phrase that Americans hear today but with a very different meaning. For the Catholic Church three decades ago, the "right to life" was a central theme to its social vision. But the right that they were envisioning went far beyond the opposition to abortion to which it has now been narrowed. Listen, for example, to Boston's Bernard Cardinal Law in the early 1980s paraphrasing the Pope: "All the great causes that are yours today will have meaning only to the extent that you guarantee the right to life and protect the human person." The Pope defined that "right to life" as:

- *Feeding the poor and welcoming refugees*
- *Reinforcing the social fabric of this nation*
- *Promoting the true advancement of women*
- *Securing the rights of minorities*
- *Pursuing disarmament, while guaranteeing legitimate defense*

"All this," he said, "will succeed only if respect for life and its protection by the law is granted to every human being from conception until natural death."[21] This promotes ideas far broader than just abortion and includes some very liberal issues.

Obviously the role of churches was multifaceted then and is multifaceted now. But when one thinks of churches in today's America, one is less likely to think of social justice and more likely to think of ecstasy, praise of God, and a narrow concept of family values, most of which have to do with reproductive functioning. Feeding the poor was not an election issue in 2004 for Catholic priests, nor were women's rights. There are few priests like the Vietnam era's Fathers Berrigan protesting the war in Iraq.[22]

The emphasis in religion now is more likely to be on feeling ecstatic through what for some has become almost an idolatrous, self-congratulatory relationship with God, which they sustain through never-ending praise of God. Bathing in God's glory takes a front seat to how one should implement the golden rule. Tackling racism or homophobia is simply not on the agenda for many churches. In fact, it is not unusual to hear some prominent religious leaders espouse bitter hatred for those who are different from themselves. What were once issues of "social justice" have somehow been transformed into "social issues," or family value issues replacing the religious values of three decades ago.

Most prominent among these, of course, is abortion. Harvard Law Professor Laurence Tribe has called abortion "the clash of the absolutes."[23] Abortion has been a long-standing debate in America. However, when the right to life of stem cells, some of which can be taken from umbilical cords that would otherwise be discarded, becomes a rationale to halt scientific work on potential cures for serious diseases and other debilitating infirmities, it reflects a profound redirection in American priorities and sense of reality. People sitting in a wheelchair become less compelling and real than a religious concept. This is a criterion for reality detached from the more concrete and palpable data on which reality has traditionally been formed, at least, until recently in America. Today, unlike thirty years ago, the "right to life" has been curtailed to the time period from conception to birth. In fighting the battle over abortion, neoconservative forces have eclipsed support for the right to life for those who have already been born. If science can be rendered submissive to religious thinking in this way, anything becomes possible.

Science once helped people establish an increasingly well-grounded reality, but it is now cast aside. Just as people no longer have to listen with any effort to the evening news, because whatever they do not like to hear they can dismiss as a product of the liberal media, they do not have to heed the latest scientific work insisting that in some critical area America needs to adopt policies that are inconvenient and not advantageous to special interests such as the oil industry. People are much freer to believe what they want to believe rather than what is real. They hear a stimulating message that they like from an authoritative voice inspired by a special relationship with God. If the message seems reassuring and the messenger feels powerful, they can make the leap of faith and pursue the more pleasurable belief. It also, however, reduces personal responsibility for forming one's own reality. It fosters dependency on others over independent thinking and promotes a downward spiral in which dependency begets greater dependency.

JUSTICE

Justice is also a profound mental health issue with significant implications for the mind. The law and the legal system are not just rules people must live by; they define reality in areas that are important to us. When justice is corrupted and people are told that what is unfair is really fair, it toys with significant elements in their reality sense. On an individual level, as already noted, false accusations that are supported by the law can have devastating results on mental stability. It can literally drive people mad.

In addition, however, on a more societal basis, a sense of justice creates feelings of empowerment. An empowered society will produce more and build a better nation. If people feel they cannot correct an injustice, it creates perplexity and often they will have a tendency to avoid even acknowledging it. They close it out of their reality sense entirely. That is one reason why an unjust system, as we observe in authoritarian nations, is mentally debilitating. Unacknowledged injustice discourages recognition of significant problems in society that need to be addressed, whether they are war and peace, social and economic justice, or environmental and economic responsibility. When people recognize on an unconscious level that their world is unjust but feel they cannot do anything about it, they shrink away from that world often into a debilitating form of social and emotional withdrawal.

For those whose circumstances force them to be aware of injustice, an unjust world is frightening and at times maddening. Anyone who has witnessed the aftereffects of false accusation cases can see this clearly. I have treated many victims of false accusation in my clinical practice and I have represented them in legal proceedings. The psychological fallout of having a world turn against you unjustly is terrifying. It is very much like what the Ingrid Bergman character in *Gaslight* experienced. One's reality is invalidated by a force far more powerful than the individual affected.

In today's America, the ability of the individual to fight injustice against larger and more powerful interests has been heavily truncated. In 1991, then-Vice President Dan Quayle gave a highly publicized speech in which he blasted the legal profession for corrupting the American economy with a plethora of frivolous lawsuits. According to Quayle, the high cost of frivolous litigation was burdening American industry and threatening America's competitive balance with the rest of the world.[24]

Over the fifteen years since that speech, "frivolous" lawsuits have been blamed for just about every consumer burden, from inadequate access to health insurance to the high price of drugs. The words *frivolous* and *lawsuits* are rarely uttered separately from each other by antilawsuit forces. Indeed, this language seems to drive any discussion about the appropriate role of litigation in American society. It is like debating the merits of "nonessential government spending." There are few adherents supporting "frivolous lawsuits." In response, there has been a plethora of legislation limiting lawsuits under the rubric of "tort reform."

In fact, the tort reform movement has had little to do with frivolous lawsuits. The main goal and the almost exclusive target of tort reform has been to eliminate the ability of small individuals with serious grievances to sue powerful corporate interests such as insurance companies, manufacturers, and drug companies. Yet for all of the criticism directed at the legal profession, the opportunity to help one individual—acting alone, with little or no resources—go into a courtroom and articulate his or her view of justice that would otherwise never see the light of day has been one of the noblest aspects of America's judicial system and a significant symbol of respect for the individual. Lawyers make it possible for everyone to "have his day in court." But after twenty years of tort reform, the American courtroom is largely closed to people of average means. It is simply too expensive. Court calendars are clogged with criminal drug arrests, domestic relations matters including divorce and custody, and the business interests of corporate America.

The poster child of tort reform has, of course, been the infamous McDonald's case in which a woman bought coffee at a drive-through window at a McDonald's, burned herself with it, and allegedly collected several million dollars for her efforts.

Although this case became the iconic evidence that things had gotten out of control with frivolous lawsuits, it, surprisingly, did not happen as it was portrayed.[25] The facts are that in 1992, a 79-year-old woman, Stella Liebeck, did, indeed, spill coffee on herself, which soaked into her clothing and scalded her. She was hospitalized for eight days with severe burns over 16 percent of her body and had skin grafts that required two years to complete. She asked McDonald's to pay her medical expenses of twenty thousand dollars. McDonald's countered with an offer of eight hundred dollars. Ms. Liebeck then sued.

Evidence presented to the jury showed that McDonald's had received over seven hundred complaints of similar burns over the previous decade and had settled several of them. The evidence also suggested that McDonald's knew that its coffee was much hotter than it had to be and that patrons would be scalded by any spill because of the coffee temperature McDonald's decided to use. McDonald's also allegedly knew its coffee would scald the throat and the esophagus if drunk as soon as it was served. A McDonald's spokesperson contended that the number of complaints did not warrant McDonald's reconsidering its coffee temperature policy and said that it had "more serious" matters to consider.[26]

Ultimately the jury assessed Ms. Liebeck's actual injury value for her two years of skin grafts at $200,000. It concluded that 20 percent of the responsibility lay with Ms. Liebeck and 80 percent with McDonald's, leading to a verdict of $160,000 for Ms. Liebeck. The jurors also concluded that McDonald's had been indifferent to its customers.

One can only presume that many of the jurors had eaten at a McDonald's at some point with their family, so the suggestion that McDonald's was reckless with the welfare of customers was upsetting to them. They voted to award $2.7 million to Ms. Liebeck as punitive damages to discourage McDonald's from continuing to neglect the safety of its patrons in the future. This figure, $2.7 million, was the amount of money McDonald's made from coffee sales every two days. This was at best a modest tap on the wrist to Mickey D's.

Nonetheless, the judge immediately reduced the award to $480,000, the amount of money McDonald's makes in coffee sales every eight hours. This made the total award from the court about $660,000. Subsequently, McDonald's appealed and the two sides settled out of court for an undisclosed sum less than $600,000.[27]

Opponents of consumers' rights to sue seized on this case as the best they could find to support a broadside attack on the general public's right to sue manufacturers, pharmaceutical companies, insurance companies, and health care providers for the death and serious injury of loved ones *even when a jury might find the defendant involved showed a reckless disregard for the welfare of the patient or consumer.*

The threat of a large damage verdict is important because of the deterrent effect it has on corporate decision making. If an automobile manufacturer is trying to decide whether to stop production of a new automobile to fix a defective part that if not fixed could put lives at risk, the company knows it will cost time and money. Regardless of the amount at stake, there are many in the business world who would no doubt do the honorable thing: absorb the cost of the lost production, and make their product safe. It is well documented, however, that there are others who have not made that same ethical decision in the past. They have been the subject of large jury awards—at least in some cases. This tends to make sure that in the future people like this "do the right thing." Without the threat of a large lawsuit, they could ignore the problem with no fear of either financial punishment or public ignominy, no matter how many people might be killed as a result. These are the cases that provide the rationale for the so-called frivolous lawsuits. It is this deterrent that the business community wants to get rid of by tort reform.

Most Americans have not noticed the chicanery behind the "frivolous lawsuit" campaign. But Connie Masters of Wichita, Kansas, did. Her son, Blake, was denied desperately needed access to a psychiatric facility when he was seriously suicidal, suffering from a very painful mental illness for which he had literally begged for treatment. After being turned away three times, he finally gave up, purchased a shotgun, curled up in his bathtub, and shot his brains out. He was eighteen.

Connie Masters filed suit against the facility that denied access to treatment for her son. Although her lawyer agreed to a contingency fee arrangement in which he received nothing if Connie did not prevail in the lawsuit, the two of them nonetheless spent

$90,000 for the expenses required to support the case, including court reporters to take depositions and experts legally required to verify the medical contentions. Fortunately for her, the jury agreed with Connie's arguments and awarded her $680,000 for her son's death.

Then tort reform stepped in. Under Kansas law, the maximum award a mother could receive for the death of her only son was capped. By the time these and other caps were applied, Connie received substantially less than forty thousand dollars. Her attorney, who had advanced the money and spent over three years on the case, received considerably less.

The question tort reform advocates fail to address is this: When corporate America runs its cost-benefit analysis on safety features that could save a child's life, what kind of value do Americans want them to factor in for a child's life? That is what tort reform is really about. It is not about frivolity.

EDUCATION

In 1961, an ultraconservative Ohio congressman, John Ashbrook, warned of a plan already drafted in the then–Department of Health, Education and Welfare that was "a blueprint for complete domination and direction of our schools from Washington, D.C."[28] At the time, the statement was dismissed by most as an alarmist overstatement from a member of the Far Right. Forty years later, a Republican president, George W. Bush, made federal control of U.S. education a reality. In 2001, the No Child Left Behind Act created strict standards for what had to be taught in public schools in America.

The Department of Education was established in 1979 over the strong objections of conservative Republicans. Expanding the role of the federal government was anathema to traditional Republican values of limited federal government and local control of schools. In his 1980 presidential campaign, Ronald Reagan made the abolition of the Department of Education a salient part of his campaign platform. Once elected, however, he did not move against the department. Instead, it became a platform for a Republican ideologue, William Bennett, to propound a set of conservative Republican values only very loosely connected to education.

If the Department of Education survived under Reagan, it flourished under George W. Bush with the No Child Left Behind Act (NCLB). President Bush turned Republican philosophy on its head. This major legislative achievement of the Bush administration was a comprehensive new set of mandatory professional standards that were imposed on all local public schools. The NCLB provides for a set of standardized tests, administered in all public schools around the country, measuring achievements in literacy, science, and mathematics and beginning in grade three. The political rationale for this approach came from the movement to make schools "accountable" for what they do and fit neatly with the need of a bureaucracy for readily discernible numbers to define quality. "Good" schools under the act are schools with students who score higher than other schools on the tests. This is now the operational definition of a good public-school education in America. This is "accountability."[29]

Since accountability means that people who do well are rewarded and those who do not do well are punished, teachers whose students do well on these tests will receive bigger raises than teachers who teach students who do less well (i.e., the disadvantaged). Schools that perform well will be publicly praised and schools that do not do well will be publicly stigmatized. In addition, their good students will be allowed to leave and transfer to other schools. In extreme cases, the state will be able to come in and take over the running of the local school that is doing poorly on the tests.

It does not require an advanced degree in human motivation to understand that teachers' pay and the implications for the schools (and the administrators that run them) make the test the focal point of the education. These tests do include some very important aspects of education that are important for any workforce, such as math concepts and reading comprehension. Things that are not measured will be deemphasized, however. These include critical thinking, creativity, writing and verbal expression, social and leadership skills, physical education, and a host of other activities that have heretofore been considered essential parts of a well-rounded education necessary for effective citizenship.

If one considers the educational needs of a future generation, there are a few points that seem compelling. First, the most dramatic educational need for the current generation of young Americans is the ability to adjust to the speed of change itself. For that they will have to develop adaptive intellectual skills, that is, skills that allow them to learn new skills. They will need to develop critical reasoning and creative learning skills to keep up with ever changing technology and new job requirements. Deemphasizing these factors in our public education system, as NCLB does, is very risky. In all probability it will create a future worker who is more likely to become obsolete.

Second, school systems are responding to the incentives that are provided. While the programs that are being taught are worthwhile, so are the programs that have been de facto curtailed by the new set of economic incentives. Teachers who teach anything other than the new requirements do so at their own risk and at their own expense, literally. The skills necessary for good citizenship—for instance, history, civics, social studies, and literature—are significantly downplayed. Since there is no measure for these skills, the deficiencies created will not show up until the next generation of Americans. These are the people who will assume the mantle of leadership of a nuclear power in a world in which many countries are armed with nuclear weapons. And, if current trends continue, many of these countries will not only be hostile to America, but they will have surpassed America on most educational measures.

Finally, there will be multiple deleterious effects on teachers as well as students. Teachers in schools with student populations who do poorly on these tests stand to lose professional advancement, both financial and otherwise. Understandably, there will be a migration of good teachers to better schools, thereby further draining the better teachers away from the inferior schools where they are so desperately needed.

In addition, however, the very identity of being a teacher will change. The hallmark of professionalism is the freedom to exercise judgment in applying the skills a professional has developed in his or her training. With NCLB, that critical component of professionalism is gone. When America shuts off the autonomous functioning of minds that it has invested thousands of dollars and years of work in developing, the country is poorer. More importantly, however, when it stops training and developing them for the future, the future takes on a decidedly grim hue.

Teachers are so overwhelmed with bureaucracy and the sheer

amount of time spent in testing that they have little left over to help a child develop an interest in literature, history, or the arts. Those, of course, are the things that build minds capable of the independent thinking necessary to make democracy work. Without that kind of independent thinking, citizens can be easily manipulated through bread and circuses and gaslighting until the social fabric and political viability of the system succumb to authoritarian demagoguery and external subjugation.

All of this is just the frontal assault on teachers from the federal government. Numerous attempts to effectively undercut the public schools through school voucher systems have also drawn heavy religious-based support in state legislatures in Georgia, Texas, Arizona, Ohio, California, Connecticut, Hawaii, Kentucky, New York, Virginia, Missouri, and New Jersey.[30]

Horace Mann's vision of an education system that creates a genuine equality of opportunity for all seemed like an inevitability in America just a few short decades ago. Now the very foundation of that dream, the public education system, is crumbling from a lack of funding, splintering from diverse religious agendas, and strangling from the grip of unwise government regulation. And yet most Americans pay strong lip service to the notion that education is the cradle for tomorrow's American mind and the challenges it must meet.

That mind is already under assault from political manipulation that undermines its effective functioning with perplexing and preoccupying matters like paranoia, sexual perplexity, and envy. But tragically, at the same time the mind is subject to such a withering assault, the traditional fortifications for the American mind, the free press, scientific rationality, the law, organized religion, and our public educational system are all succumbing to the same form of attacks and are proving less and less capable of helping us forestall the kind of national regression that some describe as a "dumbing down" of America. The effect on national policy, both now and over the coming decades, does not bode well for America's ability to survive in an increasingly competitive and complex world.

CHAPTER 10
POLICY IMPLICATIONS: THE REAL FLEECING OF AMERICA

Who are you going to believe, me or your own eyes?

—GROUCHO MARX

From a policy perspective, America is suffering under this psychological assault. America initiated a war and sent thousands of people to their deaths, maimed hundreds of thousands, displaced millions, and squandered our nation's wealth, both financial and goodwill, around the world. And just for good measure, it attacked the wrong enemy and found itself bogged down in a bloody Iraqi civil war that could have been anticipated with any study of Iraq. In the eyes of much of the rest of the world, America is now seen as an arrogant tyrant disrespectful of others with whom it shares the planet.

To some extent, these problems can be attributed to national trauma caused by 9/11 and to extraordinarily poor leadership, things to which any nation is vulnerable. But the problems confronting America will not end with George W. Bush's presidency or his war. Bush was a devastating symptom of America's problems, but the psychological disease that spawned him runs deeper.

In a democratic society, wise policy inevitably depends on voters' ability to assess their potential leaders rationally. Part of America's current national predicament is reflected in voters' failure to weigh even the most significant shortcomings Bush had as a candidate. For example, by his own admission, Bush had a severe drinking problem until his fortieth birthday, when he apparently stopped drinking altogether. He was a problem drinker during his twenties and thirties, a critical time when a professional person is learning how to exercise judgment and building a foundation of information and experience about the world that will be important in the later years of a career. The work experiences Bush had during this formative period were littered with demonstrable failure, and the fund of world knowledge and experience he acquired during these apprenticeship years was notably deficient. This was true by any standard, let alone one used to determine if an individual is prepared to lead the most powerful nation on Earth.

The American people failed to appreciate the level of immaturity that was abundantly apparent from Bush's history and demeanor before they turned over the reins of government to him. Instead, they simply overlooked the problem, opting to indulge themselves with the subtle visceral comfort they felt with Bush. Most talented young people preparing for a leadership role learn during that formative period, for instance, that challenges such as "Bring it on!"–Bush's bravado taunt to the terrorists–are rarely an effective way to manage hostility and address conflicts. Bush has now acknowledged that this was an error, but it is unfortunate that he had to learn it on the job and Americans had to pay for it with such a public relations disaster in the world community.

Regardless of Florida's recount debacle, enough Americans voted for Bush to make apparent that his fitness for office was not the significant election issue it should have been. Many attribute this to timid Democratic Party tactics, but regardless, it was also a failure for which American voters must accept some responsibility.

Close to half of Americans voted for George Bush in 2000, and a majority did vote for him in 2004. Few of America's elected leaders opposed his efforts to take America to war. Thus, whatever massive shortcomings Bush had, Americans must look further than one individual to fully explain their current predicament.

America has been making very bad decisions as a nation for several years now, and Americans have been acting frivolously with their stewardship of their nation's future. Acting as if all the responsibility falls on George Bush simply avoids acknowledging the ongoing psychological debilitation that is still threatening America's future. If the problem cannot be recognized, it cannot be addressed. Most Americans now see Iraq as a serious blunder and some appreciate the hubris that underlay the military miscalculations. But, looking past Iraq to the way the country has been functioning in other policy areas over the last two decades, the view is alarming, both for what America has been doing, and equally for what it has not been doing.

Even before 9/11, America's foreign policy was vulnerable to paranoid grandiosity. The reaction to the fall of the Soviet Union in some quarters was tantamount to drunken self-indulgence. The Soviet Union's demise was attributed to a U.S. president who coined the phrase "evil empire" to describe the Soviet Union, and in his finest movie actor swagger, demanded, "Mr. Gorbachev, tear down that wall." He initiated an enormous antimissile defense program that everyone outside the administration called "star wars." Reality played little role in formulating this program that cost billions and provided no discernible improvement in America's defensive capabilities.

While Reagan's political theater certainly had its place in articulating a firmness behind America's national defense, for a country to think that its hard-line rhetoric caused the collapse of the Soviet Union is wishful and grandiose rather than reality based. It also fed the kind of grandiosity that led to the unrealistic expectations of what America could achieve in Iraq. One conservative political economist, Francis Fukuyama, became a celebrity for a book called *The End of History and the Last Man.* Fukuyama argued that in the absence of a competing ideology with the fall of the Soviet Union, American liberal thought and democracy would now triumph worldwide.[1] As 9/11 showed, the decline of the Soviet Union was not "the end of history." America was the last man standing but it was in a fool's folly of an arms race. The country it was competing with lacked many of America's resources, making the victory less impressive than some people's self-satisfaction suggests.

This grandiose perspective was widely interpreted as saying that the United States had little to fear from the rest of the world, a feeling that made 9/11 all the more shocking. America may have hastened slightly a Soviet collapse—or it even may have delayed it slightly. To the extent Americans give themselves credit for the collapse of the Soviet Empire, however, they miss the more important lesson they need to take from that experience: empires collapse, and they can do so in a surprising hurry. *This can happen here.*

But the same problematic mechanisms, including the primitive emotional states and the self-protective and self-serving rationalizations at play in America's foreign policy, are also at play in its domestic policy. America's income distribution is growing worse, not better.[2] For many, envy and greed drive an almost exclusive focus on taxes to determine for whom they will vote. One prominent and highly successful evangelical tells his flock that the path of righteousness will also take you on a path to the bank, merging the self-absorbed enthusiasm of Gordon Gekko, the 1980s Michael Douglas character in the movie *Wall Street*, with Christian ecstasy.[3] This provides moral justification for those who have benefited from this country's vast wealth and who now self-servingly attribute their success to some presumed personal virtues they have that others less fortunate have just failed to practice. This ultimately becomes, "I got mine, they can get theirs." In a nation whose economic power has been achieved through equal individual opportunity, to deny resources needed for people to participate on an equal footing and then to rationalize it with narcissistic self-indulgence is not a winning long-term investment strategy.

But it is not just self-interest that is the problem. Investment in health care, the environment, and infrastructure–things that affect all of us–are also neglected. A national debt that had been brought under control is allowed to run wild with reckless "spend more, tax less" policies. Why don't most Americans seem concerned about this?

One of the fascinating things about the mind is that it is capable of creating different parts of itself that are compartmentalized or "split" off from other parts. *Contradictory "realities" can coexist in the same mind, each seemingly having no awareness of the other.* This "split mind" is not schizophrenia, as it is sometimes mischaracterized, but a more common compartmentalization process psychologists simply call dissociation. In very extreme cases, this phenomenon results in dissociative identity disorder (DID), formerly called multiple personality disorder, a clinical condition that has been portrayed in several movies including *Sybil* and *The Three Faces of Eve*. In DID, two or more "alter" personalities coexist as a result of a psychological defense that is present in many people, though in far less dramatic fashion.

In public policy matters, psychological dissociation lets people pursue seemingly contradictory goals, and it can make a nation seem very tolerant of hypocrisy. One can do one thing in one context and the exact opposite in another, with no apparent recognition of the contradiction.

The simplest illustration of an earlier dissociative phenomenon, often called splitting, is the young infant's image of his mother. The mother that meets the child's needs is seen as "all good." She is the perfect mother. On the other hand, when the mother is not meeting the child's needs, the child experiences the mother as "all bad." In early teenage years, when the mind is once again developmentally vulnerable to this kind of mental splitting, one sees teenage relationships fluctuate wildly from day to day. A friend who is seen as all good one day can suddenly be seen as all bad the next. The mind is simply not developed enough to integrate good and bad qualities in one image of a person. They must be one or the other, good or bad.

Sometimes in psychotherapy one sees this tendency to split in very dramatic fashion. More severely disturbed patients can rapidly shift from seeing the therapist as being all good to all bad. By keeping one part of the mind separate from the other, the patient protects himself from having to confront the perplexity that arises when he sees contradictory aspects of the same person. A weakened or perplexed mind cannot cope with the complexity required to bring the two images into one person. The image of the other person shifts back and forth with just the slightest provocation from one extreme to the other. Ambivalence and nuance is too taxing for a weakened mind. This is psychological splitting. When Bill O'Reilly, for instance, attacks a liberal guest for pointing to the complexity of an issue, he is playing to this regressive tendency in his viewers' minds.

Maturation requires the child to gradually integrate these two split off images, so that the mother who is gratifying is also the mother who is frustrating, and the disappointing friend becomes a congenial spirit who has some flaws. In other words, people learn to understand that situations are more complex than all good or all bad and to make distinctions on the basis of degree. In this process, people develop the capacity to tolerate ambivalence in relationships and to accept nuances in their understanding of social situations and complex mental tasks that require judgment.

The mental ability to tolerate the fact that most people are a mix of strengths and weaknesses is one of the most important mental developmental tasks for the child. Without it, no relationship is ever stable. But this ability to integrate contradictory images and feelings develops in differing degrees in different people. Those who have not developed it adequately have a hard time tolerating uncertainty and nuance and look to a powerful other to tell them what is real and what is not real, preferably in absolutist terms. When gaslighters exploit the difficulty that many people have in this area, it further undercuts the victim's mental health, and also makes the victim more dependent on the gaslighter.

People's view of the external world mirrors this internal process. When issues have inherent conflicts, people become perplexed. If people's psychological strength in tolerating ambiguity is low, they simplify and turn one solution into the "all good" solution, while the alternative becomes "all bad." That reduces the perplexity even if it makes for a more unrealistic view of the world. Any reconsideration of that position requires the person to reenter the state of perplexity, and so it requires tremendous impetus to make them do so. The more feeble their mind in tolerating ambiguity and nuance, the more susceptible they are to a gaslighter's distorted message. If Saddam Hussein is evil, the weakened mind is less able to make critical distinctions about the degree of threat he represents to the United States in the context of its war on terror. Simplicity rules.

This problem of splitting into unrealistically all-good or all-bad images is especially problematic for Americans when it comes to their relationship with their government. Americans tend to see government as akin to a parental authority figure. The splitting in the relationship to the government is similar to the adolescent's relationship to parents. On the one hand, people judge the government against a standard of perfection, and at the same time they express immediate disdain whenever the word *government* is mentioned. When Americans do this, it is like the adolescent who laments parental rules in one breath and then demands a twenty-dollar bill for the evening's entertainment in the next. The disdain only obscures the dependency on the parents. Americans assume their government should be there even though they are contemptuous of it. But when they elected a president who shared that contempt and eventually saw the result of his disdain in New Orleans after Hurricane Katrina, they were outraged.

The significance of this attitude was brought home to me several years ago when I heard former Indiana congressman Lee

Hamilton address a group of Washington officials on health care. He described a recent visit to his Indiana congressional district where he met with a large group of constituents to discuss the issue. He asked how many of them wanted socialized medicine. By the show of hands, none did. His next question was how many thought the federal government should pay for their health care. Every hand in the room shot up.

In addition to the psychological splitting, Americans also have a paranoid relationship with their government. America was founded on a mistrust of government. Some of America's founding fathers suffered from government-supported religious persecution. For others, their mistrust was forged by their resentment of the king's arbitrary taxation policies. The common element for most, however, was the desire to escape a government they felt unfairly restricted their lives. Today that mistrust is used by gaslighters to keep Americans from solving problems that cost wealthy Americans more money. This problem has been hampering American efforts to address major domestic policy concerns for decades, long before George W. Bush came on the scene. While Bush and other neoconservatives have certainly used that phenomenon to their advantage, they are by no means the architects of the problem.

Americans' paranoid relationship to government makes it very difficult to address problems that only government can solve. One can look at almost any domestic problem currently plaguing America from this perspective. Since I have had unique opportunities to observe and participate in health care policy from multiple vantage points over three decades, I can best discuss the problem in that context. My experience was twofold. First, I was a practitioner providing mental health care directly to patients as the health care system was beginning to transition into managed health care. Second, in the 1990s, I was one of a relatively small number of actual health professionals who served in a significant advocacy role in Washington while the health care reform issue was playing out in the first Clinton administration. Through a series of circumstances, I had the opportunity to work in some capacity or other with most of the major players in that health care effort in the administration, in the insurance industry, and in Congress. While inevitably, of course, I can only understand my own piece of that huge elephant, I think I saw some aspects of the process that shed light on why America's psychological vulnerabilities will continue to make it difficult for it to address any domestic policy crisis, including health care, even in a post–George W. Bush era.

The history of health insurance reform or national health insurance goes back to the 1940s when current Michigan congressman John Dingell's father proposed to use Social Security to cover hospital and physician expenses for workers and retirees. At that time, a majority of Americans clearly supported the idea. Some estimates of public support were as high as 74 percent. These were Americans who, for the most part, had been rescued from the Great Depression by government and were less inclined to view it as the bogeyman than possibly any other generation of Americans.

When President Truman tried to revive the idea immediately after WWII, the Red menace was on everyone's mind. The American Medical Association organized a campaign and defeated the proposal by convincing the American public that the idea was "socialist" and would lead to a government takeover of medicine.

In the early 1970s, Senator Edward Kennedy and President Richard Nixon appeared ready to compromise on a national health insurance plan that used the private sector and ran the program through employer-based insurance plans administered by the private health insurance companies, as opposed to the strictly government-run system Kennedy originally proposed. The Watergate scandal preempted any legislative action and the opportunity was lost. For the next two decades, efforts to fix health care were largely centered in the private sector in the managed care movement. Managed health care was brought to us by the private sector.

In the early days of employer-based health insurance, health care costs were not a significant problem. They were just a "fringe benefit" of employment. By the 1980s, they had become a significant cost problem that was growing worse. When the *Wall Street Journal* reported that General Motors was spending more on health care for its employees than it was on steel for its automobiles, the problem of rising health care costs got the attention of everyone paying for the cost of health care—employers, labor unions, and government officials in particular. By the late 1980s, health care expenditures had grown to 8 percent of the gross national product. Today, even under the managed health care regime, with all of its promises of savings, costs have grown to 16 percent of gross national product.[4] It was certainly understandable that everyone would look for ways to reduce costs.

However, as health care's price had gone up, its significance as a benefit to employees and government beneficiaries had also risen. This created a political and public relations dilemma. How could business and government leaders cut health care costs without incurring the negative fallout that reducing benefits would entail? Traditional mechanisms of cost control–such as increased deductibles, increased copayments, or increased subscriber share of premiums–would obviously have created adverse reactions that no one wanted to face. If there was a way to cut costs without incurring the public relations fallout of doing so, it was an idea whose time had come. This idea was "managed health care," or "HMOs." Few domestic policy issues so embodied gaslighting as the evolution and implementation of managed health care. And it had nothing to do with George W. Bush.

At its inception, managed care deftly used its right hand to point to the comparative advantages between managed and traditional indemnity insurance. Eager to present itself as providing better health care to prospective patients, HMOs emphasized that there were no co-insurance payments and no deductibles, and routine physicals were free, as were doctor visits.

While this was being used to distract the audience's attention, a new cost-containment mechanism was being developed with the unwatched left hand. That mechanism was the financial conflict of interest that drives every managed care system. *The single most important fact about managed care is that the person at the top stands to make money to the extent they are successful in denying people care no matter what the reason.* It is that incentive system that permeates everything in managed care.

To implement the cost control, a new concept was subtly introduced into the health care system, a veritable wolf carefully dressed in sheep's clothing. The sheep's clothing is called "medical necessity," a phrase that introduces the cost-containment mechanism in a manner that lets it slide unnoticed past the distracted eye of the audience still listening to the comparison of traditional indemnity insurance and managed health care. Managed care promised to provide "all the care that's medically necessary." When one hears it, the inflection is on the phrase "all the care," and the phrase "medically necessary" is rolled out as a statement of the obvious. As most doctors are now all too painfully aware, the judgment of what is "medical necessity" is the wolf that devours the unsuspecting patient. The question is what is and what is not "medically necessary." In addressing that issue, one invariably meets with a wide range of clinical sophistry that has but one objective: to deny care.

Managed health care came to the Research Triangle of North Carolina where I was practicing at the time in the 1980s in a very peculiar form that has typified the deception that has now infiltrated health care financing in the private sector. A public education campaign, dubbed "Health Vote," was started by an ostensibly public education group to educate people, through TV and print media, on the dilemmas created by rising health care costs. People were educated on alternative ways to combat rising health care costs. Some involved draconian rationing of health care. Managed health care, on the other hand, was described as a system of care that limited one's choice of doctors to those who promise to be efficient in the provision of services and not give you unnecessary care. At the end of the educational campaign, people in the Triangle area were given the opportunity in a straw vote conducted by the local newspapers to indicate their personal preferences among options ranging from several very undesirable solutions like rationing to managed care, as defined above. The results would presumably help guide public and private employers how to restructure health care coverage in their employee benefit plans.

Upon investigation, however, it was revealed that the funding for the Health Vote public education campaign came from public utility companies and other large employers eager to hold down the cost of health care. Health Vote was really designed to make it appear that managed health care was something desired by their employees, obscuring the fact that it was initiated by cost-conscious employers. In short, it was a campaign designed to make it appear that there was a groundswell of support for managed health care among educated consumers.

This attempt to obscure the real support for managed health care has typified managed health care's deceptive history. The cost containment of managed health care is powerful. In the old fee-for-service system, there were three players. The patient and the doctor essentially went into the room and decided how much of the third-party insurer's money they would like to spend on health care services for the patient and income for the doctor. The answer was invariably "a lot." Under managed health care, the money was given to a fourth party, the HMO, by the payer. The fourth party was asked how much of the money they wanted to give to the patient and doctor on the one hand, and how much they would like to retain in corporate profits on the other. The fourth party's answer was obvious.

The "beauty" of managed care was that it let government and business out of their dilemma of how to cut costs without appearing to cut benefits. Managed care could be promoted to the beneficiary as providing better care—in fact, all the care that was "medically necessary." Furthermore, when compared to traditional insurance cost mechanisms, it appeared to save the beneficiary considerable money.

The managed health care companies argued that under managed care, there were other ways to save money as well. They could keep people well by applying preventive health care programs. Prevention, combined with economies of scale and sound management practices, would enable them to provide what care people did need for less money. Of course this played into Americans' belief in the efficiency of the private sector, and by virtue of that it seemed plausible.

What the subscribers were not told, however, is that the managed care system had far more powerful mechanisms for cost control that were not brought to their attention. Under the managed health care system, the more care that is *denied,* the more profitable the business. The manager of the health care program was placed in direct financial conflict of interest with the patient: every dollar authorized for treatment was a dollar that came out of their profit margin. It really was no more complex than that.

Not surpisingly, pseudo-treatment-based rationales for denying care were quickly developed to rationalize the denial of care for not meeting the "criteria" for medical necessity. The phrase *medical necessity* itself was not something that really even existed in the medical field prior to the onset of managed care. The phrase was designed to make it seem that the insured will get the care that their doctor felt was necessary.

It was a ruse. The phrase simply meant that the managed care company reserves the right to define what care they will provide and what care they won't. This was the covert cost control in managed health care. Few managed-care companies provided any of the preventive care that they originally promised, and "medical necessity" became a very austere concept, as doctors learned to their increasing dismay.

The problem for the insurance company was compounded because of the very high overhead they faced, making expenditures on actual treatment even more problematic. When one tallies the cost of the bureaucracy needed to monitor the care being provided, the costs of advertising in the competitive marketplace, and the profit investors expected, there was remarkably little left over for actual health care. Further complicating the financial picture was the fact that health care became a very speculative growth industry. Highly leveraged buyouts occurred at breathtaking speed, adding corporate debt management expense to the already high overhead.

My actuarial and auditing sources say most mental health managed companies take 40 percent of the total premium dollar for overhead and profit. Some have been as high as 70 percent.[5] The fleecing of the American health care dollar is not occurring in vast and wasteful government bureaucracies. It is occurring in vast, wasteful, and exploitative private health insurance bureaucracies. While statistics on this vary, none supports the notion that the government is as inefficient as the private health insurance industry.

Managed health care was built on the gullibility of the human mind and was made possible by the mind's capacity to "split." Managed care began with a demagogue's most fundamental lure: "You *can* always get what you want." The proponents of managed care said that one *could* have all the health care they wanted despite the growing costs of the health care system. America did not have to pay more taxes or cut more benefits. It did not have to resolve the ideological rifts that currently block it from moving

to any of the government-based alternative health care systems
available. It played on people's capacity for self-deception and
their wish that they need not confront their conflicts.

But managed care has left America with another problem. Both
managed care and private fee-for-service systems leave 44 million Americans uncovered by any health insurance, especially
those who are most in need, the sick. This problem is inherent to
a private profit-driven insurance system, whether it is indemnity
or managed care. It is dynamically impossible to create a system
in which everyone is covered but where profit margin is the goal.
One makes profit by excluding the sick or failing to treat them.
Both run directly contrary to the policy objectives of the system,
to get care to those who need it.

In 1985 at an American Psychological Association Board of
Professional Affairs dinner meeting, a prominent Capitol Hill
committee staffer who was one of the major architects of the
current managed-care regime described the next five-year expansion of managed care. When I asked him what plan they had for
dealing with the inevitable problems with quality of care that the
financial conflict of interest of managed care would create, he
smiled and said, "Well, I guess we'll just wait until people scream."

People have screamed. The impact of all of this hit particularly
hard in the mental health area and particularly on life-and-death
mental health situations. Jimmy was a thirteen-year-old boy living
in a middle-income suburban community. His father had died
from pancreatic cancer when Jimmy was seven years old. Childhood depression after such a loss oftentimes does not appear until early adolescence. Adolescents, because of their mind's limited
capacity to process and tolerate painful feeling states, often show

signs of mental illness in the form of aberrant behavior, typically stimulation-seeking behavior that is designed to ward off the painful feelings of depression. Though Jimmy had rarely gotten into trouble before his teenage years, he started taking his mother's car to go joyriding with friends late at night after she was asleep. He was caught by the police and sentenced to a few days in juvenile detention, where he was incarcerated with violent youth offenders much older than he was. His boyish appearance and long hair made him a potential target of homosexual assaults, which terrified him. He was released after forty-eight hours with the stern admonition that if he were caught again he would have a much lengthier stay.

After that, Jimmy's mother routinely slept with her car keys to make sure that they did not fall into Jimmy's hands. But when Jimmy was confined at home, he became agitated and violent, and on one occasion his mother had to call the police. The police officer who answered the mother's call quickly saw that Jimmy was in need of mental health treatment and sent him to a nearby psychiatric hospital. Jimmy was admitted on a Tuesday afternoon.

On Wednesday the hospital treatment team met and concluded that Jimmy needed a two-week inpatient stay, during which time he could establish a therapeutic relationship in the hospital and begin medication to help him better control his behavior. The hospital's concern was that Jimmy's behavior made him a danger to himself and to others; it was not safe for him to be out of the hospital. On Thursday morning, less than twenty-four hours later, the treating psychiatrist wrote a discharge order for Jimmy: "Does not meet criteria. Needs to be discharged today." The medical record indicates that there had been a phone call from the managed health care company late Wednesday afternoon. Jimmy was sent home.

To this day, Jimmy's mother does not know how Jimmy obtained keys to the car, but he did. He picked up some friends around midnight. They were spotted by the police. Presumably terrified of being returned to juvenile detention, Jimmy let his friends out of the car so they could run off into the woods. He then took off at breakneck speed down a slippery winding road, with the police in chase. He failed to negotiate a turn and crashed the car, killing himself at the age of thirteen.

Of course we hear about all of the frivolous lawsuits filed in this country. The managed health care industry, with a few exceptions, is immune from litigation under a federal statute that has been interpreted to preempt lawsuits for direct liability against managed health care treatment decisions. Under that statute, people who are denied care can sue for the cost of the service they should have been provided, but they cannot sue for the damage they suffer as a result of that care being denied. In Jimmy's case, that would have been the cost of two weeks in the hospital.

I wish I could say that Jimmy's care was an isolated failure of the managed health care system. During the 1980s and into the 90s, America moved from a system of health care that was wasting money to one that wasted both money and lives. This is the current private sector health system in America. The fact that this was established to avoid the inefficiency and loss of freedom Americans assumed would accompany a national health insurance system is tragic.

By the time the Clintons came to the White House in 1993, American health care was truly a mess. In addition to the estimated 44 million Americans who lacked health insurance entirely, "cherry-picking" by the insurance industry–people who were healthy got insurance but those who were sick were denied it–suggested that millions more would lose their insurance unless something was done about guaranteeing coverage to people who fell ill. The problem was how to do this, given the American public's inability to free itself from long-standing but false assumptions that the government would be worse than the private sector in guaranteeing health insurance coverage. The group assembling the Clinton health care plan, led by Hillary Clinton and Ira Magaziner, made an unprecedented effort to involve all the players in this vast sector of the American economy to reform the system.

For most Americans it is an article of faith, adhered to no matter what the empirical reality, that the ideology of a free market health care system is preferable to a government-financed health care system. In this *belief* system, the benefits of having a private health insurance system operating under free market forces seems so apparent to everyone it is not even questioned. For many Americans, these are the principles of private market performance:

- *Governed as it is by competition and the profit motive, the private health insurance system will keep the overhead costs of health care to a minimum and avoid the waste, not to mention the corruption, of publicly run health care plans.*
- *The public will benefit because the competitive pricing of a private free market economy guarantees lower health care costs than a government plan.*
- *The public does not have to trust in the insurer's beneficence because with free market competition, the insurance company knows that if*

it fails to provide quality care people can take their business else-
where.

Because Americans accept these statements as articles of faith, America is now the only advanced nation in the world without a national health system. In their analysis, however, the government is never compared in a meaningful way to the private sector. Is the government wasteful and occasionally corrupt? Yes, of course it is. Is it as wasteful and corrupt as the private health insurance industry? Not by a long shot. Does managed health care really provide the quality of care the axioms of free market competition suggest it will? Many Americans have had that question answered the hard way.

The health care reform initiative of 1993 was an attempt to restructure one-seventh of the nation's economy, the portion that is spent on health care services. It affected literally trillions of dollars. Needless to say, it brought Washington lobbyists out of the woodwork, not the least of which was the Health Insurance Association of America, a lobbying group funded by health insurance companies. It had a stunning effect on outcome.

A key committee in health care reform was the House Ways and Means Health Subcommittee. At the beginning of health care reform, it was chaired by California democrat Fortney "Pete" Stark. The ranking minority member was a highly respected Republican congressman from Cincinnati, Willis Gradison. The minority staff member serving the Republicans on the committee was a veteran Hill staffer by the name of Charles "Chip" Kahn. Both minority members were extremely knowledgeable about health insurance matters in Congress. And, of course, given their years of service, they were well connected in congressional circles.

In a stunning move, the Health Insurance Association of America simply hired both Gradison and Kahn right out of their congressional positions. Mr. Gradison became president of HIAA and Mr. Kahn worked for him. This was done right in the middle of the health care reform legislative effort.

The next salvo from the health insurance lobby was a $12 million advertising campaign represented by "Harry" and "Louise," two actors whose real names were indeed Harry (Johnson) and Louise (Claire Clark). They starred in a series of campaign ads that bombarded Americans in key congressional districts night after night. Ostensibly a typical American couple, Harry and Louise read the Clinton health care plan, which, of course, most Americans had never done and would never do. Harry and Louise concluded that the plan was a "vast government bureaucracy." Their apprehension triggered off the bogeyman of big government. "Government bureaucracy" translates into "government inefficiency." The Clinton health care plan was made to seem un-American. Louise said, "Having choices we don't like is like no choice at all." Harry: "They choose." Louise: "We lose."[6] After all, we all know the government is incompetent, inefficient, and corrupt. We all know it so well, we do not even really need to look, see, or think.

There was a largely unrecognized irony to these Harry and Louise ads. One of the major inefficiencies in the American health care system is that American consumers as a group are really unable to negotiate prices with the major health care providers. This is the primary reason, for example, Americans pay such dramatically higher prescription drug prices than other countries that have some type of national health plan. The Clinton plan addressed this problem by proposing to set up "health alliances" that could negotiate prices and benefit packages with the insurance industry on behalf of consumers as a group. The alliances were to be set up in each state and function like consumer cooperatives in their purchasing power.

This, of course, gave them clout commensurate with the insurance industry. Naturally it was anathema to the health insurance industry and large medical supplier groups. It was these alliances that Harry and Louise successfully mischaracterized as a "vast government bureaucracy." They were in truth consumer cooperatives that would have let the American people have purchasing leverage against the large corporate players in health care, like health insurance companies and pharmaceutical manufacturers. The insurance industry, however, gaslighted the public. They misled them into believing that the alliances were a giant government bureaucracy. The industry convinced the American public to shoot themselves in their collective foot by opposing the plan.

The administration made no countervailing assault against the private health insurance industry. What was in truth a commendable effort to bring some measure of rationality to American health care, to blend the public and private sectors, went up in flames. The legislative momentum that is so difficult to generate on issues of this magnitude was lost. In what I have always seen as a great act of historical revisionism, both Chip Kahn and conservative columnist Robert Novak have attributed the failure of the health initiative to Hillary Clinton's intransigence. That is not what I saw.

In 1996, Senators Ted Kennedy (D-MA) and Nancy Kassebaum (R-KA) took what was left of that momentum to pass the Health Insurance Portability and Accountability Act of 1996

(HIPAA), a well-intended measure designed to solve two of the major problems affecting health care: preexisting conditions and portability of health insurance. The 1996 bill was proof that "the devil is in the details." The exceptions and exemptions written into the bill effectively eviscerated the protections for preexisting conditions, and most Americans were unable to afford the exorbitant rates for portability. Today the only operationally significant part of the legislation is a series of record-keeping "accountability and privacy" guidelines that have only added to the billions of dollars of health care administrative costs in this country.

Most Americans adhere with quasireligious zeal to the notion that any government bureaucracy is worse than a private, profit-making one. This belief blinds them to the facts. America's *private* health insurance bureaucracy is extraordinarily bloated and astonishingly inefficient. The United States spends 50 percent more on health care costs per capita than any other nation in the world.[7] This is not because Americans are using more services, and it is not because America has more lawsuits, as opponents of meaningful reform allege. The Johns Hopkins Bloomberg School of Public Health's Department of Health Policy and Management dispelled those two myths. "We can't blame the United States' higher health care costs on limiting procedures in other countries or the elevated number of law suits filed in the United States," writes Peter Hussey, Ph.D., coauthor of the study. "As in previous years, it comes back to the fact that we are paying much higher prices for health care goods and services in the United States. Paying more is okay if our outcomes are better than other countries. But we are paying more for comparable outcomes," writes Gerard Anderson, Ph.D., a professor at the

Bloomberg School of Public Health.[8] The private, free market sector has failed in health care.

What *is* a considerable factor in health care costs is the inefficiency of the private health insurance system. In fact, private health insurance administrative costs are *four times* what Medicare's administrative costs are. The duplication, the screening, and the coordination of benefits determinations combine with high CEO salaries, advertising, corporate profits, and leveraged debt service to make the private sector much less efficient administratively. And because there are no long-term incentives to engage in preventive treatment, health care costs continue to go up.

Nor has the private sector's emphasis on managed health care provided the promised health care savings. The Kaiser Family Foundation reports that U.S. increases in health care spending as a percentage of gross domestic product are higher than the increases in any other country.[9] America's costs are not only going up, they are rising faster than anywhere else.

When it comes to quality of care actually delivered in America's private insurance system, most Americans believe they are receiving the best health care available in the world, even if it does cost a bit more. They are not. The World Health Organization ranks the U.S. thirty-seventh in national performance in health care.[10] This puts the United States behind most European nations and Japan as well as Chile, Colombia, Saudi Arabia, and Singapore. We do not have more doctors' visits or services than many of these other countries.[11] Studies consistently show Americans are paying hundreds of billions of dollars a year to subsidize a terribly inefficient private health insurance system that could be converted with relative ease into a system that covers all Americans,

pays for all prescription drugs, and allows us to implement meaningful preventive care, all with the savings realized by getting rid
of the "efficient" private health insurance industry.

Why is America stuck in the unenviable position of spending far
more on health care than any other nation and yet getting far less
than most? The answer lies in America's attitude toward government. Americans have taken primitive feelings, ones that people
often project onto strangers or foreigners, and projected them
onto the very notion of government itself. Americans are so mis-
trustful of government–not any particular government, just the
concept of government itself–that they are unable to use the primary tool available to fix problems that only the government can
fix.

   During the debate on the Clinton health care plan, HIAA
hired a pollster named Bill McInturff. "In those early focus
groups," he recalled, "people wanted health care to pass." However, the focus groups also showed that "people don't believe the
federal government can get anything done." McInturff convinced
all those opposed to the Clinton plan to call it "government
health care," not "national health insurance."[12]

   In fact, America is so paralyzed by a paranoid reaction to government that it is incapable of addressing many of the serious
problems that confront it. These problems are not being solved
by the private sector, nor can they be. America is stopped by its
own myths: that the invisible hand of the free market will correct
its problems and that the government would only interfere with
that process if it became involved in it.

   Americans' attitude about government splits off the notion of
government from their notion of themselves. Americans need to

learn the corollary to Pogo's widely recognized maxim, "We have met the enemy, and he is us." If America is going to move forward on health care, not to mention other large social issues, Americans must recognize that "the government is us." And we do not have to be an enemy to ourselves.

It is impossible to make a case that government-run health care would be even remotely as incompetent, inefficient, or corrupt as private health insurance. And yet, if Americans acknowledge that possibility, their mind has to contend with a much more complex world, in which one cannot make policy decisions simply on the basis of a black-and-white test predicated on simplistic notions about government involvement. But if Americans are unable to learn to do this, they are then vulnerable to the kind of exploitation that victimized them with the Clinton health initiative.

With the defeat of the Clinton health care plan, Americans were left with the privately run health care system. It has delivered precisely what Americans feared they would get from a government-run plan: an inefficient health care system that denies Americans control of their own health care and fails to provide any health care access to 44 million Americans. There is no better illustration of the manipulation of reality in domestic American policy than the advent of managed health care and the insurance industry's successful defeat of health care reform.

The health care issue will come around again. It has to because so many are suffering. Conservative forces will first of all try to co-opt the momentum into further tax deductions for employers. If this fails, they will do the same thing they did with prescription drugs for the elderly: turn it into a giant federal subsidy not for the sick, but for the private health insurance industry.

They will do so by waving the specter of "government-run medicine." Gaslighters love the bogeyman.

The private health insurance industry is a dinosaur America cannot afford to subsidize any longer. It has been too costly, too inefficient, and too inhumane. Its existence is not due to any divine principle such as a "free market economy" or "private enterprise." Instead, it is an exploiter of America's own immature attitude toward government. As the health care debate so vividly illustrated, private health insurance is a symptom of that immaturity and does not fulfill any of the benefits attributed to private enterprise.

We can curse the government all we want, but that will not facilitate efforts to develop a cost-effective heath care system accessible by all, especially those most in need. For this we need collective national action. Our government *is* our collective national action.

CHAPTER 11
THE POLITICS OF REALITY: BATTLEGROUND STATES

Senator Obama and Senator Clinton want to surrender. They want to wave the white flag. They want to set a date for withdrawal. My friends, that means surrender, and I will never surrender as president of the United States!

—Senator John McCain

It's a Washington where George Bush hands out billions in tax cuts year after year to the biggest corporations and the wealthiest few who don't need them and don't ask for them—tax breaks that are mortgaging our children's future on a mountain of debt, tax breaks that could've gone into the pockets of the working families who needed them most.

—Senator Barack Obama

In his first inaugural address in 1993, President Clinton confidently declared, "There is nothing wrong with America that can't be cured by what's right with America." That is far less certain now than it was in January 1993. It is not because the problems are so overwhelming; it is because the American mind is in such disarray.

The battleground psychological states of sexual perplexity, envy, and paranoia can each in their own right have politically significant effects on the American voters. But when they are all in play at the same time, the synergetic effect can be politically explosive. If one appreciates the power of the three battleground states, it is easy to see that anyone who understands these forces and is inclined to manipulate them can do great evil.

America's predicament is dire; it is not hopeless. At the present time, the psychological forces that shape our view of reality have been almost the exclusive province of gaslighters who have used their understanding to divide America, start a disastrous and needless war, stifle social progress, and steal both America's national treasury and its national resources.

It is important to notice, however, that these psychological forces in and of themselves are not necessarily evil. These dimensions of the mind that I have discussed throughout this book can be harnessed for either good or for evil. Paranoid mechanisms are the sensitivities that enable us to understand each other. Sexuality is the means by which we love our partner and create our children. And envy creates our motivation to work and be productive.

If Americans have the wisdom to select leaders who want to harness these forces to make it a more effective nation, there is an enormous opportunity these battleground states provide. They are battlegrounds, however, and they cannot be converted to constructive purposes without a fight.

President Franklin D. Roosevelt's famous first inaugural address delivered to a frightened nation declared, "The only thing we have to fear is fear itself." It epitomizes the constructive role leadership can play during national emotional crises. FDR identified the fear and allayed it so that it would be less psychologically problematic and less likely to cripple rational faculties. First with the Great Depression and then with World War II, Roosevelt channeled America's fears into constructive action. Domestically, the result was Social Security and a host of New Deal programs that still form a safety net for millions of Americans. Internationally, he redirected America's fears away from its traditional isolationism that would have been so disastrous to the world at that time. In his confident presence and personal willingness to confront problems head on, he gave a troubled nation confidence. In contemporary America, one gets the sense the pathos of the Great Depression would have been used as an excuse for more tax cuts for the rich and the Nazi menace a reason to stifle dissent, turn the country into an incompetently run police state, and attack a South American country on behalf of U.S. business interests.

Contrary to popular misconception, anger and rage are not necessarily bad emotions. The question is simply how they are used and for what purpose. In World War II, America directed its anger over being attacked against both Japan and Adolf Hitler, with spectacularly beneficial results. In addition, after the peace, an exhausted war-weary nation had the presence of mind, and the psychological sophistication, to understand the importance of reconstructing postwar Europe with the Marshall Plan. We also acknowledged the tragedy of our paranoid failure to support the League of Nations after World War I by actively promoting the United Nations.

Certainly on other occasions, leaders with vision have helped channel potentially vulnerable emotional states into constructive action. President Kennedy's space program helped Americans convert their fear and self-doubt over the Soviet Union's launching of Sputnik into a constructive venture that restored American confidence. Alternatively, that fear could have been projected, making the Soviet Union seem even more menacing and America even more frightened. Obviously this could have had dire consequences for the world as well.

Without the astute emotional management exemplified by Roosevelt and other presidents, paranoid dynamics can play havoc on a world stage. The problem is compounded if the world has bad, unstable, or inept leaders. The national leaders involved in the invasion of Iraq and the "axis of evil" have been George W. Bush, Saddam Hussein, Mahmoud Ahmadinejad of Iran, and Kim Jong Il of North Korea. As different as these four are from one another, none will find their way into psychological case studies as models for the mitigation of worldwide paranoia.

Today Americans have many legitimate reasons to be angry and frightened. The question confronting America is why fear and resentment from so many legitimate grievances are not channeled into constructive action as they have been in our past.

Why are Americans *not* enraged about their predicament with oil? Why are American youths dying in a foreign country to ensure a steady flow of oil when it is now possible for us to find alternative energy sources? Even if it were necessary, why should the oil industry profit from the situation? Why shouldn't the oil industry rather than gays be attacked for America's national predicament? Such a campaign would constructively channel rage, enhance feelings of personal adequacy, and increase feelings of security. It would also be based in reality.

In May 2007, top pharmaceutical executives acknowledged that they deliberately marketed a pain medication, oxycodone, claiming that it was not addictive even though they knew it was. These highly paid executives knowingly sold a medication for pain that they knew could cause hundreds of thousands of users to incur something far worse than the pain the medication was trying to stop: drug addiction. They did this dressed in the garb of respected members of America's private health care industry that is trusted more than the federal government. And yet their "punishment" was a fine.[1]

This is from the same industry that successfully lobbied to make the Medicare prescription drug bill for the elderly a financial windfall for themselves at the expense of America's elderly and American taxpayers. Their primary competition for this opportunity to exploit the public was the health insurance industry. The pharmaceutical lobbyists prevailed, however, and got the better of the health insurance industry in the process. The pharmaceuticals took a page from the Health Insurance Association of America's own playbook and hired Louisiana congressman Billy Tauzin away from Congress to lead their lobbying effort in Washington. Prior to his new position, Rep. Tauzin had been chairman of the congressional committee that oversaw and regulated the pharmaceutical industry.

Now, Americans pay excessively high prices for drugs, much higher than people in other countries pay for the same medications made by American companies. In the case of oxycodone, the medication is deliberately mischaracterized to mask the addicting effects of the medication. When people fall ill with drug addiction from the drug, the managed health care insurance company denies them the care they need. When they then die or suffer serious injury in many states, neither they nor their family can sue the pharmaceutical manufacturer or the HMO because such lawsuits have been successfully mischaracterized as "frivolous."

A few people Americans elected to public office to protect them from this state of affairs have simply parlayed the people's trust into a lucrative job with the health insurance industry or the pharmaceutical industry lobbying their former colleagues. The industries generate still bigger profits from our health care system, which people naively believe is efficient because it is run by the private sector. Even when an event such as the oxycodone scandal is uncovered, the executives simply have to give back some of the money in the form of a fine. My former client who spent time in prison for stealing a small quantity of food from a 7-Eleven to feed his three sons asked me why this is fair.

The legitimate resentment that all of this should create is obfuscated with negative advertising that channels hatred into a mixing pot of envy, sexual perplexity, and paranoia, which is then used in the service of supporting the continued exploitation of Americans. Homosexuals are having sex in a way that makes people anxious, and it is seeping into people's houses right through the TV screen. On July 8, 2007, terrorists are arrested in New Jersey, and while they more closely resemble the Keystone Cops than menacing terrorists, the media attention and public alarm rekindle the fears of 9/11. It is hard to focus on the complex workings of health insurance or pharmaceautical companies mischief when one is struggling to manage this kind of anxiety.

And yet the strangest part of it all is the comparative quiet about the whole state of affairs from "the other side." Why have Democrats been so slow to rage?

In May 1966, I drove from Cambridge, Massachusetts, to New Haven, Connecticut, to represent Harvard College in the annual triangular debates between Harvard, Princeton, and Yale. The debates typically took place at the end of the academic year, with each school sending a two-person team to one of the other schools while another two-person team stayed home to debate a visiting rival from the third school. As an underclassman, I drew the assignment of going to New Haven. This was less desirable not only because of the travel, but because based on the long history of the event, the home team had a remarkably lopsided chance of winning no matter which school it was. Despite the hallowed halls of ivy's reputation for academic integrity, some cynically attributed this to the fact that the home team always selected the judges.

The debate was preceded by a dinner with seating arranged in commingled groups of four. I sat with one of the Yale debaters, a very lean, dark-haired, seemingly nervous, slightly aloof fellow from a very exclusive New England prep school; one of the judges, a friendly and affable attorney from New Haven; and a younger member of the Yale debate team, not debating that evening, who was also quite outgoing and politically very liberal.

The reason I remember the evening so clearly is because of what happened after dinner. I got up to give the first speech, known as the "first affirmative" in the debate world. I was to make the case for the proposition that America should reduce its foreign policy commitments around the world and present a plan for how to do that. Each of the first four speeches was limited to ten minutes. They were followed by four five-minute rebuttals. When I sat down, the "first negative" speaker turned out to be the rather serious Yale debater with whom I had tried with only moderate success to have a conversation at dinner. He began his attack saying, "The gentleman from Harvard has hit the bull's eye. But, alas! It was with a wet noodle."

The comment was greeted by a bit of an awkward rustling in the small audience. I think for most it had a "clang effect." It was an attempted joke without context and, more importantly, it had the contrived air of something borrowed from some very dated oratorical text. It was, for sure, not "cool" by contemporaneous debate standards. I am absolutely certain that but for that comment, I would not have remembered the evening at all.

By the time this same Yale debater, John Kerry, debated George W. Bush in 2004 with the fate of the Western world possibly riding in the balance, he was in my opinion a much better debater than one might have anticipated based on his performance that night in New Haven forty years earlier. It was, however, humorous to hear Republican spin doctors in the predebate publicity try to lower expectations for their candidate by calling Kerry the greatest college debater "since Cicero" and mythologizing the "famous" Yale debate program.

Yale did not even field a team in what was nationally recognized as intercollegiate debating. Instead, it had a very limited debate program conducted largely as a club sport, with limited exhibition public debates. But if it suited Kerry's opponents to make it appear their candidate was a David going against the Goliath, "Cicero Kerry," what was reality to stand in the way? Yale simply did not have such a program, and John Kerry was not easily confused with Cicero.

One of the intriguing things about projection is that if you look carefully at unfair accusations and trace them back to their source, you will find that they oftentimes are present in the accuser himself. This makes some sense. The accuser, in manufacturing an attack, has to be creative, and he draws on his own unconscious for the creative material with which to attack. The more unfounded the accusations, the more likely they are to be a derivative of his own unconscious rather than any objective reality. In effect, the false accuser finds his own shortcomings in his own unconscious and projects them onto the other person. The childhood retort that I am rubber and you are glue has some foundation in this context.

After watching John Kerry's inability to counterattack George Bush on the Swiftboat allegations (and later his inability to deliver a joke), I wondered if the wet noodle joke in New Haven might not have been an apt illustration of this principle. Kerry's comment about the wet noodle that struck me as somewhat inept forty years ago did not seem so funny in the spring and summer of 2004 when his inability to respond to the Swiftboat attack or the allegations of being a flip-flopper unfit to lead were psychologically reinforcing the notion to the country that George Bush was more qualified to lead and more decisive than Kerry. Kerry's inability to throw a counterpunch during those long 2004 spring and summer months actually turned George Bush into a credible alternative candidate, despite the monstrous debacle that was Iraq.

Kerry's use of the term "wet noodle" was not done with any particular malice or mean-spiritedness. In fact, it might have portended better for America if it had been based in anger. Instead, I think it reflects a terrible inability progressive forces have had in launching a counterattack to right-wing psychological manipulations. If Karl Rove really did say he was history's actor creating his own reality, he was correct. Americans gave him that power, but the truth is, he was not tested by someone else presenting an alternative reality—a reality that derives from a very different mind-set than Karl Rove's. There is a reason for this.

Neoconservative groups understand the principles of a political reality constructed on the basis of how the mind really works as opposed to how people assume it works. Progressive political figures have been a paradigm shift behind. Progressives have clung to an antiquated form of political marketing. Their strategy is reminiscent of what a prominent psychoanalyst, Erich Fromm, characterized as "the marketing personality." The marketing personality's motto is "what you want, I will become." Marketing-personality candidates listen to opinion polls about existing public attitudes and, like the general rushing to catch up to his troops, try to lead by presenting the position that their marketing techniques tell them their target audience wants.

The strategy worked for President Clinton in 1992 and 1996 partly because there were few obvious dangers on the horizon in 1992 other than economic ones, and partly because of his opponents. George H. W. Bush had the appearance of someone who was almost entirely out of touch with everyday life, famously exemplified by his astonishment at supermarket laser-checkout machines. He was never able to dispel the wimp factor and won the election in 1988 primarily because Dukakis was made to appear to be even more of a wimp. Clinton's second opponent, Bob Dole, was similarly unable to give voters a sense of engagement and vitality. (Ironically, he became a happy spokesman for Viagra after the 1996 campaign.)

Strategically, progressives have tried to find the political center and cater to it, rather than address the critical need the public has had for a "reality." The current political battleground over reality has had only one team competing. Such singularity does not guarantee victory because that one competing team may blunder so badly that it self-destructs periodically. Overall, however, the future belongs to it—unless it is joined on the battleground by a competitor able to articulate a vision of reality that understands the mind and helps it shape a meaningful reality itself. When Lee Iacocca asks where all the leaders have gone, as he does in his recent book,[2] the answer is "gone to marketers every one." When will they ever learn?

This does not mean, of course, that polls do not have a place in current political campaigns. Of course, they do. A poll can tell people which way the wind blows and that is invaluable information to have. But there is another fact that is more fundamental: it is people's notion of reality that makes the wind blow in the first place and determines the wind's direction.

The problem is that there is a new paradigm in politics. It is the politics of reality. It is a battle that will be won by whoever controls the relevant battleground states, the most prominent of which are paranoia, sexual perplexity, and envy. With new technology and greater understanding of the human mind, a very determined, maybe even desperate out-group have fought their way to center stage in American politics, and they are doing the kind of long-term strategic planning that suggests they intend to be there for a while.

Americans, especially moderate and liberal Americans, can stomp their feet or naively assume that because things are deteriorating so precipitously that surely they must change for the better. They believe that Americans who have been gaslighted in the past will not be so vulnerable to it in the future.

Occasionally the political winds will appear to support that proposition. Indeed, sometimes things become so bleak that people will temporarily reject the gaslighters. The tenure of any successor progressive regime, however, will most likely be short-lived and power will be quickly returned to the gaslighters, because the gaslighters, once out of office, will be back on the offensive and able to play on the inevitable discontents that plague any society.

What is the solution? Of course, the struggle between wise government and unwise government is Sisyphean in nature. But there are factors of the mind that cannot be ignored. When people are in a battle with those who address the mind on a very deep level and manipulate it, they also have to be able to access that mental state and do battle with the gaslighters on the real battleground. I do not say this in a cynical way at all. Implicit in all political differences is a point of view. I have mine and you have yours. Hopefully, the points of view we each have are sincere and determined in good faith. They then have to be fought for. There is ample opportunity to do this honestly. In fact, a tremendous advantage one has against gaslighters is that the gaslighters are being dishonest. When that is exposed aggressively, it works against them.

The battleground states can work in support of better government. Envy is a necessary part of the human condition. While in some ways it is an ugly emotion and many people do not want to soil their hands with it, it is also the hunger that makes us strive. All human achievement as well as much destructive human aggression is a reflection of envy. What Americans strive for, however, is very much up for grabs. But there are options. For example, Americans can be angry at health insurance companies or they can be angry at the government. It simply depends on who makes the better case and who better appreciates the depths and nature of envy. There are many ways to do this, but it cannot be ignored.

Conservatives have been correct in their appreciation of the family values issue. And it is not just coincidental most of them pertain to sex and reproduction. Strong family values are a big help in fighting sexual perplexity because of the support they provide to sexual identity stability and combating sexual fears. But the real pressure on the American family is not values, it is economic. I am not saying it *should* be that way, I am saying it *is* that way. And given these pressures, a populist uprising is a very strong possibility latent in the American emotional psyche. One can create a very appealing and badly needed program to provide real support for the American family by redirecting the envy away from gay bashing and reproductive matters and toward solving problems that would actually make a substantive difference in Americans' lives.

This is not something that can be done with dispassionate policy discussions. Nor will it be suggested by any poll. John Edwards was alert to the importance of envy in his 2004 presidential bid with his "Two Americas" theme, and he parlayed it into the vice presidential nomination despite being a long shot contender at the start of the primary campaign. He was clearly muzzled during the general campaign. Immediately after the concession speeches, he said that the next Democratic candidate had to believe "in his whole being" in the Democratic message the candidate was delivering. Edwards had seen the future in his own primary campaigning and had been forced to straddle the past in the presidential race. But he at least had intuited how to reach voters in their battleground states.

If the presidential candidate is not reaching the voter in the battleground states of envy, paranoia, and sexuality, he or she is simply not touching the voters at all. It is like playing not to lose.

Sometimes you can win that way, but when you are up against someone who is playing to win at all costs and who understands the battleground states, you will win far less often.

These same battleground issues need to be addressed and fought out within all the critical institutions that support the independent functioning of the mind. Catholics seem clear that the right to life begins at conception. But why do so many priests now support de facto the notion that the right to life *ends* at birth? Why do so many evangelical Christians let their vision be truncated to sexual matters and ecstatic pleasure rather than to Jesus's real work of feeding the poor, casting the money changers out of the Temple, and standing firmly against a judgmental society? And who said that God favored Adam Smith and the invisible hand of free market economies?

Ultimately Americans want hope. That is not a vision that the neoconservatives offer. There is no vision of a Great Society, nor is there any notion that it is even Morning in America. What the gaslighters offer is a profoundly nihilistic society where the most one can hope for is an illusory respite from fear and anxiety. One can try to assuage anxiety with material goods, stimulation, or religious ecstasy, but each of these ultimately becomes like a drug requiring more and more so that the analgesic can stay ahead of the pain. Ultimately, there is a psychological crash that in the present era can wreak tremendous havoc on millions of people and potentially even destroy America. This is the result of the gaslighted mind.

When the mind is strengthened, however, it has a very different subjective experience. A mind that is not perplexed and that is not in flight from itself can live comfortably within itself, not only free from terror but filled with the extraordinary internal richness of its own existence, a richness created in the free and flexible recesses of the mind.

Such a mind can attend to its own cravings and manage its own envy, establish an equal relationship with a significant other that is mutually self-enhancing, and use its understanding and sensitivity toward others to facilitate peaceful coexistence. This sense of equanimity can also maximize the mind's tolerance for uncertainty, letting it respond to crises with appropriately measured steps. It is an antidote to perplexity.

There is an old *Far Side* cartoon that shows a dinosaur giving what appears to be a state of the union address to a distinguished-looking audience of fellow dinosaurs. He says, "The picture's pretty bleak, gentlemen. The world's climates are changing, the mammals are taking over, and we all have a brain the size of a walnut."[3]

Is this America?

NOTES

1. THE ASSAULT ON THE AMERICAN MIND: GASLIGHTING

1. Gaslighting in the mental health community first arose in contexts like the movie in which a gaslighter was trying to drive a spouse crazy. See, for example, V. Calef and E. M. Weinshel, "Some Clinical Consequences of Introjection: Gaslighting," *Psychoanalytic Quarterly* 50, no. 1 (1981): 44–66. However, Seattle psychoanalyst Theodore Dorpat, M.D. discussed gaslighting in the context of relations between psychoanalysts and patients in his book, *Gaslighting, the Double Whammy, Interrogation and Other Methods of Covert Control in Psychotherapy and Analysis* (New York: Jason Aronson, 1996). In her book *The Sociopath Next Door* (New York: Broadway, 1995), Dr. Martha Stout explained how unrecognized sociopaths frequently use gaslighting with devastating effect on victims. More recently, a book by New York psychotherapist Dr. Robin Stern, *The Gaslight Effect* (New York: Morgan Road Books, 2007), described the effect of gaslighting in relationships. Victor Santoro in *Gaslighting: How to Drive Your Enemies Crazy* (Port Townsend, Wash.: Loompanics Unlimited, 1994) provides a semi-tongue-in-cheek book about how to gaslight one's enemies.

2. *The Iraq Study Group Report: The Way Forward—A New Approach,* cochairs James A. Baker III and Lee H. Hamilton (New York: Vintage Books, 2006).

3. Gingrich, *Rediscovering God in America* (New York: Thomas Nelson, 2006).

4. Ben Evans, "Gingrich Admits to Extramarital Affair," Associated Press, March 9, 2007.

5. Bill O'Reilly and Charles Flowers, *The O'Reilly Factor for Kids: A Survival Guide for America's Families* (New York: Harper Entertainment, 2004); Howard Kurtz, "Bill O'Reilly, Producer Settle Harassment Suit," *Washington Post,* October 29, 2004.

6. Evan Thomas, "I Am Addicted to Prescription Pain Medication," *Newsweek,* October 20, 2003.

7. Stephanie Simon, "Haggard's Church Finds Evidence of Strange Behavior Before Downfall," *Los Angeles Times,* March 18, 2007.

8. William Bennett, *The Book of Virtues* (New York: Simon & Schuster, 1993).

2. THE MIND: REALITY SENSE, PERPLEXITY, AND REGRESSION

1. Associated Press, "Falwell Says Christians Shouldn't Focus on Global Warming," August 6, 2007.

2. Marshall McLuhan, *Understanding Media: The Extensions of Man* (London: Sphere Books, 1967).

3. Pope John Paul II appointed a commission to study the case. In 1984, the commission published a series of essays in newspapers entitled *Galileo Galilei: 350 Years of History*. In it they wrote, "The judges who condemned Galileo committed an error."

3. STATES OF CONFUSION: PARANOIA

1. Remarks of Karl Rove at the New York Conservative Party meeting, June 22, 2006. Transcript in http://www.washingtonpost.com/wp-dyn/content/article/2005/06/24/AR2005062400097.htm.

2. R. Steel, "Endgame," *New York Review of Books,* March 13, 1969.

3. Bob Woodward, *Plan of Attack* (New York: Simon & Schuster, 2004).

4. McCarthy made political hay over the Red menace. Hoover allegedly needed an excuse to do something other than fight the mob he feared might expose his suspected homosexual relationship with his chief aide and roommate, Clyde Tolson. Some assert that Meyer Lanksy had picture proof of Hoover's homosexuality.

5. Hisham Matar, "Seeing What We Want to See in Qaddafi," *New York Times,* February 5, 2007.

6. *Encarta Encyclopedia,* S. V. "Iran–Iraq War."

7. Yossi Melman and Meir Javendanfar, *The Nuclear Sphinx of Tehran: Mahmoud Ahmadinejad and the State of Iran* (New York: Carroll & Graf, 2007), 89–90.

8. Fred Barnes, *Rebel in Chief* (New York: Crown, 2006), 58, 60.

9. "The First Gore–Bush Presidential Debate," *Commission on Presidential Debates,* October 3, 2000, http://www.debates.org/pages/trans2000a.html.

4. STATES OF CONFUSION: SEXUAL PERPLEXITY

1. Amanda Schaeffer, "The Family Unplanned," *Slate,* November 21, 2006, http://www.slate.com/id/2154249.

2. The Third Gore–Bush Presidential Debate," *Commission on Presidential Debates,* October 17, 2000, http://www.debates.org/pages/trans2000c.html.

3. Donald G. McNeil, "Taboos, Globally Speaking; Like Politics, All Political Correctness Is Local," *New York Times,* October 11, 1998.

4. Ben Evans, "Gingrich Admits to Extramarital Affair," Associated Press, March 9, 2007; "Livingston: I was Running for Speaker, Not Sainthood," *New York Times,* December 18, 1998; David Talbot, " 'This Hypocrite Broke Up My Family': Henry Hyde, the man who will sit in judgment on President Clinton, confirms that he carried on a secret affair," *Salon.com,* September 16, 1998, http://www.salon.com/news/1998/09/cov_16newsb.html.

5. Bush told reporters, "If the person has violated the law, that person will be taken care of." "Bush Welcomes Probe of CIA Leak, *CNN.com,* February 11, 2004, http://www.cnn.com/2003/ALLPOLITICS/09/30/wilson.cia/. (In light of the commuting of Scooter Libby's sentence, it now appears the president may have spoken with double meaning.)

6. Vice President Dick Cheney on *Meet the Press,* October 18, 2006.

7. Gilbert Burnham et al., "Mortality After the 2003 Invasion of Iraq: A Cross-sectional Cluster Sample Survey," *The Lancet* 368, 9545 (October 21, 2006): 1421–28.

8. The End of a Revolution," *Time,* October 16, 2006, 30.

9. The assault on Cleveland was used by the Republicans to try to offset Cleveland's high ethical standing and to minimize the difference in ethical reputation between Cleveland and his opponent, Maine senator James Blaine, whose reputation for dishonesty sparked the famous mugwump defection in the Republican Party. Cleveland, a bachelor, did not dispute having a sexual liaison with the unmarried woman, but he reportedly took financial responsibility for the child because he knew that of the several men who had been with the woman, he was the only bachelor.

10. John Harris, *The Survivor: Bill Clinton in the White House* (New York: Random House, 2005), 403.

11. Joe Conason, "Don't Blame Clinton," *Salon.com,* January 15, 2002, http://dir.salon.com/story/politics/feature/2002/01/15/clinton/index.html.

12. Alfred Kinsey, Wardell B. Pomeroy, and Clyde E. Martin, *Sexual Behavior in the Human Male* (Bloomington: Indiana University Press, 1998).

13. It is often overlooked, but Freud himself explicitly opposed the characterization of homosexuality as pathological or as reflecting any moral depravity.

14. Charles Socarides, *The Overt Homosexual* (New York: Grune and Stratton, 1968).

15. "US Military's Gay Policy 'Costly,'" *BBCNews,* February 25, 2005, http://news
.bbc.co.uk/2/hi/americas/4296325.stm.

16. James Moore and Wayne Slater; *The Architech: Karl Rove and the Master Plan
for Absolute Power* (New York: Crown, 2006), 40–41.

17. Ibid.

18. Remarks at Conservative Political Action Conference, March 2, 2007. Video
available at http://www.cnn.com/video/#/video/politics/2007/03/02/sots
.giuliani.cpac.cnn.

19. See, for instance, www.Boycott-Hollywood.us.

5. STATES OF CONFUSION: ENVY

1. Evans-Novak Political Report, *HumanEvents.com,* week of October 25, 2006,
http://www.humanevents.com/article.php?id=17709.

2. Melanie Klein, *Envy and Gratitude* (New York: Basic Books, 1957).

3. Diane Barth, "The Role of Self-Esteem in the Experience of Envy," *The American Journal of Psychoanalysis* #48, 3 (1988): 198–210.

4. Anne MacDonald Maier, *Mother Love, Deadly Love* (New York: St. Martin's
Press, 1994).

5. Truman Capote, *In Cold Blood: A True Account of a Multiple Murder and Its Consequences* (New York: Random House, 1965), 302.

6. "House Sergeant-at-Arms Ordered Pelosi Plane," July 28, 2007, http://www
.msnbc.msn.com/id/17035721/.

7. James Moore and Wayne Slater, *The Architect: Karl Rove and the Master Plan for
Absolute Power* (New York: Crown, 2007), 188.

8. Nicholas Confessore, "Welcome to the Machine," *Washington Monthly*
(July/August 2003).

9. Rush Limbaugh, *The Way Things Ought to Be* (New York: Pocket Books, 1992),
40. Although Limbaugh says that he was making a point by being absurd, he also
says that he meant every word.

10. Ibid., 78.

11. Ibid., 253.

12. Ann Coulter, *Slander: Liberal Lies About the American Right* (New York: Crown
Publishers, 2002), 16.

13. Ibid., 30.

14. Ibid., 6.

15. CBS News, *Ronald Reagan Remembered,* ed. Ian Jackman (New York: Simon & Schuster, 2004).

16. Joe Conason and Gene Lyons, *The Hunting of the President: The Ten-Year Campaign to Destroy Bill and Hillary Clinton* (New York: St. Martin's Press, 2000).

17. "The Second Gore-Bush Presidential Debate," *Commission on Presidential Debates,* October 10, 2000, http://www.debates.org/pages/trans2000b.html.

18. Jacob Weisberg, *Bushisms,* (New York: Fireside, 2004). Originally quoted in *The Economist,* June 12, 1999.

6. THE GASLIGHTERS: ARCHITECTS OF FALSE REALITIES

1. Drew Westen, *The Political Brain: The Role of Emotion in Deciding the Fate of the Nation* (New York: Public Affairs, 2007).

2. Larry Tye, *The Father of Spin: Edward L. Bernays and the Birth of Public Relations* (New York: Crown Publishers, 1998). (All information concerning Edward Bernays is from Tye's excellent biography.)

3. The commercial is available at the Museum of the Moving Image in New York, New York. It is also available online at http://livingroomcandidate .movingimage.us/election/index.php?nav_action=election&nav_subaction= overview&campaign_id=168.

4. David Greenberg, *Nixon's Shadow: The History of an Image* (New York: Norton, 2003), xxii.

5. "Bush's Most Valuable Player," *Time,* November 14, 1988.

6. Candidate ads: 1988 George Bush "Revolving Door," *InsidePolitics,* http:// www.insidepolitics.org/ps111/candidateads.html.

7. "Fighting the Wimp Factor," *Newsweek,* October 11, 1987.

8. "The Second Bush-Dukakis Presidential Debate," *Commission on Presidential Debates,* October 13, 1988, http://www.debates.org/pages/trans88b.html.

9. "Bush Calls for Ban on Same-Sex Marriage," *CNN.com,* February 25, 2004, http://www.cnn.com/2004/ALLPOLITICS/02/24/elec04.prez.bush .marriage/.

10. Joshua Green, "Karl Rove in a Corner," *The Atlantic,* October 2004.

11. James Moore, and Wayne Slater, *Bush's Brain: How Karl Rove Made George W. Bush Presidential* (New Jersey: Wiley, 2003), 130.

12. Moore and Slater, *The Architect,* 255.

13. Ibid., 6.

14. Green, "Karl Rove in a Corner," October 2004, http://www.theatlantic.com/doc/200411/green/3.

15. Ron Susskind, "Faith, Certainty, and the Presidency of George W. Bush," *New York Times Magazine,* October 17, 2004.

16. Moore and Slater, *The Architect,* 104.

17. Frank Rich, *The Greatest Story Ever Sold: The Decline and Fall of Truth from 9/11 to Katrina* (New York: Penguin Press, 2006), 45.

18. "Photographic Manipulation," *SourceWatch,* September 9, 2006, http://www.sourcewatch.org/index.php?title=Photographic_manipulation.

19. Richard A. Davis, "The Anatomy of a Smear Campaign," *Boston Globe,* March 21, 2004.

20. "McCain Hired Swift Boat Advertising Firm Designed to Attack Veterans," *New York Times,* February 4, 2007.

21. "Anonymous Critics Aim at Romney," *TheState.com,* March 31, 2007, http://www.thestate.com/mld/thestate/16805857.htm.

22. Ibid.

23. Moore and Slater, *Bush's Brain,* 33ff.

24. Green, "Karl Rove in a Corner."

25. Paul Brooks, "Hinchey Sees Hand of Rove: They Set Him Up," *Times Herald Record,* February 22, 2005, http://archive.recordonline.com/archive2005/hinchey2.htm.

26. Susan Page, "Norquist's Power High, Profile Low," *USA Today,* June 1, 2001.

7. FOX NEWS: SPEAKING POWER TO TRUTH

1. "Roger Ailes," *SourceWatch,* http://www.sourcewatch.org/index.php?title=Roger_Ailes#Working_For_Big_Tobacco.

2. "Study Criticizes Anti-Smoking Ads," *Seattle Times,* December 18, 2006, http://seattletimes.nwsource.com/html/health/2003482961_tobacco18m.html.

3. Nancy Kingsbury and Laurie E. Ekstrand, *ONDCP Media Campaign: Contractor's National Evaluation Did Not Find That the Youth Anti-Drug Media Campaign Was Effective in Reducing Youth Drug Use,* Report to the Subcommittee on Transportation, Treasury, the Judiciary, Housing and Urban Development, and Related Agencies, Committee on Appropriations, U.S. Senate, GAO-06-818 (Washington, D.C.: U.S. Government Accountability Office, August 2006), 6.

4. Lawrence Wright, *Remembering Satan* (New York: Knopf, 1994).

5. George Lakoff, *Whose Freedom: The Battle over America's Most Important Idea* (New York: Farrar, Straus and Giroux, 2006), 10.

6. Richard Berke, "The 2000 Campaign: The Ad Campaign; Democrats See, and Smell, Rats in G.O.P. Ad," *New York Times,* September 12, 2000.

7. *Outfoxed: Rupert Murdoch's War on Journalism,* DVD, produced and directed by Robert Greenwald (New York, N.Y.: The Disinformation Company, 2005). See 3:41 of disc and 4:22 of disc.

8. Ibid. See 2:34 of disc and 1:39 of disc.

9. Thomas E. Patterson, *Doing Well and Doing Good* (Cambridge: Joan Shorenstein Center at Harvard JFK School of Government), December 2000.

10. Ibid, 3.

11. FOXnews.com, March 6, 2007.

12. MSNBC.com, March 6, 2007.

13. See daily ratings at http://www.mediabistro.com/tvnewser/.

14. James McCartney, "News Lite," *American Journalism Review,* June 1997, 19–21, quoted in Patterson, *Doing Well and Doing Good,* 3.

15. Thomas E. Patterson, *The American Democracy* (New York: McGraw Hill, 2001), 309–11, quoted in Patterson, *Doing Well and Doing Good,* 3.

16. Pew Research Center for the People and the Press, *Public Knowledge of Current Affairs Little Changed by News and Information Revolution,* April 15, 2007.

17. Patterson, *Doing Well and Doing Good,* 3.

18. Patterson, *Doing Well and Doing Good,* 9.

19. "American Fathers and Their Children," *FOXNews.com,* January, 29, 2007, http://www.foxnews.com/printer_friendly_story/0,3566,248127,00.html.

20. *Outfoxed.* See 7:07 et seq. of disc.

21. Doreen Carvajal, "For News Media, Time Introspection," *New York Times,* April 5, 1998, 28, quoted in Patterson, *Doing Well and Doing Good,* 12.

22. *Outfoxed.* See 5:58 of disc.

23. *Outfoxed.* See 5:50 of disc.

8. THE RELIGIOUS RIGHT: FAITH-BASED REALITY

1. Kevin Phillips, *American Theocracy: The Peril and Politics of Radical Religion, Oil, and Borrowed Money in the 21st Century* (New York: Penguin, 2006), 193.

2. Paul Thigpen, *Guidelines for Catholic Voters* (Huntington, IN: Our Sunday Visitor, 2004).

3. Rob Boston, "The Theocratic Agenda Is Heading for a Statehouse Near You," *AlterNet, Church and State,* March 10, 2007.

4. Sigmund Freud, *The Future of an Illusion* (New York: Norton, 1961), 42.

5. Karen Armstrong, *A History of God: The 4000-Year Quest of Judaism, Christianity, and Islam* (New York: Knopf, 1993), 357.

6. Robert J. Lovinger, *Working with Religions Issues in Therapy* (New York: Jason Aronson, 1984).

7. Matt Bai, "The Multilevel Marketing of the President," *New York Times Magazine,* April 25, 2004.

8. Leonard Cohen, "The Story of Isaac," in *Stranger Music* (New York: Pantheon Books, 1993).

9. J. Rodman Williams, *The Pentecostal Reality* (Grand Rapids, Mich.: Zondervan, 1996), http://www.regent.edu/acad/schdiv/williams/pent1.html, 1–2.

10. Ibid., 3.

11. Ibid., 2.

12. "Robert Bellarmine: Letter on Galileo's Theories, 1615," in *Modern History Internet Sourcebook,* http://www.fordham.edu/halsall/mod/1615bellarmine-letter.html.

13. Gingrich, *Rediscovering God in America.*

14. Brian C. Mooney, "Giuliani Continues His Conservative Shift," *Boston Globe,* August 13, 2007.

15. David Kuo, *Tempting Faith: An Inside Story of Political Seduction* (New York: Free Press, 2006), 168–70.

16. Ibid.

17. Ibid.

18. Ibid.

19. Ibid.

9. THE ASSAULT ON PROFESSIONALISM

1. Walter Cronkite, *A Reporter's Life* (New York: Knopf, 1996), 258.

2. "About the *Media Research Center,*" *Media Research Center,* http://www.mediaresearch.org/about/aboutwelcome.asp.

3. "Examining the 'Liberal Media Bias' Claim," press release, *Fairness & Accuracy in Reporting,* June 1, 1998, http://www.fair.org/index.php?p=2447.

4. Joe Conason, *Big Lies: The Right-Wing Propaganda Machine and How It Distorts the Truth* (New York: St. Martin's Press, 2003), 34.

5. Stephen Colbert, 2006 White House Correspondents' Association Dinner speech, April 29, 2006, http://politicalhumor.about.com/od/stephencolbert/a/colbertbush.htm.

6. See, for instance, the Media Matters Web site, "NBC's David Gregory Accused of Partisanship for Confronting White House with ISG Findings," *Media Matters,* December 8, 2007, http://mediamatters.org/items/200612090004.

7. See relevant Media Research Center CyberAlerts on their Web site, http://www.mediaresearch.org/archive/cyber/welcome.asp.

8. Colin Powell press conference, Cairo, Egypt, February 24, 2001, quoted in Al Franken, *The Truth (with Jokes),* (Boston: Dutton, 2005), 44.

9. Condolezza Rice, interview with Wolf Blitzer on CNN, July 29, 2001, quoted in Franken, *Truth,* 44.

10. President George W. Bush speech at Cincinnati Museum Center, October 7, 2002, quoted in Franken, *Truth,* 46.

11. "Saddam 'Had No Link to Al Qaeda,'" *BBC News,* September 9, 2006, http://news.bbc.co.uk/2/hi/americas/5328592.stm. In this headline, they are quoting a U.S. Senate Intelligence Committee report released on September 8, 2006. Quoted in Franken, *Truth,* 44.

12. Keith Olbermann, "Inside the World of Rupert Murdoch," *MSNBC.com,* June 29, 2007, http://www.msnbc.msn.com/id/19504943/.

13. "Fahrenheit 911 Viewers and Limbaugh Listeners About Equal in Size Even Though They Perceive Two Different Nations, Annenberg Data Show," National Annenberg Election Survey release, Annenberg Public Policy Center Web site, August 3, 2004, http://www.annenbergpublicpolicycenter.org/Downloads/Political_Communication/NAES/Release_fahrenheit_20040803.pdf.

14. Ibid.

15. Dennis Prager, "Why Liberals Fear Global Warming More Than Conservatives Do," *Realclear Politics,* June 20, 2006, http://www.realclearpolitics.com/articles/2006/06/why_liberals_fear_global_warmi.html.

16. "Shaping the Message, Distorting the Science," testimony of Sheldon Rampton to the Committee on Science and Technology of the U.S. House of Representatives, March 27, 2007, http://www.prwatch.org/node/5899.

17. Ibid.

18. "Former Bush Aide Who Edited Reports Is Hired by Exxon," *New York Times,* June 15, 2005.

19. "Shaping the Message, Distorting the Science."

20. See the Church of the Reconciliation (North Carolina) Web site, http://www.churchrec.org.

21. "Letter," *Diocese of Lansing.org,* May 13, 2005, http://www.dioceseoflansing.org/bishop/bishopletters/05_13_05.html.

22. Daniel and Thomas Berrigan were two Jesuit priests known for their radical opposition to the Vietnam War.

23. Laurence Tribe, *Abortion: The Clash of Absolutes* (New York: W. W. Norton, 1992).

24. Julie Johnson and Ratu Kamlani, "Do We Have Too Many Lawyers?" *Time/CNN,* August 26, 1991, http://www.time.com/time/printout/0,8816,973684,00.html.

25. "Liebeck v. McDonald's Restaurants," *Wikipedia,* http://en.wikipedia.org/wiki/Liebeck_v._McDonald%27s_Restaurants

26. Ibid.

27. Ibid.

28. Joseph R. Larson, "Countdown to Socialism in America," *Citizens for a Constitutional Republic,* http://www.citizensforaconstitutionalrepublic.com/larson_Count_Down_To_Socialism_In_American.html.

29. Personal communication from Dr. Toni Thompson and Dr. Pamela Winton, April 2007.

30. Boston, "The Theocratic Agenda."

10. POLICY IMPLICATIONS: THE REAL FLEECING OF AMERICA

1. Francis Fukuyama, *The End of History and the Last Man* (New York: Penguin, 1992).

2. Brian K. Bucks, Arthur B. Kennickell, and Kevin B. Moore, "Recent Changes in U.S. Family Finances: Evidence from the 2001 and 2004 Survey," *Federal Reserve Bulletin* 92 (February 2006).

3. Michael Luo, "Preaching a Gospel of Wealth in a Glittery Market, New York," *New York Times,* January 15, 2006.

4. Centers for Medicare and Medicaid Services, "National Health Expenditure Projections, 2006–2016," http://www.cms.hhs.gov/NationalHealthExpendData/downloads/proj2006.pdf.

5. J. Wrich, personal communication, December 2001.

6. David S. Broder and Haynes Johnson, *The System: The American Way of Politics at the Breaking Point* (New York: Little, Brown, 1996), 205–6, 207.

7. Centers for Medicare and Medicaid Services, "National Health Care Predictions"; Paul Krugman, "A Healthy New Year," *New York Times,* January 1, 2007.

8. Peter Hussey, "U.S. Still Spends More on Health Care Than Any Other Country," *Science Daily* (July 12, 2005), http://www.sciencedaily.com/releases/2005/07/050712140821.

9. "Health Care Spending in the United States and OECD Countries," *Kaiser Family Foundation,* January 2007, http://www.kff.org/insurance/snapshot/chcm010307oth.cfm.

10. Phineas Baxandall, "How U.S. Health Care Stacks Up Internationally," *Dollars and Sense,* no. 235 (May/June 2001).

11. Ibid, 2.

12. Broder and Johnson, *The System,* 205–6.

11. THE POLITICS OF REALITY: BATTLEGROUND STATES

1. "Purdue Pleads Guilty in OxyContin Case," *Chemical and Engineering News* 85, no. 20 (May 11, 2007), http://pubs.acs.org/cen/news/85/i20/8520news10.html; "OxyContin Maker, Execs Guilty of Deceit," *ABC News,* September 13, 2007, http://abcnews.go.com/Business/wireStory?id=3160486.

2. Lee Iacocca with Catherine Whitney, *Where Have All the Leaders Gone?* (New York: Scribner, 2007).

3. Gary Larson, *The Far Side,* 1985, http://www.ittc.ku.edu/workshops/Summer 2004Lectures/Global_Climate_Change_04.pdf.

BIBLIOGRAPHY

Armstrong, Karen. *The Battle for God: A History of Fundamentalism*. New York: Random House, 2001.

Barnes, Fred. *Rebel in Chief: Inside the Bold and Controversial Presidency of George W. Bush*. New York: Crown, 2006.

Bennett, William. *The Book of Virtues*. New York: Simon & Schuster, 1993.

Broder, David S., and Haynes Johnson. *The System: The American Way of Politics at the Breaking Point*. New York: Little, Brown, 1996.

Brodie, Fawn. *Jefferson: An Intimate Portrait*. New York: W. W. Norton, 1974.

Capote, Truman. *In Cold Blood: A True Account of a Multiple Murder and Its Consequences*. New York: Vintage, 1993.

Conason, Joe. *Big Lies: The Right Wing Propaganda Machine and How It Distorts the Truth*. New York: St. Martin's Press, 2003.

——. *It Can Happen Here: Authoritarian Peril in the Age of Bush*. New York: St. Martin's Press, 2007.

Conason, Joe, and Gene Lyons. *The Hunting of the President: The Ten-Year Campaign to Destroy Bill and Hillary Clinton*. New York: St. Martin's Press, 2000.

Coulter, Ann. *The Church of Liberalism*. New York: Crown, 2006.

——. *Slander: Liberal Lies About the American Right*. New York: Crown, 2002.

Cronkite, Walter. *A Reporter's Life*. New York: Knopf, 1996.

DeVos, Rich. *Compassionate Capitalism: People Helping People to Help Themselves*. New York: Dutton, 1993.

Dorpat, Theodore, M.D. *Gaslighting, the Double Whammy, Interrogation and Other Methods of Covert Control in Psychotherapy and Analysis*. New York: Jason Aronson, 1996.

Fainaru-Wada, Mark, and Lance Williams. *Game of Shadows: Barry Bonds, BALCO, and the Steriods Scandal that Rocked Professional Sports*. New York: Gottham Books, 2006.

Frank, Thomas. *What's the Matter with Kansas: How Conservatives Won the Heart of America*. New York: Henry Holt and Company, 2004.

Franken. Al. *Lies and the Lying Liars Who Tell Them: A Fair and Balanced Look at the Right.* New York: Dutton, 2002.

Freud, Sigmund. *The Future of an Illusion.* New York: W. W. Norton, 1961.

Fromm, Erich. *The Heart of Man: Its Genius for Good and Evil.* New York: Harper & Row, 1964.

Fukuyama, Francis. *The End of History and the Last Man.* New York: Penguin, 1992.

Gingrich, Newt. *Rediscovering God in America.* New York: Thomas Nelson, 2006.

Gore, Al. *The Assault on Reason.* New York: Penguin, 2007.

Greenberg, David. *Nixon's Shadow: The History of an Image.* New York: W. W. Norton, 2003.

Grotstein, James S. *Splitting and Projective Identification.* New York: Jason Aronson, 1993.

Hamilton, Lee H., and James A. Baker III. *The Iraq Study Group Report: The Way Forward: A New Approach.* New York: Vintage, 2006.

Harris, John. *The Survivor: Bill Clinton in the White House.* New York: Random House, 2005.

Hofstadter, Richard. *The Paranoid Style in American Politics and Other Essays.* Cambridge, Mass.: Harvard University Press, 1996.

Iacocca, Lee, with Catherine Whitney. *Where Have All the Leaders Gone?* New York: Scribner, 2007.

James, William. *The Varieties of Religious Experience.* Mineola, N.Y.: Dover, 2002.

Kernberg, Otto F., M.D. *Ideology, Conflict, and Leadership in Groups and Organizations.* New Haven, Conn.: Yale University Press, 1998.

Kinsey, Alfred, Wardell B. Pomeroy, and Clyde E. Martin. *Sexual Behavior in the Human Male.* Bloomington: Indiana University Press, 1998.

Klein, Melanie. *Envy and Gratitude and Other Works 1946–1963.* New York: Free Press, 1975.

Kuo, David. *Tempting Faith: An Inside Story of Political Seduction.* New York: Free Press, 2006.

Lakoff, George. *Don't Think of an Elephant: Know Your Values and Frame the Debate.* White River Junction, Vt.: Chelsea Green Publishing, 2004.

——. *Whose Freedom: The Battle over America's Most Important Idea.* New York: Farrar, Straus and Giroux, 2006.

Levy, Paul. *The Madness of George W. Bush: A Reflection of Our Collective Psychosis.* Bloomington, Ind: AuthorHouse, 2006.

Limbaugh, Rush. *See, I Told You So.* New York: Pocket Books, 1993.

———. *The Way Things Ought to Be.* New York: Pocket Books 1991.

Lippmann, Walter. *Public Opinion.* New York: Simon & Schuster, 1997.

Lovinger, Robert J. *Working with Religious Issues in Therapy.* New York: Jason Aronson, 1984.

Maier, Anne MacDonald. *Mother Love, Deadly Love.* New York: St. Martin's Press, 1994.

McLuhan, Marshall. *Understanding Media: The Extensions of Man.* London: Sphere Books, 1967.

Melman, Yossi, and Meir Javendanfar. *The Nuclear Sphinx of Tehran: Mahmoud Ahmadinejad and the State of Iran.* New York: Caroll Graf, 2007.

Minutaglio, Bill. *First Son: George W. Bush and the Bush Family Dynasty.* New York: Times Books, 1999.

Moore, James, and Wayne Slater. *The Architect: Karl Rove and the Master Plan for Absolute Power.* New York: Crown, 2006.

———. *Bush's Brain: How Karl Rove Made George W. Bush Presidential.* Hoboken, N.J.: Wiley, 2003.

Moore, Richard. *The Creation of Reality in Psychoanalysis: A View of the Contributions of Donald Spence, Roy Schafer, Robert Stolorow, Irwin Z. Hoffman and Beyond.* New York: The Analytic Press, 1999.

O'Reilly, Bill. *The O'Reilly Factor: The Good, the Bad, and the Completely Ridiculous in American Life.* New York: Broadway Books, 2000.

O'Reilly, Bill, and Charles Flowers. *The O'Reilly Factor for Kids: A Survival Guide for America's Families.* New York: Harper Entertainment, 2004.

Phillips, Kevin. *American Theocracy: The Peril and Politics of Radical Religion, Oil and Borrowed Money in the 21st Century.* New York: Penguin, 2006.

Rich, Frank. *The Greatest Story Ever Sold: The Decline and Fall of Truth from 9/11 to Katrina.* New York: Penguin, 2006.

Santoro, Victor. *Gaslighting: How to Drive Your Enemies Crazy.* Port Townsend, Wash.: Loompanics Unlimited, 1994.

Segal, Hanna. *Introduction to the Work of Melanie Klein.* New York: Basic Books, 1964.

Shawcross, William. *Murdoch: The Making of a Media Empire.* New York: Simon & Schuster, 1997.

Shrum, Robert. *No Excuses: Confession of a Serial Campaigner.* New York: Simon & Schuster, 2007.

Stern, Dr. Robin. *The Gaslight Effect: How to Spot and Survive the Hidden Manipulation Others Use to Control Your Life*. New York: Morgan Road Books, 2007.

Stout, Martha. *The Sociopath Next Door*. New York: Broadway Books, 1995.

Tribe, Laurence. *Abortion: The Clash of Absolutes*. New York: W. W. Norton, 1992.

Tye, Larry. *The Father of Spin: Edward L. Bernays and the Birth of Public Relations*. New York: Crown, 1998.

Weisberg, Jacob. *Bushisms*. New York: Simon & Schuster, 2004.

Western, Drew. *The Political Brian: The Role of Emotion in Deciding the Fate of the Nation*. New York: Public Affairs, 2007.

Woodward, Bob. *Plan of Attack*. New York: Simon & Schuster, 2004.

——. *State of Denial*. New York: Simon & Schuster, 2006.

Wright, Lawrence. *Remembering Satan*. New York: Knopf, 1994.

INDEX